FIREWORKS

Fireworks

George Plimpton

Photo editor Margaret Mathews

DOUBLEDAY & COMPANY, INC.
Garden City, New York
1984

By George Plimpton

THE RABBIT'S UMBRELLA (juvenile)
OUT OF MY LEAGUE
WRITERS AT WORK, Vols. I–VI (ed.)
PAPER LION
THE BOGEY MAN
AMERICAN LITERARY ANTHOLOGY, Vols. I–III (ed.)
AMERICAN JOURNEY: THE TIMES OF ROBERT F. KENNEDY (with Jean Stein)
PIERRE'S BOOK (ed.)
MAD DUCKS AND BEARS
ONE FOR THE RECORD
ONE MORE JULY
SHADOW BOX
SPORTS (with Neil Leifer)
SPORTS BESTIARY (with Arnold Roth)
EDIE: AN AMERICAN BIOGRAPHY (with Jean Stein)
D.V. (with Christopher Hemphill)

BOOK DESIGN BY LAURENCE ALEXANDER

Library of Congress Cataloging in Publication Data

Plimpton, George.
Fireworks.

Includes index.
1. Fireworks. I. Title.
TP300.P55 1984   662'.1   83-20565
ISBN: 0-385-15414-3
Copyright © 1984 by George Plimpton

For Jimmy Grucci

Acknowledgments

The artwork which comprises such a major part of this volume was collected by Margaret O. Mathews. I am greatly indebted to her. She would want me to mention two fireworks aficionados who were of particular assistance to her: Orville Carlisle, who has a fireworks museum in the back of his shoestore in Norfolk, Nebraska, and Betty Brightlow, who is the curator of the Du Pont Collection of the Eleutherian Mills Historical Library in Greenville, Delaware. My own research was greatly helped by Steven Cassorla, who offered me the use of his considerable file on pyrotechnical matters. I am especially grateful to Robert G. Cardwell, Robert M. Winokur, and Michael T. Swisher, all members of the Pyrotechnics Guild International, who studied the text of this book for errors with the care they would give the making of an aerial show. Mr. Swisher provided the "Further Reading About Fireworks," which readers will find on page 267. Of particular inspiration and help, of course, have been the professional fireworks people: David Opperman, the executive secretary of the American Pyrotechnics Association, John Serpico of International Fireworks, the Souza family of Pyro Spectaculars, and especially the Gruccis from Bellport, Long Island. I would be remiss in not mentioning Jacqueline Kennedy Onassis, of Doubleday, who after watching a display of fireworks rise from Central Park in New York felt that such artful beauty deserved some written words.

CONTENTS

"What are fireworks like?" she had asked.

"They are like the Aurora Borealis," said the King, "only much more natural. I prefer them to stars myself, as you always know when they are going to appear . . ."

OSCAR WILDE
The Remarkable Rocket

The great thing was to do it yourself—just the nudge of a lighted punk to a fuse, a small commitment that seemed such an insignificant act, and yet the result was so decisive and visible . . . the sudden puff of a colored ball emerging from the long tube of a Roman candle, the quick rush and fading hiss of a rocket, the popping busyness of lawn fountains that smoked and sputtered and sent the family cat scurrying under the upstairs bed. Anyone could do it. Even "the snake in the grass," that curious pellet that elongated and convoluted into a length of gray-black ash, had its quality of mystery. Whoever lit it suddenly had that extraordinary alchemist's gift of turning an inert object into something else. And fireworks provided a sort of equalizer, especially for those kids who were not good at sports, and were taken last on the pickup teams, and knew they were doomed to spend most of the long summer afternoons in the far reaches of right field when they were not stepping up to the plate and striking out. They too on the Fourth of July had the capacity to create something just as satisfactory as a ball caught up against the fence, or a base hit—and make a big racket about it besides . . . with only the requirement of nerve enough to reach forward with the punk to the brightly papered device on the lawn and touch it to the fuse to set the thing off.

I always thought it was the best day of the year. It was in the middle of the summer, to begin with, and when you got up in the morning someone would almost surely say, as they did in those times, that it was going to be a "true Fourth of July scorcher." School had been out long enough so that one was conditioned for the great day. One's feet were already leather-hard so

Two scenes of an old-fashioned family Fourth of July. Charming as these scenes are, the lack of safety precautions would indicate why anti-fireworks legislation began to be passed. (Both, The Bettmann Archive, Inc.)

that striding barefoot across a gravel driveway could be done without wincing, and yet not so insensitive as to be unable to feel against one's soles the luxurious wet wash of a dew-soaked lawn in the early morning. Of course, the best thing about the day was the anticipation of the fireworks—both from the paper bag of one's own assortment, carefully picked from the catalogues, and then, after a day's worth of the excitement of setting them off, there was always the tradition of getting in the car with the family and going off to the municipal show, or perhaps a Beach Club's display . . . the barge out in the harbor, a dark hulk as evening fell, and the heart-pounding excitement of seeing the first glow of a flare out there across the water and knowing that the first shell was about to soar up into the sky.

Christmas was all right, but it was over too quickly, and was almost inevitably fraught with dashed hopes. Rather than the Savage .475 Special rifle (complete with barrel scope) that one had specifically asked for, the "big present" turned out (the heart sank as one noticed the conformation of the package under the Christmas tree) to be a dartboard. Grandmother—one had counted on her—inevitably turned up at the house with a Norwegian sweater she had bought "especially" on a cruise that summer through the fjords.

The Fourth of July had none of these disappointments . . . unless it rained, which I do not ever remember happening until fireworks were banned and when it did not make any difference. The day was always bright.

A big part of it when I was growing up were what rightfully became the bane of the fireworks industry—the cherry bombs and silver salutes. They were the first objects, after a scout knife, matches, and one's first BB-gun, that a youngster was truly lectured about—vociferously, the admonishing tone, the dire warnings about what the cherry bomb could do to fingers or eyes. I can remember the helter-skelter flight after nervously lighting my first cherry bomb off a stick of punk, peering around the corner of the tree at the steam-like smoke in the grass, and starting at the violent report.

There were various accessories that could be used with a cherry bomb. I remember an iron device like a football kicking-tee on which one balanced a tennis ball; when the cherry bomb went off underneath, it knocked the ball straight up, far above the elm trees and the rooftops, finally just a speck in the sky; the great thing was to circle under the ball with a baseball glove as it began to rematerialize; there was time enough to construct an entire mental scenario—the last out of the World Series, a "loud" foul as they used to say, and a lot depended on its being caught because the bases were loaded, and there was the business of waving everyone off that responsibility, shouting out to one's five-year-old sister, standing by on the lawn, wide-eyed, with a lollipop in her mouth, "I've got it! I've got it!"

There were other uses for the cherry bomb that I heard about among school chums but never had the nerve to try: with its lacquered and thus waterproof fuse, the cherry bomb was a favorite for lighting and flushing down a toilet at school to see what would happen; the inevitable was a pipe bursting a floor or two below with devastating effect, particularly if a class happened to be in session. Fortunately, the bulk of those devices were around in mid-summer when schools were not in session. It was obviously not an experiment one wanted to try in one's own house.

On the Fourth, there were other, more refined items that also utilized a sharp bang. One of my favorites was the SOS Ship—a squat, cardboard ocean liner, about five inches long, with people painted standing along the rail; belowdecks their faces peered out of round portholes; it was a craft quite suitable for launching in a pond or a swimming pool; it had a single funnel with a fuse sticking out of the top which, when lit, caused (according to the catalogue) "A Shrill Siren Whistle Followed by Several Loud Reports Ending in Complete Destruction of Ship." For a young boy, there was something agreeably satanic to hold the destiny of these painted people in his hand and to launch them on their last journey—one could see their immobile passive faces staring imperturbably out of the portholes as the liner bobbed out into the pool while above them the ship's funnel began to send out its last despairing shriek.

A companion piece was a cardboard fire engine that did more or less the same thing, including an equally cataclysmic finale which was described in the catalogue as "A Whistle Followed by a Brilliant Flash of Flame, Ending in Complete Conflagration of Fire Engine." Only in the fertile minds of fireworks designers could the notion exist of a fire engine exploding and burning up!

There was a whole series of self-destruct items—a "Gothic Castle," among them, and perhaps the most bizarre—"A Wild Elephant . . . A Ferocious Beast That Belches Fire, Goes Mad and Destroys Itself!"

The prices were within a youngster's fiduciary parameters. For example, for five dollars in 1935, from the American Fireworks Distributing Co. in Franklin's Park, a suburb of Chicago, one could order a "Children's Assortment," which included four boxes of sparklers, twelve Python Black Snakes, twelve pounds of various-sized firecrackers, a Catherine wheel, firepots, and Roman candles—a total of fifty-six listed items!

What one chose was carefully culled from brightly colored pamphlets printed on cheap straw-colored paper with illustrations that could hold the attention of a boy for the better part of a day. Once again, they were at least as exciting as those that arrived in the weeks before Christmas. The Christmas catalogues were geared for adults and they seemed to emphasize kitchen appliances and chinaware, all at enormous expense, whereas the items in the

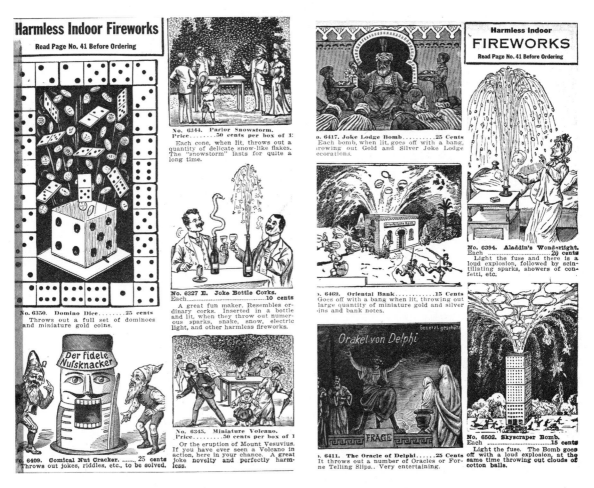

Such ads for "Harmless Indoor Fireworks" enjoyed wide appeal for generations of America's youth. (The Bettmann Archive, Inc.)

Fourth of July catalogues were not only mostly within one's own means but they were absolutely consistent and to the point: everything in there was calculated to terrify mothers.

The catalogues had a hyperbolic style (an "Octopus shell" had twenty-four tentacles) that kept one lingering on a page—the imagination ignited by the bright illustrations and the carny prose. "Tom, Dick, and Harry," the description might read, "a red-hot trio! Tom—a powerful No. 2 Flash Bomb; Dick—a beautiful No. 3 Star Shell; Harry—a big No. 3 whistling aerial bomb. Touch a match to it and away goes Tom with a big noise, sailing high in the air before he bursts with a loud report. Dick follows with a terrific shower of beautiful stars. Then away goes Harry with a screaming whistle before he bursts in the air with a big bang. New. Different. Sensational. Order plenty!"

While the copy was always flamboyant and hypnotizing, perhaps the first suspicions in a youngster's mind that one should not believe everything one read came from these catalogues. Even if "Tom, Dick, and Harry" did everything one hoped of them out there on the lawn, there were other items that did not live up to expectations. "Extra-Large Python Snakes," the description would proclaim. "Just light one of the pellets, and out comes a black *snake*, little by little, until it reaches a length of 3–4 feet!"

I lit perhaps thirty of them—all when I was about ten years old—perhaps the first firework item to which I was ever allowed to touch a piece of lighted punk; and even though I watched their performance prudently, as usual from behind a tree, I never saw one of the "snakes" produce more than half a foot of length until—in a quite touching final convulsion that looked more like a death than a birth—the thin piping of gray-black ash would shrivel up and collapse upon itself.

So one learned to be careful about catalogue copy. The choices were made with great care. A couple of weeks before the Fourth, the fireworks themselves arrived. Parents inevitably took the packages and hid them away somewhere, but usually they could be ferreted out and the devices within lined up to be gloated over.

They were inevitably, in their flamboyant colors, pretty, but there was always that fine fringe of danger one was aware of. Indeed, if one learned to suspect the sales pitch in a fireworks catalogue, perhaps the first English sentences that one truly absorbed were those on the items themselves: *Do Not Hold In Hand After Lighting,* or (even more awe-inspiring) *Lay On Ground— Light Fuse—Get Away . . .* these were among the first positive indications to a youngster that the written language was of use in imparting extremely important information.

The Fourth itself always seemed to be the longest day of the year. So much went on: when one's own allotment of daytime fireworks was done— the cherry bombs, the smoke bombs, the parachute shells, and so forth—there were friends with theirs to join down the block. Twilight was awaited eagerly, since the bulk of one's "best" fireworks were for use in the darkness. The colored stars rose from the lawns up above the trees.

And then, of course, there was the professional show. Not only did these soft summer evenings have perfect weather, but perhaps they were the first community gatherings one experienced in childhood—the first instance of communal activity. The crowd had gathered for a common purpose. There was the occasional pop of a firecracker at its perimeter, or perhaps a sparkler or two fizzing and spitting a shower of sparks amid the scampering of children; then at the end of the dock or across the baseball diamond where the scaffolding with the lances outlining the American flag was discernible in the gathering darkness, a red flare suddenly glowed. Expectant murmurs sifted through the crowd, the flare dipped, and then there was the thump of the first canister of the evening going up, the faint flutter of its passage, and the faces turning to the sky in expectation of what was going to happen up there.

One of the first truly romantic figures to my mind was the man who was responsible for that, the pyrotechnist or, as he was known, the "fireworks man." He was only seen once a year—unlike a soldier or a fireman, or a baseball player, who were ubiquitous enough so that after a while they tended to be run-of-the-mill. The fireworks man, on the other hand, was not only seen once a year, but it was at night, and just for an instant . . . coming ashore from the fireworks barge and striding down the dock, or appearing across the country-club lawn from the distant firing-line. Somehow, I remember the fireworks man as solitary, aloof, coveralled, perhaps sooty, staring straight ahead as he came, perhaps reflecting back on the trench-war violence he had just been a part of, indeed responsible for, and he seemed oblivious to us as we sucked back, wide-eyed, to let him pass: "The fireworks man! The fireworks man!"

The first pyrotechnician I actually came to know—long after those childhood years—was a man named John Serpico. He was the proprietor of a small manufacturing plant—the International Fireworks Co.—in North Bergen, New Jersey. I had found his firm's name in the telephone directory and phoned to ask if I could come out to his plant and buy fireworks from him to set off a minuscule display at a friend's country home where I was spending the weekend—thinking of what I was bringing as a rather unique house present. Serpico was hesitant. After all, the entire fireworks situation has changed. Shortly after the war the anti-fireworks laws in many states, including my own, New York, had become extremely stringent; all commercial fireworks, even Roman candles and sparklers, were banned. The crack of fireworks heard during the Fourth, the occasional whiz of a bottle rocket, were illegal fireworks, either smuggled into the state or purchased off the back of a bootlegger's station wagon. Thus Serpico had no commercial fireworks for sale, and it was improper both for him to give professional fireworks to an amateur and for me to set them off without a license and permission from the local authorities. But I think Serpico appreciated my passion for fireworks; he must have sensed it in my voice over the phone. He also learned that I had been a demolition specialist in the Army, which meant that I would be careful and concerned with safety factors. He agreed to provide me with a small allotment and a mortar from which to fire them.

His compound was a forlorn stretch of land, flat and heat-blasted, fronting on the cattail marshes of the New Jersey swamps—a collection of small buildings and trailers in which aerial shells were either being made or in storage. There were two animals on the premises which served to symbolize the wasteland quality of that melancholy place: a large police dog with three legs and an almost apoplectic temper—he crashed endlessly against a length of chain trying to get at strangers—and the other a crippled goat—it too had a missing leg, as if to be thus handicapped was the conditional trademark of the International Fireworks Co. The goat was far more placid than its canine companion. It browsed among the frames of the American flag set pieces out in the sun, hopping oddly from one dusty clump of grass to the next.

15

Serpico himself had a large purple splotch on one cheek which one might have supposed was firework-related, but was, in fact, a birthmark. He took me on a tour of the sheds. He showed me an aerial shell—a round canister, in dimensions not unlike a biscuit tin, wrapped in brown kraft paper and utterly functional-looking compared to the brightly designed fireworks prepared for the public. It had a black fuse at one end encased in a length of brown tubing, and at the other—he turned the shell over to show me—the base which contained the propellant charge to eject the firework from the mortar and up into the air. What then happened, Serpico went on to tell me, was that the shell, tumbling end over end as it went up into the night, had a time fuse inside which burned until its fire reached the bursting charge that broke open the canister at the top of its climb and ignited small cubes of a mixture of oxidizers and fuels called "stars." These would spray into the air and burn in the familiar patterns of the aerial display.

The containers Serpico made at his plant ranged from three to twelve inches in diameter—the twelve-inch shell being a projectile that weighed up to a hundred pounds and was shot out of a huge mortar a small boy could hide in, with iron handles on the side so that two men could lurch it into position. The half dozen shells that Serpico gave me were four inches across the top, one of them—which he told me was a "three break and report"—was two feet in length; it seemed mammoth and forbidding. He gave me a railroad flare to light the shells and a single mortar to fire them from. Although I knew that there was not the slightest danger, no matter how hard the box of shells was jostled, I remember wincing as I drove away and bounced across the railroad tracks at the far end of Serpico's compound.

When I arrived at his country place my host was somewhat surprised. "Ahem," he said, looking at the small carton of shells. "What do I do with these things?"

His wife said, "This doesn't mean jail, does it, or anything like that?"

"There are only about four or five in there," I said. "When it's dark, I'll go out in the field and set them off for you."

I dug the mortar in. Their little house-party came out to watch from the patio. I could see the glow of their cigarettes. I lit the railroad flare and touched off the first shell—a break and report—scampering from it, a bit panicked, through the meadow grass; first there was the thump of the propellant charge driving the shell out of the mortar, and then above I heard the pop of the canister opening; I looked up to see the curved spray of red and blue, and quickly, the flash of the report, the boom echoing in the hills . . . feeling then, for the first time, the extraordinary exhilaration and sense of self-fulfillment that comes with setting off a large professional shell.

I thought about the pleasure of it afterward as I stalked around the kitchen. There is a kind of delicious trepidation involved. First, after lighting the fuse, there is sometimes a wait before the shell—with a kind of *harrumphing* sound— leaves the mortar whose iron clangs with the sudden blow of the propellant charge. Until this happens, the mind races with the worry that the shell may refuse to budge. It will have to be removed. So the relief when the shell goes up is considerable. Even then, it takes so long for a large shell to reach its apogee—up to four or five seconds—that an additional worry takes over. One waits, looking up into the darkness, until the possibility occurs that the shell is coming back down, this awful projectile, invisible in the night, what pyrotechnicians refer to as a "black shell" . . . and then just as one thinks about scurrying desperately for cover, far up the shell snaps open in its huge enveloping umbrella of stars, so intensely beautiful that it invariably produces a cry of delight, partly in appreciation of the shell's aesthetics, but also in relief that the thing has gone off properly.

It is an infectious practice. After a while, friends would step out of the shelter of the patio, or come out onto the beach, wherever, and ask if they could set one off. I would give them firm and rudimentary instructions: "Just keep the body away from the top of the mortar . . . above all, don't look down in there to see if anything's going on!"

Some were nervous. The first sight of the mortar-pipe with the fuse drooped over the edge of its mouth, just barely visible in the twilight, the hissing of the railroad flare, sparks dripping molten to the ground, and the uncertainty of what the ignition would do to this somnolent device waiting out of sight, like a beast in its lair, was extremely unsettling to them; they tended to approach the fuse in a low, tense crouch, poised for flight, as if offering a morsel to a leopard. Sometimes, safely behind them, I called out, "Remember Ralph Waldo Emerson: 'As soon as there is life, there is danger!' "

Of my friends, the writers seemed to be the ones who most enjoyed the sensation of setting off a shell, especially those who were having difficulty with their own work, and suffering the so-called "writer's block." I understood why, I thought: it was the frustration of not being able to put on paper what was so vivid in one's mind—the agony of confronting Mallarmé's blank page—compared to the simple act of igniting a fuse and immediately producing a great chrysanthemum of color and beauty high above, punctuated with a splendid concussion, while below, people would gape in wonderment and call out "Wow!" It was the kind of reaction that writers always hoped for with their own work but never received in such visible and adulatory form. The best one could expect from a reader was a low *hmmm,* whereas a firework could produce loud "Ohhs!" and "Ahhs!" Often, having sent up a shell and seeing it perform, an author would run up in the darkness and ask to try another—a bigger one, this time, a "huge Jap shell, please!"

I remember Norman Mailer at one of our July fireworks parties in the Hamptons. He wanted to fire a shell. He had his bourbon drink in a blue glass, really more a *vase,* the sort of receptacle one usually finds in the back of a kitchen cabinet when everything else in the house, even the plastic cups, has been commandeered. He held the drink in one hand, safe out behind him, and he approached the fuse with the railroad flare in the other. The mortar held a six-inch Japanese shell. I watched him—struck again by the grotesque attitudes that people get into when faced with igniting a shell. In his case, he seemed not unlike a scientist intent on catching a lizard by the back of the neck. The shell came out almost instantaneously. His surprise at the shock of its emergence—a six-inch shell of that type weighs about eight pounds—toppled Norman into a complete backward somersault through the sawgrass. Astonishingly, the blue vase remained upright as he pinwheeled around it; not a drop of bourbon splashed out. He got up and took a sip and asked if he could do another. "Do you have anything slightly larger?"

Of course, there were the occasional traumas. Fireworks were, after all, dangerous enough if ill-used, and even, on occasion, unpredictable if used properly. On one occasion at our house in the Hamptons, which is on the sea, a large eight-inch shell fired at our annual summer fireworks party sailed back from the beach in a fog-laden wind and burst lower than it should have. One of its stars, still burning, dropped in among the spectators, landing on the upper arm of a Chicago broadcasting executive. It burned through his sweater, giving him a nasty singe indeed . . .

After being treated at the Southampton Hospital, he went home to Chicago with a large Band-Aid on his wound and then—a man I had never met before (he had come as the guest of a friend)—he sued me for eleven million dollars.

The process-server himself was rather embarrassed by the enormous sum. After he had served me the paper, he hung around my office at the *Paris Review,* a rather rumpled older man, I remember, who said that in his many years of this nasty business he had never served a paper of such mammoth proportions. "Did a building blow up?" he asked.

The incident got into the press. I told a newspaper reporter that anyone who had an arm valued at eleven million dollars should be pitching for the Chicago White Sox. The executive was not amused. He let it be known that he had been "burned from head to foot"—somewhat of a jump from his original complaint that he had a scar "three and a half inches long and two inches wide."

Not long after, I met a famous litigation lawyer at La Costa, the Teamster resort north of San Diego; he had read about the lawsuit in the newspapers. He asked me to dinner. We drove to the restaurant in his Rolls-Royce. His clients included some of the great names in the entertainment world, though his early years in the law had been—he made me understand—in the lower echelons of the legal society. He had done a lot of work in Chicago.

"Who is representing you?" he asked.

"My father's firm."

He knew the name, but he was not in the least agreement that a corporation law firm—which my father's is—was right for the job. "No, no, wrong. You should get a good tough Court Street lawyer to do the job."

I did not know what the term meant.

". . . somebody who'd really want to mix it up with this guy. Put him on notice. Counter-sue. Your father's firm is too gentlemanly to do that sort of thing."

My friend tapped the steering wheel of his Rolls-Royce. "And if none of that works," he said, *"I'll put in a call to some people in Chicago!"*

A slightly whimsical depiction by the American artist Winslow Homer of a Fourth of July celebration in 1868 and of what every displayer of fireworks fears most—one of his aerial pieces dropping back into the crowd. In this case, it is a rocket (see far right). (The Bettmann Archive, Inc.)

I have wondered what that extreme measure might have entailed. I imagined the scenario as being something out of the film *The Godfather*—along the lines of the famous scene of the horse head in the bed—except that, in this case, the intimidation would have been done far more subtly. And presumably with fireworks. The television executive would arrive back from his day's work to find a brightly colored fountain fizzing mysteriously on his lawn; or late at night, the colored ball of a Roman candle would soar up past his bedroom window, or an SOS Ship would start screaming in his bathtub. Investigating a strange hissing sound, he would open up the cellar door and look down the steps to discover a long length of fuse slowly burning off toward something behind a pile of empty suitcases in the corner . . .

None of this happened, of course. The matter was settled out of court, the man being paid a small pittance by the insurance company.

Despite the unpleasantness of this incident, my obsession with fireworks continued. During the Lindsay Administration in New York City, I kept pestering the mayor and other officials to allow more fireworks shows, especially in great barrages out of Central Park, to such a degree that the mayor finally made me his fireworks commissioner, a completely bogus designation which is not on the city rolls but one which I have perpetuated through succeeding administrations and a title which I answer to at the drop of a hat.

I got to know a number of fireworks people in the metropolitan area—in particular, the Grucci family from Bellport, Long Island. They allowed me to help choreograph shows for them—an international exhibition fired from Central Park, Venetian Night in Chicago, shows at Shea Stadium on Fireworks Night, Ronald Reagan's Inauguration, and the Brooklyn Bridge Centennial, among others. It was a great stroking of the ego to choreograph a large fireworks show. It allowed the chance—since the shells were sent up by electrical impulse—to put extraordinary effects in the sky, which were witnessed not just by folks sitting around on the lawn but by literally over a million people roaring in excitement at what they were seeing.

And yet, curiously, the small, more intimate shows are the ones I remember most vividly. I remember one in particular that John Serpico, my first mentor, and I did in the mountains of Vermont—an occasion to mark the graduation of the class of 1975 from Bennington College. I had been asked by one of the members of that class, a tall, lovely girl named Pamela Morgan, if there was any point in trying to persuade her senior tutor to let her do her senior thesis on the history of fireworks. I had said, "Of course! What a remarkable framework on which to put so much! And what a novel and clever way to present history! Think of the great personages who had been obsessed by fireworks—Queen Elizabeth, Peter the Great, Louis XIV, Queen Victoria, John Adams, ever so many."

Alas, her tutor did not share my enthusiasm. She ended up doing her thesis on the poems of Paul Éluard.

But perhaps imbued by my enthusiasm for fireworks, she was able to convince her senior committee that her class should choose some kind of pyrotechnic event for its graduation, rather than the perfunctory rock-'n'-roll band.

I obliged. John Serpico and I drove up into those lovely mountains with a van of shells. On the slope just down from a long expanse of lawn that stretched back to the college buildings, we dug in the mortars. The commencement was in the evening. Where we waited, we could hear the speeches drifting across the lawn. When they were done, I stepped forward and through a megaphone I read off a list of the graduating seniors as, behind me, John Serpico lit a shell for each one. Sometimes, to speed things along, I would read off ten names in a row and when I had done howling their names through my megaphone, Serpico would light a quick-match fuse to send a whole flight of shells up simultaneously, bouquets bursting in great profusion over the lawns.

There was a vague attempt in some cases to match a firework with the character of the student graduating: the harum-scarum performance of a Korean hummingbird shell for the class cutup, the lovely comet shells for the class lovelorn, a huge chrysanthemum for Pamela Morgan herself. The college dean—a brassy disciplinarian, apparently—got herself a sharp single report (what some fireworks people call a maroon) and nothing else, and from the lawn, after the echoes of that shell had drifted away, booming in the hills, I could hear the thin sound of laughter.

The long echoing of the reports coming off those dark blue hills must have resembled the sounds made when General John Burgoyne came through with his Loyalists and Hessians in the fall of 1777 and ran into the Green Mountain Boys. The hills collected the reports and hid them in their folds and ravines, and then suddenly released them, quite a time after, so that it seemed that what had produced the sound was some agency other than ours. When the display, and its final echoes, finally died away, it was replaced by the faint high calls of the students celebrating, flower bouquets tossed in the air in picayune imitation of the great fireworks' burgeonings just moments before, and I could see many couples standing in embrace on the expanse of that vast lawn— slender forms just barely visible now in the gathering darkness.

PAMELA MORGAN I am sorry about that tutor. I guess he doesn't have much of a feel for fireworks.

It's not uncommon. He may have been startled by a Krazy Kat jumper, or some such pyrotechnic device, and hid under the bed with the family cat on some Fourth of July long ago. But the time taken on your thesis surely has not been misspent. When you overhear someone down the length of the dinner table mention Paul Éluard, you can lean abruptly forward and say, "Ahem." You will have much to discuss.

P.M. Can't we talk about pyrotechnics? Tell me about their history. Is it true that the Chinese invented fireworks?

Alas, it is not clear. For years that was thought to be the case. Alan St. Hill Brock, a member of the great Brock dynasty of pyrotechnicians in England and the author of a history of fireworks, had a theory that a Chinese cook toiling in a field kitchen in ancient times happened to mix together those most common of ingredients—sulfur, charcoal, and potassium nitrate, or saltpeter, as it is more commonly known. Brock picked a cook because all these elements are found around a kitchen fire—saltpeter as a salt substitute, sulfur as a flammable solid, and, of course, charcoal from charred wood. The cook noticed that, when ignited, the pile burned with a combustible force considerably more hearty than the burning of a bunch of sticks. Furthermore, the cook, or whoever, discovered that when these ingredients were enclosed, say in a length of bamboo stopped up at both ends, the combination exploded rather than burned . . . producing a loud report perfect for frightening off spirits, celebrating weddings, battle victories, eclipses of the moon, and the beginning of the New Year, and so forth. The mixture (its chemical notation is KNO_3) is what we know as gunpowder.

But what the Chinese did not figure out at that start, apparently, was how to use gunpowder to fire a projectile out of a barrel.

P.M. Who was responsible for that?

Gunpowder for use in a gun was supposedly (according to Brock) perfected at Freiburg im Breisgau, Germany, in the thirteenth century, by a Franciscan monk named Berthold Schwarz, also known as Black Berthold, or often the "Powder Monk." He is said to have made his discovery while trying to invent a type of gold paint. I have seen an illustration of Berthold at work in his laboratory dressed in his monk's habit *just* at the moment of "Eureka!"—starting back in alarm from an erupting mortar which has just tossed a pestle in the air. The figure of the devil, smiling vaguely, hands crossed at his chest, is in the background looking on.

Although the burghers of Freiburg im Breisgau have celebrated their native son by erecting a statue to him in the town square, many authorities consider him a fraud. J. R. Partington, a British professor of chemistry, in his monumental *History of Greek Fire and Gunpowder,* thought that the "Powder Monk" was invented by someone who for some reason wished to place the origin of gunpowder and cannon in Germany—the "Powder Monk" never existed. Partington believes that gunpowder was known to the Chinese by the end of the Mongol Yüan dynasty (A.D. 1206–1368) and was used specifically at the Mongol siege of the city of Kai-feng Fu, the capital of Honan, where the Chinese were described as defending their city with "arrows of flying fire."

But no one knows for sure. Almost every medieval nation takes credit for the marriage of gunpowder and the gun—the English, French, Turks, even the Hindus.

P.M. When did the Chinese figure out that you could use gunpowder to shoot a bullet?

There is a rather touching account of the Dutch sailing up the Pearl River in the sixteenth century toward what is now Canton. They were met by a flotilla of Chinese junks crowded to the gunwales with wizards shouting imprecations and shooting off fireworks, which they felt should have done the trick and driven the intruders away. The Dutch, very likely roaring with laughter, eventually touched off a cannon. The cannonball went skipping up the river toward the Chinese, dimpling the water as it came, and aboard the junks all the shouting and snapping of firecrackers and the puffing of balls of fire from the bamboo tubes stopped abruptly. There was silence on the river, except for the reverberating of the Dutch cannon, and then I've always imagined one of the wizards slapping his brow and saying, "Hau-aa!" the Chinese equivalent of "Ah-ha!" or "Oh-ho!", realizing just then as he watched the cannonball disappear upriver what ramifications had been missed with their invention.

P.M. That is a very sad story.

Well, the Chinese were really not *that* innocent. With their invention they built incendiary bombs fired from catapults into towns, and the defenders in those towns dropped similar devices off the parapets onto the attackers be-

BERTHOLD, SCHVVARTZ,

A portrait of Berthold Schwarz shows the "Powder Monk" at work in his alchemist's laboratory. (The Granger Collection)

low. And once they saw cannon, the Chinese were very quick to adapt. Guess who helped them cast their first cannons—the Jesuits!

And then, the Chinese, being identified with the invention and first use of gunpowder, were obviously its first victims. An early sixteenth-century legend tells the tale of Wan-hu, an inventor who built a rocket-vehicle consisting of two kites, a propelling mechanism made up of forty-two rockets, and a seat for himself. When the rockets were fired simultaneously, the kites, the seat, and Mr. Wan-hu all disappeared without a trace in a loud explosion!

P.M. That is also a sad story.

Fireworks are full of such things. But let us say as follows: that black powder was discovered quite likely in the East, where it was used ceremonially, much as fireworks are today. Then it became increasingly involved, es-

FOLLOWING PAGES *A mock battle designed by French fireworks master Abraham Fabert, complete with airborne, fire-breathing dragons, girandoles, and fire-touched swords, took place in front of Sainte Chapelle in Paris during the seventeenth century. (Roger-Viollet)*

pecially in the West, in Europe, with military usage—first with rocketry, and then with guns. There may have been a cannon or two at the battle of Crécy (1346). In the 1500s, armies began to have their gunpowder specialists. They were rather shunned people. Gunpowder did not travel at all well. Its bouncing on the back of a mule tended to separate the components, with the saltpeter, the heaviest component, sinking to the bottom of the cask. So the powders had to be mixed on the field of battle—hardly the safest of places to do such a thing, not only for the mixers but also for anyone who happened to be passing by, friend or foe—so the gunpowder specialist was a man not only to avoid but traditionally a repugnant and somewhat feared figure. What he did was beneath dignity. Most were not even professional soldiers, but were specialists referred to—and one would have to assume in a derogatory way—as "artists." In fact, the French used civilian "artists" in their artillery complexes up until about 1800.

About the only pleasant time these beleaguered people enjoyed was when a victory had to be celebrated. The custom was to do that with fireworks. As far back as 1532, Charles V, the ruler of the Holy Roman Empire, had "fireworkers" in his army whose particular function was to put on victory displays. The emperor was a timid man—known for his great fear of mice and spiders—and, though he was a brave warrior, one imagines him taking much more pleasure in the victory fireworks than in the hair-raising seesaw proceedings of battle that led to the celebration.

P.M. How did you know he was scared of mice?

I read that somewhere. I can tell you almost nothing else about Charles V. It's the sort of thing—that business about the mice and spiders—that refuses to rid itself from my mind. Peter the Great, who was almost seven feet tall, was petrified of cockroaches. Why can't I forget that and simply remember that he was a great fireworks fancier?

P.M. Which he was?

Absolutely. He designed the fireworks show that celebrated the treaty and final peace after twenty-one years of war with Charles XII of Sweden. He often lit the fireworks himself; indeed, he initiated the ceremony of setting off fireworks on New Year's Eve. Apparently, he simply *loved* noise. He dined in the blare of military bands. Once, when Catherine, his consort, had secretly built a country home for him fifteen miles from St. Petersburg, she arranged that when she raised her glass to toast the master of the new house, at the *exact* second the glass touched his lips, eleven cannon hidden in the garden would suddenly boom out just beyond the french windows. She knew he would like that.

Some authorities believe that the tsar's delight with loud noises may have been formed during his earliest moments: when he was born (on May 30, 1672), for three days, starting at one o'clock in the morning, not only were cannon fired from the Kremlin walls, but every great bell in the city pealed

This seventeenth-century French engraving shows the kind of "machine" that artificiers used on water—which they chose not only for reasons of safety but also because their displays were enhanced by the reflections. (Roger-Viollet)

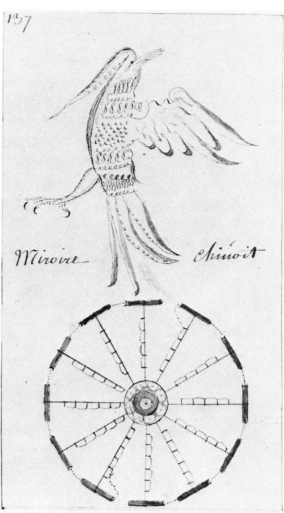

On occasion the master pyrotechnists recorded their "recipes" for fireworks. This title page of a French recipe book, left, is dedicated to Colbert, a minister in the court, by the artificier *or fireworks master to a royal artillery regiment. Right, shows his design for a* miroire chinoit *from which this stylized bird will soar. (Courtesy, Hagley Museum and Library, Wilmington, Delaware)*

incessantly . . . an awesome din, since Moscow at that time had sixteen hundred churches. As a young man Peter played the drums. He enjoyed shooting off salvos of artillery. He especially enjoyed experimenting with elaborate and often dangerous fireworks. During the celebration of his son Alexis's birth in 1690 he put on a display which lasted for five hours during which a five-pound rocket fell back to earth and killed a distinguished Russian nobleman. The tragedy did not seem to deter the tsar's enthusiasm for fireworks in the *slight*est, either at the time of the show (the boyar was simply removed and the display went on) or in the future: he kept perfecting his pyrotechnical displays, including elaborate set pieces. In 1693, introduced by a fifty-six-cannon salute, he put on a huge fireworks scenario which included a fiery portrait of Hercules prying open the jaws of a lion. Oh yes, his great passion was fireworks. And dwarfs.

P.M. You certainly have a lot of technical facts at your fingertips. How do you remember all this stuff?

Notes. You'll notice that I am constantly fidgeting with these scraps of paper spread out here on the table. There are only one or two things about fireworks that truly I have memorized thoroughly.

P.M. Such as Charles V's fear of mice.

Exactly. And also you can ask me the formula for a firework known as "the snake." It's a little black pellet. When you light it, it magically grows into a vague replica of a serpent. It has various names—"Pharaoh's serpent egg," being one of them, I recall.

P.M. What is the formula for a "Pharaoh's serpent egg"?

I'm glad you asked. It is $(NH_4)_2Cr_2O_7$. I have always wanted someone, unprompted, to ask me that. I have written the formula down on a tablecloth hoping the person opposite would ask, "Hey, what's that interesting-looking thing you've written down there?" Instead, they always say, "We're going to be late for the movie. Oughtn't we to go?"

P.M. You mentioned when you were urging me to do my thesis on fireworks that Louis XIV built Versailles because of a fireworks show.

I may have been pressing my case just a bit. But it's true that in 1661 Louis XIV—he was a young man then—was invited to an extraordinary housewarming party given by his finance minister, Nicolas Fouquet, at Vaux-le-Vicomte near Fontainebleau. Very famous evening. Fouquet invited six thousand people, fed them all an incredible feast, gave away such gifts as diamond tiaras and saddle horses, and entertained them with ballets and fireworks—this at a time when the young king was selling off his own belongings to help finance his armies. For misuse of the public funds Fouquet was clapped in jail. Did you know that he was one of the candidates for the true identity of the Man in the Iron Mask? But apparently the king's greatest impression from the evening at Vaux was to give him an idea of what Versailles *could* become. He removed a lot of the material things at Vaux—tapestries, paintings, ornaments, statues, and over a thousand orange trees that he set about Versailles in silver boxes—but, more important, he also took the artisans who had been responsible for Vaux . . . Le Nôtre, the landscape genius, Le Vau, the architect, Le Brun, the overall artist, the chef who had fed all those battalions of knights; and surely he took the grand vizier, Vigarini, who had been responsible for the fireworks. These people all went to work

Louis XIV instituted a tradition of fireworks in the gardens of Versailles. During the summer of 1676, displays went on for five consecutive evenings. This engraving depicts the spectacle that took place on the fifth night of the event—aquatic fireworks in the Canal and rockets bursting over a tall, stately obelisk in honor of the French king. Authorities have suggested that the squiggly lines in these engravings represent the aerial shells, the time fuses turning as the shells rise, whereas the straighter lines trace the paths of the rockets. (Roger-Viollet)

on the little "card castle" built by his father, Louis XIII, at Versailles and they made it one of the masterpieces of civilization. All because of a lovely spray of rocket tails.

P.M. I see what you mean by pressing your case.

Well, certainly fireworks became one of the major distractions at Versailles. By 1664, Vigarini was happily at the peak of his career. That year, for example, he provided the climactic scene of a huge festival entitled "The Pleasures of the Enchanted Isle" to which Louis XIV invited six hundred guests. These people enjoyed a three-day program of banquets, ballets, theatrical comedies by Molière, music by Lully . . . all this leading up to a pyrotechnical battle between three sea monsters, an illumination of the Palace of Enchantment by fireworks, and the eventual eruption in an upward flare of pyrotechnics of the entire island! Very grand stuff indeed.

Heavens! Time itself was announced by fireworks at Versailles at one period. There was a kind of sundial in the maze off the King's Garden equipped with a magnifying glass, and when the sun reached the meridian its beams ignited a lifting charge under a maroon, which went up into the noon sky and exploded.

P.M. You mentioned Vigarini. Were most of the pyrotechnicians Italian?

Almost invariably. For example, the best-known name in French fireworks today is Italian in origin—Ruggieri—just as, equivalently, in America, the Gruccis, the Zambellis, the Rozzis are among the most famous fireworks firms. The Ruggieris have been in France for centuries. Originally from Bologna, the family settled itself in Monteux. The patriarch of the family, Claude-Fortuné Ruggieri, was an early experimenter with rockets. In Paris he staged a number of displays in which mice and rats were sent aloft by rockets and came down under little parachute canopies. Imagine the terror of sitting out having lunch in the garden of the *pension*—quite unaware of M. Ruggieri's rocket experiments—and having a mouse drift down and land next to you in a parachute harness!

P.M. Think what it would have done to Charles V!

Ruggieri even had plans to send up a small boy attached to a rocket cluster; he too was to be equipped with a parachute, Ruggieri was careful to point out to the authorities, but the French police intervened and this particular experiment was never carried out.

P.M. Were the Italians the only ones involved with fireworks?

From the sixteenth to the eighteenth century, not only Italy but also the German principalities were the two areas of the Continent most noted for their displays. Their pyrotechnical styles tended, though, to be quite different. The Italians emphasized what was called the "machine"—often known as the "temple"—landscaping their shows with elaborate, ornamental structures, usually in the form of buildings, which were decorated with paintings, usually of allegorical figures, flowers, and lamps which were cut out in silhouette to glow from behind. Fountains were also constructed, set about with statues of fantastic animals. Very rococo and romantic. One of the pleasures of going to a fireworks show was to inspect the machine, as one might go on a modern-day "house tour."

The main reason for the emphasis on the machine in the early days of fireworks history was that the artisans did not have very much to work with for their fireworks—sulfur, saltpeter, charcoal, antimony, and few varieties of zinc and iron filings—amber was the primary color—which was why so much effort went into the intricacies and ingenuity of the machines themselves. Some of the machines were truly immense.

Let me scrabble around in this pile. Somewhere I have a picture of a typical machine. Ah, here we are:

(Roger-Viollet)

This elaborate wedding-cake structure was built for a display of fireworks for Louis XIV. You can see how enormous—as well as ornate—the structure was by noting the scale of the people walking around at its base. The symbol of the Roi Soleil—a cartoon-like sun—is set over the entrance. One of the virtues of the machine was that it was a wonder on its own. There must have been some spectators who preferred the machine to what was eventually, when evening fell, fired from it.

The Germans, on the other hand—of the so-called Northern School, most of them from Nürnberg—tended to rely more on the fireworks themselves. They also had a kind of centerpiece from which the fireworks were displayed, but it was much less elaborate than the machine. Usually it was a large figure made of scaffolding, appropriate to the occasion (a Cupid for a wedding), which was covered with paper with the fireworks themselves inside. When it came time for the display, the device was swung apart, rather like opening a vast steamer trunk, and the fireworks set on the scaffolding inside were ready for firing. The obelisk was a particular favorite since it had no specific meaning and was suitable for any occasion.

One of the most famous graduates of the Northern School was a Swedish soldier-of-fortune named Martin Beckman. He became the "fire master" of England. He designed a number of spectacular shows, including the coronations of James II and Charles II, both on the Thames. Because of his skills, Beckman was a gentleman of considerable substance. He lived in the Tower of London; indeed, one night there he was responsible for the apprehension of Captain Blood when in 1671 that gentleman tried to steal the Crown Jewels; Blood actually had the royal crown under his coat when Beckman tackled him to the ground.

Here is an example of the sort of thing Beckman did. It is a representation of his display for the coronation of James II in 1685. It was performed in front of a great banquet. Apparently the guests, or perhaps the servants, were not of the highest quality. Afterward, it was discovered that much of His Majesty's silverware—including forks, knives, spoons, and saltcellars—was missing. A plaintive advertisement appeared in the London *Gazette* a week or so after. Under an announcement of the missing silverware, it read: "Whoever have found the aforesaid or any part of it, are desired to bring it to His Majesty's Pantry at Whitehall, and they shall be rewarded for their pains."

Actually, the picture shows the influence of both the Northern and the Southern schools. Two obelisks are visible, as well as allegorical figures, including, in the lower-right foreground, Father Thames astride a spouting dolphin leading a long line of cygnets—symbols suggesting the nation's hopes for a fecund monarch.

For someone in Beckman's time the art of pyrotechnics, surprisingly for an art so seemingly haphazard, was highly stylized and formalized. Casimir Simienowicz in *The Great Art of Artillery* (1650) published long essays on proper pyrotechnical etiquette. He explained the exact procedures for celebrating victories, weddings, honoring kings, observing saint's days, and so forth. For example, for coronations, Simienowicz advised that "Princes . . . may be very

A Representation of the FIRE-WORKS upon the River of Thames, over againſt WHITEHALL, at their Majeſties CORONATION A°. 1685.

PATER PATRIÆ · MONARCHIA

(BBC Hulton Picture Library)

Reasonably reminded . . . of the . . . Incertitude of Prosperity, by a Sight of the *Wheel of Fortune.*"

P.M. Do you do this sort of thing in your own choreography? Did you have a Wheel of Fortune in the Inauguration display for Ronald Reagan?

Alas, I had not read Casimir Simienowicz's *The Great Art of Artillery* in time to remind the President in fireworks of the incertitude of prosperity. It might have been appropriate. An aide would have whispered in his ear what the Wheel of Fortune symbolized when it appeared in the show. I doubt the President would have understood it on his own.

But he would have known had he lived in the seventeenth century. The earliest fireworks shows in Europe were not only very carefully planned, they meant something to the audiences in terms of allegory and symbol. Thus the firemaster was in part a theatrical producer.

Allegorical statements were still being made as late as 1814. That year, in Green Park, in London, the principal attraction of a great fireworks show was the Grand Metamorphosis of the Castle of War into the Temple of Concord. After a great amount of pyrotechnic fury and smoke, the machine, a very elaborate structure rather like a fancy top-heavy birthday cake, was revealed as the Temple of Concord, decorated with allegorical paintings lit from within so the crowds could see them in the darkness. The paintings bore such titles as "Peace Restored to Earth."

Charles Lamb saw this display, and I have a note here about what he wrote to William Wordsworth. It will give you some sense of the displays at the turn of the century, really not too far removed from what we have today. "The fireworks were splendid," he reported, "the Rockets in clusters, in trees and all shapes, spreading around like young stars in the making, floundering about in Space, (like unbroken horses) till some of Newton's calculations should fix them."

P.M. What's that about Newton's calculations?

Well, I think that was Lamb's way of suggesting that what goes up must come down . . . even fireworks.

Incidentally, *The Times* of London didn't like that show at all. Its critic wrote in a kind of high moral dudgeon: ". . . the chief fault of the amusement . . . was its insufferable length, in consequence of the wearisome repetition of the same fireworks. Whatsoever is not the subject of reason and sanctioned by its high ordinances cannot bear to be seen often."

P.M. Wasn't the 1981 fireworks show in London to celebrate the wedding of Princess Diana and Prince Charles patterned after a great fireworks show centuries before?

It was indeed—and an ill-fated choice it turned out to be. The authorities should have known better. The original took place in 1749—celebrating the peace treaty signed at Aix-la-Chapelle ending the War of the Austrian Succession. Celebrations took place throughout Europe, though in a number of instances one would hardly call them celebrations. The most horrific one was in Paris—and let me refer to my notes here—where, according to contemporary accounts, "there were forty killed and nearly three hundred wounded by a dispute between the French and the Italians, who, quarreling for precedence in lighting the fires, both lighted at once and blew up the whole."

Incredibly, very much the same sort of thing happened at the English celebration in London. An enormous machine had been built over a four-month period in Green Park. Designed by Cavalieri Servadoni, it was 410 feet in length

Casimir Simienowicz, the Lieutenant General of the Ordnance to the King of Poland and the author of the classic Great Art of Artillery *(1650), designed this Bacchus atop a wine barrel for a wedding celebration. At the appropriate time, this delightful machine would open and the fireworks hidden inside ignite. (Courtesy, Hagley Museum and Library, Wilmington, Delaware)*

The extraordinary sight that greeted spectators at the International Naval Festival at Portsmouth, England, in 1865. The rockets were fired in barrages from the Allied Fleets, their superstructures illuminated, anchored at nearby Spithead. (The Mansell Collection)

and 114 feet high—from which eleven thousand fireworks of different kinds and characteristics were to be fired while Handel's *Music for the Royal Fireworks,* especially composed for the occasion, was to be played.

The fireworks for the great show were made by Gaetano Ruggieri, the Italian forebear of the famous pyrotechnic firm that later settled itself in France. Ruggieri came from Italy with his fireworks. He found he was to share the responsibility of firing the show with a number of others: the firemaster, one Captain Thomas Desaguliers, Charles Frederick, the comptroller of the Woolwich Depot, the Royal Train of Artillery, as well as two professional local pyrotechnicians. All had equal authority. All issued orders at once. Inside the machine the English, this time, got into an argument with the Italians, apparently over the best method of igniting the show, and, while this was going on, an explosion occurred in the North Pavilion, which almost consumed the entire structure. Cavalieri Servadoni became so enraged at the sight of part of his magnificent machine going up in flames that he drew his sword on the first pyrotechnician he could find, Charles Frederick, and was disarmed and arrested as a result. He was taken to the Tower, where in those grim surroundings he apologized and was allowed to go free.

There were a number of other tragedies: a man fell off the machine to his death; a boy tumbled out of a tree and also died; a man lost his balance and fell into a pond where he drowned. Another tragedy was avoided when a quick-witted bystander ripped the clothes off a young girl who had been set afire by a wayward rocket. Horace Walpole, who was a witness, described it: "She would have been destroyed if some person had not the presence of mind to strip her clothes off immediately to her stays and petticoats."

Well, it was *this* frenetic occasion which the authorities decided to copy for the wedding of Prince Charles and Lady Diana. They didn't have the people tumbling out of trees and into the pond, nor the petticoat girl, but they planned the burning of the North Pavilion and an eighteenth-century fire engine to put out the flames. By all accounts, the show was a disaster. The machine was undersized—only 300 feet long and 40 feet high as compared to the original's 410 by 114 feet—and, moreover, it was a two-dimensional structure, described as "a slab of cardboard," rather than the three-dimensional 1749 structure. The critic on the *Evening Standard,* Russell Davies, scored it: Wedding 6, Fireworks 0.

I have some pictures here of the original 1749 display [see next four pages]. The first shows the great machine and the fireworks choreography as it was supposed to look, with the great sun surmounting all. At the Royal Wedding in 1981, the replica of the sun came in for a lot of criticism; it was suspended from a cherry picker, which was perfectly visible behind it, and so was a man turning the sun with a crank, outlined in flame like Loge in *Das Rheingold.* Very bad form, considering that in 1749, over two centuries before, the sun performed on its own.

The original machine was an object of great curiosity. A newspaper account of the time wrote: "the crowds were so numerous . . . that two persons had their arms broke in passing the gate by Buckingham House and several others were much hurt. On the Surrey shore the populace pressed so hard to get in the boat that some were obliged to be thrown overboard to cool their zeal." No wonder the evening was laced with tragedy!

The next picture shows the fire in the north wing. You can spot the fire engines, or what used to be called "water engines" in the eighteenth century. The king and his royal retinue withdrew while this unexpected *divertissement* was going on. It was this episode that the promoters of Prince Charles's wedding thought would be interesting to re-create in 1981, and perhaps it would have been, except that the north wing of the castle refused to burst into flame. A set of antique fire engines suddenly appeared, nonetheless; hoses were waved at a nonexistent fire and then the contingent, as one of the newspapers put it, "mercifully withdrew into the obscurity from which it had appeared."

Many of the twenty-five tons of fireworks which were supposed to go up that night in 1749 were left unexploded. These were either bought or confiscated by the Duke of Richmond, no one is quite sure which, and about

FOLLOWING FOUR PAGES *(BBC Hulton Picture Library)*

A VIEW *of the* FIRE-WORKES *and* ILLVMINATIONS, *at his* GRACE t...
Perform'd by the direction of Charles Frederick

Fix'd Sun.

Regulated Piece of 5 Mutations.

Tritons.

Vertical Wheel.

Spirals with Horisontal Wheel.

Vertical Sun.

Battery of Marons.

Pots d'Aigretts with Fountains

No 1. Pavillon beautifully illuminated.
2. The Duke of Richmonds House.
3. The Boats and Barges for the Aquatic Fire-workes.
A. His Majestys Barge.

Vûe des FEUX d'ARTIFICE et des ILLUMINATION...
sùr la TAMISE, et vis a vis de son I...

of RICHMONDS at WHITE HALL and on the River Thames, on Monday 15 May, 1749.

Corded Mortars with Air Ballons
D.° with Saucissons.

Flights of Sky Rocketts

Pots de Brin.

Water Rocketts.

Jatte d'eau.

Water Ballons
with 3 Stages of Lights

Vertical Illumination

...cés par Monseigneur le Duc de RICHMOND de LENOX et d'AUBIGNY.
Lundi le 15.ieme de Mai 1749. Sous la direction de Mons. Frederick.
à Londre.

1. Le Pavillon magnifiquement Illuminé.
2. L'Hotel de Monsig.r Le Duc de Richmond.
3. Les Bateaux employées aux Feux d'artifices Aquatique.
4. Barque de sa Majesté.

three weeks later he invited an intimate group of friends to a garden party at Whitehall on the Thames where he had them set off. The picture on pages 46–47 shows what an extraordinary event it must have been. Horace Walpole, who was among the guests, was moved to write: "Whatever you hear of the fireworks, that is short of the prettiest entertainment in the world, don't believe it; I have never passed a more agreeable evening."

P.M. What were the colors one saw in the sky in the early days of fireworks?

Up until the 1830s the colors were fairly limited—mostly tails of burning charcoal and iron filings—amber-like colors. Zinc metal powders produced a greenish blue. Eight parts of saltpeter and one part each of sulfur and antimony produced a whitish color with a blue tinge to it. Potassium chlorate was established as an ingredient in the 1840s, and after that, color advancement was swift, with blue being the last shade to be added to the spectrum.

P.M. Why haven't great painters been associated with fireworks? I don't mean painting them but designing displays.

Well, some have. Bernini. Michelangelo. According to Vasari's biography of Leonardo da Vinci, the artist created a great lion which was designed to walk a few steps, roar, and then out of its chest a display of flowers and birds would burst—all of this done largely with the use of various types of fireworks. Vasari mentions that this odd beast was "to be compared with any of the great accomplishments by this Master Artist."

P.M. Are there great differences in a country's fireworks?

Each nation's shells have their own characteristics. The French are famous for the preciseness and depth of their colors, and the careful aesthetics of their multi-break shells. They make wonderful Roman candles. The Brazilians, well, their fireworks are remarkably sharp in color (especially blue) and full of novelty, with stars that dart and change color; the best Canadian shells are the willows—long thick-tendriled descents of spray, usually of magnesium, that bloom in the sky with just the smallest puff of an explosion. Lovely! The most interesting British shells are the hummingbirds—streaks of light that zip helter-skelter in the sky with a thin, high whistle; Americans specialize in multi-break shells that give birth to one cluster after another as the shell falls, the crowds on the slopes of the hills counting the bursts, ". . . one, two, three . . ." Italian shells usually incorporate noise, a great deal of noise. At Italian feast-day celebrations nothing pleases the guests at the long tables set out under the trees as much as an evening of cannonading with maroons, aerial bombs that go off with a bright, noisy flash. "Don't worry too much about color. Think *bombardment!*"—*that* is the Italian feast-day dictum for pyrotechnicians.

The shells from the Orient are round rather than cylindrical. When they break open they fling out a quick thistle-like radial burst of stars very much like the spread of peonies or chrysanthemums, which indeed the shells have come to be named after. A fancy Japanese shell of that variety will have a tag on which is handwritten in spidery script: "Twice Color Changing Chrysanthemum with Pistils, Silver Tail and Ascending Comets."

The names of Oriental shells are even fancier at their place of origin. In China, shells have such splendidly evocative names as "Golden Monkey Plays an Umbrella," "Dragon Chasing a Bull, with Silver Rain and Thunder" or "Monkeys Invade the Heavenly Palace and Chase Out the Tiger." Sadly, such fancy names do not usually survive in the United States. Charles Anderson, a major importer, told me that he thought the names were too exotic for home consumption. That one about the monkeys invading the palace had been changed to "Sky Monkeys." Some of them had been all right. There was one called "Flower Scattering Child" that survived importation.

P.M. Well, I should hope so. It's too bad we don't have titles to help show us what's going on up there.

I'm afraid that imagination counts a bit more than those titles. Seeing that particular Sky Monkey shell, I don't think you'd jump up and say, "Oh, look there go the monkeys! And, see, there's the tiger!" Incidentally, I have always thought that would be a wonderful position to retire to—thinking up names for Oriental fireworks shells. You'd become a specialist and travel around to different fireworks factories in China; at night you'd sit in a bamboo chair in the middle of a field with a notebook on your knee and they'd send up these great chrysanthemums for you to name. You'd say, "I'm not inspired. Send up another one just like the last." So they'd do that, and after some pondering you'd write down "The Great Frog Leaps Off the Lily Pad and Frightens Ten Silver Minnows" or "The Blue Ox Comes Down the Turnpike." I'm getting carried away. Ask me another question.

P.M. Are you really the fireworks commissioner of New York City?

It is, I'm afraid, a bogus title. There is no such position on the city rolls. I am not even a dollar-a-year man. I invented the position during John Lindsay's tenure as mayor. Being unable to accept a post in his administration, I was asked what I'd like to do; I told the mayor blithely that I'd like to be his fireworks commissioner. He agreed, possibly because there is no such thing; and, feeling as if I had been tapped lightly on the shoulder by a sword, I rose and left Gracie Mansion with a strong sense of mission. I have stayed on. As you know, all commissioners are required to send in a letter of resignation upon changes of administration. I do not do so. I have rationalized that to resign from a position that does not exist would throw City Hall into confusion, so I usually write them that I am sorry but I am refusing to resign.

P.M. Doesn't that put quite a strain on City Hall to receive this stubborn note?

It doesn't appear so. They've never written back. In any case, it's a position I relish. If anyone says, "Commissioner!" or indeed anything like it, I tend to wheel around.

P.M. What are the duties of the so-called fireworks commissioner?

Promote, promote, promote! Ticker-tape parades and feathery plumes from fireboats have always been New York City's traditional celebratory devices. I would like to add fireworks in a big way to the repertoire. I see myself calling the authorities to say, "Did I not read in the *Times* this morning that the King of Thailand will be passing through on the way to a vacation in the Grand Tetons? Should this not be heralded by a fireworks display off the Cloisters?" That sort of thing.

P.M. Can one take a solid diet of fireworks, night after night?

It's true that some authorities think that fireworks can be too much of a good thing. Reminiscing about the fireworks of his youth in fifteenth-century Siena, Vannoccio Biringuccio observed that fireworks were not only expensive but also "endured no longer than the kiss of a lover for his lady, if as long . . . and thus should be reserved only for very special occasions of rejoicing." I am not of that school. I tend to side with the Maltese, who set off fireworks at the slightest pretext. Their use should be constant. After all, to borrow the analogy of the kiss, it has been my experience that one forgets what it was like very quickly, and has to try it again almost immediately. I'm surprised at il signor Biringuccio, and an Italian, too!

P.M. You were saying the other day that fireworks have often been used to symbolize romance and love . . .

Well, I was thinking especially of Hollywood directors, who have on occasion used fireworks to illustrate the consummation of a love affair. Do you remember Cary Grant and Grace Kelly in *To Catch a Thief,* their union symbolized by a great crash of fireworks outside their balcony overlooking the harbor of Monte Carlo? The only thing wrong with that scenario, it has always seemed to me, is that any normal couple would be out on the balcony enjoying the fireworks, and not inside tumbling around on a bed.

In New York a couple of winters ago, I tried to use fireworks to help a cousin of mine, Fred, who was having a *crise de coeur.* Fred was desperate over a young woman who had, I believe, an eye for someone else. Things were not going at all well. I called him one day and said I had something in mind that was sure to impress her. I had organized a display of Chinese aerial shells to help celebrate the opening of an exhibition at the Metropolitan Museum. The fireworks were planned to go off at exactly nine-thirty from the meadow behind the museum. My suggestion was that my cousin should be ambling along Fifth Avenue just at nine-thirty, perhaps arm in arm with his date, so that he could glance down at his watch. At exactly nine-thirty he should prepare some appropriate thing to say ("Tina, I have put together a little surprise for you . . . just to show you how much I feel about you . . .") because I promised him that precisely then, *whoosh,* a curtain of Chinese shells would rise from just behind the museum, their bouquets high above bathing the avenue in pale rose. There had been no publicity about the display so it would come as a complete surprise. Very likely, the girl, whatever her feelings, would have had to say *something* . . . like, "Oh, Fred, you shouldn't have done it!"

The timing was off. At first, Fred, late himself, hurried the girl to Fifth Avenue somewhat against her will ("What are we going *there* for?—it's cold"); once there he wondered if perhaps the fireworks had already gone off. Finally, he asked a passerby, "Has anything, er, gone on here?"

The pedestrian gave him a startled look and hurried by.

"Fred, what in God's name are we doing out here?"

"What time is it?" he asked.

"What *is* wrong with you?"

Just then, the barrage went up. It had been delayed five minutes or so by the Museum officials. At the rush of sound from the darkness of the park, Fred's date started abruptly. The heel of her shoe went over on the cobblestones of the pavement, straining her ankle slightly, and she let out a sharp exclamation of pain. She was looking down at her foot as the fireworks began to blossom above. She asked to be taken home so she could get an ice pack on her ankle.

Fred was never able to convince her that there was any connection ("the little surprise") between their being in front of the Museum on that cold winter's night and the fireworks show. "The way my luck was going," Fred told me, "even if she hadn't hurt her ankle, we would have gone to a discothèque and she would have sprained it *there!*"

P.M. That is a sad story too.

It was probably all for the best. Anyone who cannot shake off the pain of a sprained ankle and enjoy a flight of Chinese shells probably isn't worth the pursuing.

P.M. What is the future of fireworks in the country? What do you think will happen?

The great change will be, I'm sure, in the choreography. The older generation of fireworks people used to say that the industry was a very simple one: "You make the fireworks in the winter and shoot 'em up in the summer"—that is to say that on the Fourth of July both professionals and amateurs simply reached for the next device at hand in the box and set it off. About the only consistent choice in the professional shows was that the biggest shell in the box was always the last to go up, and then, of course, it was time to light the American flag set piece, or the one that wrote out *Good Night* so that everyone knew the moment had come to pack up the blanket, collect the children, and head for home.

But in the future, the artist will become far more involved. With electrical firing, he will work at establishing extraordinary patterns and effects in the sky, until finally spectators will recognize fireworks for what they could well be described as—an eighth art. And that will mean we'll see a lot more of them! Perhaps every Tuesday night. Surely during the summer. And perhaps even through the winter!

I will tell you one more sad story. A few years ago I went to see Charles Revson, the great cosmetics tycoon. I had a tremendous concept about fireworks for him, so I thought. I was ushered into his penthouse apartment. It overlooked Central Park. The room was quite dark, I remember, but the curtains had not been drawn so that one looked out on the park and the lights of the West Side beyond. He was a very elderly gentleman. He sat in a deep leather chair opposite me with an aide standing to one side with an open notebook and a pencil poised.

I started out by saying that I had come to talk to him about fireworks and a far-flung campaign for his empire.

"Oh yes," he said.

"The point is, sir," I said, "that the night sky is essentially rather boring. It is *very* boring when it is cloudy and moonless, because frankly—"

"There's nothing much to look at," Mr. Revson said, nodding from his chair.

"Exactly. Even when the cloud cover lifts, there's not all that much to relish—the stars, of course, but they're small and never surprise you by being out of position, or doing anything interesting. They simply persist. Planets—"

"What about the moon?" asked the old gentleman, somewhat wearily, I sensed.

"Yes, but the moon," I said, "while grand, especially when full, is also predictable; it's worth not more than a minute or two of concentrated gazing. It shows only one side of itself. Shooting stars turn up every once in a while, but even the Pleiades showers in August are thin and haphazard. The constellations are too difficult to figure out. The Southern Cross is an enormous disappointment. Satellites behave like the navigational lights of extremely small slow-moving airplanes. Comets are not at all what they look like in children's books, and besides, the great ones only turn up every 150 years or so. So the point is that the night sky—"

At this point there was an interruption—a soft tap on the door. The aide looked up from the pad on which he had written nothing. He moved silently to the door where a message of some sort was whispered to him; he returned, blank-faced. Mr. Revson would apparently be told later.

I said: "My feeling is that the situation up there could be improved. The idea is to think of the night sky as a kind of canvas waiting for somebody to work on it. Your empire, Mr. Revson, which is dedicated to beautification and cosmetics, could graduate from the human face"—I winced at this awkward bluntness—"and move on"—I pointed up—"to the heavens themselves!"

I coughed. "What I thought, sir, was that Revlon could sponsor, every week, a big fireworks show out of the Central Park reservoir here in New York."

"Fireworks out of the reservoir?" He sounded astonished.

"They'd be fired off barges, sir. Revlon Night, perhaps every Tuesday in summer, would become a tradition in New York. I see no reason why, under the sponsorship of Revlon, fireworks shows could not spread across the country—caravans of them, moving across the landscape like old-time circuses or road shows—pulling into town on a summer afternoon with the word everywhere that the *Revlon fireworks people have come to town!* That might be a nice, catchy slogan: *Revlon's come to town!* In the evening the municipal park would fill up with people carrying food baskets, and guitars, and along about nine o'clock, the mayor would get up on the bandstand to thank Revlon, and then behind him, just as his last words were dying away, the first shell of the evening would thump up to start beautifying the night sky, trailing a thin tail of sparks after it. At the end of the show, the letters *R E V-L O N* would hang in the sky briefly. People would cheer the name. TV broadcasters would mention the event on the evening broadcasts. Then, on the show would move to the next town. Sir," I said to Mr. Revson, "you would become America's commissar of fireworks."

I gave all this, as they say, quite a reading. But it didn't seem to elicit any sort of response, even from the man standing there with the pencil. He never moved it. The awful thought crossed my mind that perhaps I had the wrong Mr. Revson, that perhaps this gentleman was the head of an automobile accessories company—mufflers or something . . .

P.M. You've gone quiet on me. What happened then?

Well, I finally took my leave. Mr. Revson didn't say so, but it was perfectly obvious he thought I was completely daft.

In the United States the fireworks families are almost invariably Italian in origin—the Zambellis, who settled in New Castle, Pennsylvania; the Gruccis in Bellport, New York; the Rozzis in Loveland, Ohio, among the best known. Oddly, there has never been love lost between fireworks companies. The competition is intense. In the old days, the wives, armed with shotguns, would patrol the mortar lines to scare off rivals who might sneak in to cut or tamper with the fuses—their hope to disrupt the show in the chance of getting the contract the next year.

The "boss" or patriarch of a family regarded his pyrotechnic formulas, or what are quaintly known as "recipes," as secrets to be closely guarded. Though he probably never knew the chemical notations in the first place, if asked he often would give the chemicals the wrong names and percentages— just in case "spies" had been sent around by his competitors. One wonders if an especially unscrupulous fireworks manufacturer might not leave a spurious but combustible combination of chemicals on a notepad, just lying around in the hope it would be swiped and a competitor's factory would go up in a detonation as a result.

The fireworks clan I came to know best were the Gruccis. They lived near New York in Bellport, Long Island, and fired most of the shows in and around Manhattan. Sometimes they let me help them plan a display; I would visit the compound and sit around and talk about fireworks. They knew I had friends from other families in the fireworks field. Sometimes I'd get a quizzical look. "You ever met any of the Zambellis?"

The patriarch of the family, Felix Grucci, was born in 1905; he looks twenty years younger than his age—a full, sleek crop of black hair, a strong, somewhat high gravelly voice with a faint Italian inflection, though in fact he does not speak the language of his forebears. He has nothing to show for the danger of being in the explosives business but a missing fingertip and the slightest of hearing impediments; on occasion he cocks his head to hear bet-

This highly complex control panel strung with wires for electric firing contrasts sharply with earlier methods of hand-fired shows dating from the sixteenth century. Here, members of the Grucci family, Butch, Jimmy, and Felix, Sr., discuss final plans with the author for a fireworks display in New York City's Central Park. (Photo © Ken Clark, 1978)

ter. His favorite expression has always been, "Things aren't what they were, I'm telling you." In the compound he would take me off to look at the electric control panels which are used to fire displays automatically; he never put his hands on them that I ever saw, or ever touched a switch. He would motion at them, and shake his head somberly. "Look at this! I'm telling you, things aren't what they were."

The Grucci family came from a town in Apulia, on the Adriatic side, named Bari, "which the best fireworks people came from—the *very* best," Felix told me. His mother had fired shows on feast days and had won a prize from the king of Italy for a fireworks spectacle carried up in a balloon. One of the family legends was that the exodus of the Gruccis to the United States was hastened by the complaints of neighbors harassed by the constant noise of explosions and whose hens—so they said—refused to lay eggs as a result.

The first Grucci shop was set up in Hagerman, a town on Long Island which is now called East Patchogue. Felix was fourteen at the time. All the work was done outside, with just about everything, including fuses, flares—what were called "parade torches"—lances, and the paper casings made on the premises. Other than the Fourth of July, the jobs were usually feast days: St. Anthony, St. Liberata, Our Lady of Mount Carmel. The day started with an effigy of the saint being carried through the Italian neighborhood, and the *patroni* coming down the porch steps to pin money to the saint's clothing to help pay for the festivities. The parade ended in a nearby field, with the tents up, and the long tables, and the fireworks to come later in the day. The fireworks were largely flights of salutes with the Italian burghers pounding their fists among the plates and wineglasses and shouting for more noise.

For five hundred dollars, the feast-day audiences got ten ground pieces, about twenty aerial shells—four to six inches in diameter—and then a finale rack made up of ninety-six three- and four-inch shells. To light the shells, the Gruccis used strips of burlap bag twisted into a cigar-like shape which when ignited would smolder; if twirled in the wind or blown upon, the strip—which was called a "stuppine" in Italian—would glow sufficiently to ignite a fuse.

In the Depression years Felix went down to Florida with his uncle to see if they could make a go of things. "We did little shows here and there around Miami," he told me. "We did one at the Kennel Club which Al Capone saw. He sent for us and said *he* wanted one."

"Was he specific about what he wanted?" I asked.

"Oh yes," Felix said. "He wanted ten ground pieces—wheel-turners and pinwheels, a palm tree made of lances, and then he wanted a set piece of two dogs racing. He was crazy about the dog track. We were going to suggest a Statue of Liberty set piece, but my uncle and I didn't think it was very appropriate."

"No," I agreed. "I doubt patriotic themes were high on his list."

Felix suddenly asked: "You don't think I'm going to get into any trouble telling you this about Capone?"

I assured him that it had all happened nearly fifty years before.

"You can't be too sure about these people," Felix said. "They worshipped him down there," he went on, almost as if to be on the safe side. "He'd send his people around to the Italian stores in Little River to buy them out of everything on their shelves, and then distribute the stuff to the poor."

"Did you have any aerial shells for his show?" I asked.

"We had fifteen or twenty aerial bombs," Felix said. "And then we had six racks with seventy-two shells in them for the finale. It was a good show—worth about two or three thousand dollars, which was a lot of money in those days when anywhere along Biscayne Bay you could buy coffee and a couple of fried eggs for fifteen cents."

"Was Capone wearing a white fedora?" I asked.

Felix looked puzzled.

Felix Grucci (left) and the Grucci clan (above) of the famous Bellport, Long Island, family. (Woodfin Camp & Associates, © John Marmaras, 1980)

"A hat," I continued. "I never can think of Capone's head without a hat on it, a white one, even indoors."

"It *was* indoors where my uncle and I talked with him, but he wasn't wearing a hat. He had his people standing around. Some of them were wearing hats, and probably guns too. Capone said to me, 'You get the permit to shoot the show and I'll do you good.' But we couldn't get the permit. We saw all these officials. The mayor. But something was up. The Feds had their eye on him. You know what I think?" Felix asked, leaning forward, "I think that right in the middle of the fireworks show—all that noise—Capone was going to have some poor guys bumped off."

"Who?" I asked.

"Listen," he said conspiratorially, "when that gang was killed in that garage up there in Chicago on Valentine's Day, Capone wanted an alibi. That's a pretty good alibi—to have a big fireworks show going up when you want your guys to bump somebody off in another town."

In 1931, Felix and his uncle left Florida and returned to New York. They settled their fireworks firm in Bellport. Situated in a large compound near the railroad tracks, the firm has slowly prospered; indeed, the names the company has given itself since the 1930s would suggest its increasing stature: originally it was called Suffolk Novelty Fireworks Co., then Pyrotechnics Products; after that, New York Pyrotechnics Products, followed by International Pyrotechnics, and finally, most recently, after considerable family discussion, it was decided to follow the lead of fashion designers—"Ties by Sulka," and so forth—and now one refers to the company as "Fireworks by Grucci." That is how the family members answer the phone at the compound.

The complex is typical of the fireworks compounds I have seen. It consists of twenty-five separate workshops. For safety's sake the workshops stand apart from each other by thirty yards or so, each brightly painted in white with red trimming. At the side of every entrance is a copper plate set in the outside wall which everyone who enters the building must touch in order to ground themselves and thus eliminate the chance that a spark might jump from one's person to the worktables. The procedure becomes an ingrained habit. In winter, of course, the danger of static electricity increases sharply. Apparently, women tend to carry more electricity than men. They are never allowed to brush or comb their hair on the job. The rules at the Grucci compound are that no one can ever wear silk underwear.

About two thousand shells a week are made at what the Gruccis call "the shop"—ranging from two-inch to twelve-inch. A twelve-inch shell takes about fifteen man-hours to make—including the five hours of the finishing process of drying and curing.

Fourteen employees, many of them Gruccis, work in the compound at various stages of fireworks manufacture. Fifty family members, five generations of Gruccis, are involved in varying degrees in the business. Many of them, who have other jobs, are called in to help during the heavy demands of the Fourth of July. It would be hard to imagine marrying into the Grucci clan without taking on an all-consuming passion with fireworks.

In the spring of 1978, Felix (Butch) Grucci, Jr., the younger of the patriarch's two sons, got married to a pretty girl, Madelene, from Rocky Point, Long Island, about fifteen miles from Bellport. I was asked to attend. The ceremony was scheduled for the early afternoon. I asked if there would be fireworks. Of *course,* there'd be fireworks. The Grucci males performed as ushers, about eight of them, wearing velvet cutaways, ruffled dress shirts, and large, black-felt top hats that all seemed a half size too large, and were kept from sliding down to the bridge of the nose only by the barriers of the eyebrows, so that, afterward, in the formal wedding photographs, everyone seems to be peering out from under lids. All of the ushers carried ebony canes.

I had hoped that when the newlyweds emerged from the church, the Gruccis would fire off some daytime fireworks which at that time I had never seen. The Japanese are famous for them—a shell that goes up and releases varicolored puffs or ribbons of smoke, or a stream of flags drifting down from parachutes. Sophisticated models spew out paper replicas which, cleverly weighted around the base, balloon out into recognizable shapes as they descend—elephants, buffaloes, giraffes, samurai, boxers, and so forth. The Gruccis had planned to fire off something of this sort—they had a few of these shells in their warehouses—but apparently the fire marshal of Rocky Point was not sympathetic to the notion of giraffes or buffaloes or anything else drifting down into his precinct. He was persuaded to allow "just a salute or two," surely not aware that what the Gruccis meant by that innocent request was going to sound more like an artillery barrage.

The Gruccis arrived with a few racks of salutes—that is to say, shells which go up and perform in loud reports. Japanese fireworks brochures speak of salutes as being useful for "invigorating" a crowd. The racks were set up behind the athletic field next to the church. Just as the wedding party appeared at the church door after the ceremony, I happened to notice a jogger out on the athletic track. He was just coming around the curve, middle-aged, bouncing along in a gray sweat suit, running easily, but puffing slightly, noticing the crowd coming out of the church door, marveling perhaps at the big black top hats and the ebony canes, and then behind him—it must have seemed just aft of his eardrums—the sharp, concussive reports of the salutes began to go off. He jumped; he was "invigorated," he behaved like a man who has suddenly got it into his head that he is being pursued by something; he got moving at top speed down the track, not daring to look back, his rear end drawn in slightly like that of a cartoon character on the run, and it was not before fifty yards or so that he stopped, puzzling over what it was that had so abruptly disturbed the equanimity of his afternoon's run.

The people in Bellport, the home ground of the Gruccis, have become accustomed to this sort of thing over the years. Almost every evening at five o'clock, the Gruccis "test" their products. A sharp explosion in Bellport, or a faint shudder of the earth, or a quick electric-like flash over beyond the railroad tracks is simply understood by the citizens to be that "the Gruccis are at it again."

In 1979 the Gruccis decided to try to enhance their standing in the fireworks industry, and publicize their company at the same time, by accepting an invitation to the most renowned of the world's fireworks' competitions—the annual tournament that takes place over in Europe in Monte Carlo every summer. There was great controversy in the Grucci clan whether to go. It was a risk, of course. The entries—limited to five every year—are all by invitation. Those who accept are the ranking fireworks companies of the world—Ogatsu of Japan, Ruggieri of France, Brocks of England, Brunchu of Spain, among them, each of whom realizes the prestige of the award. They perform with their best. Yet even the Japanese, despite the rare beauty of their skills, have never won at Monte Carlo. Felix Grucci was extremely pessimistic. He had discovered that an Italian company was competing. "I don't know why we're thinking of going—not with the *Italians* in there."

A fireworks competition is a rare event in the United States. In a field so competitive, no company dares risk its reputation coming in second; the best an entrepreneur could hope for would be to get a number of American fireworks companies to cooperate in an "exhibition."

In other parts of the world, on the other hand, competitions are a matter of course. The great nightly displays in Valencia in Spain during the feast of St. James are fired by individual companies competing for prestige and a fifty-thousand-peseta prize. Japan has many competitions. In England, the first fireworks competition took place in 1863. It was organized by Charles Thomas Brock, the third son of William Brock, the founder of the famous firm. The contest took place at the Rye House, which is near Hoddesdon in Hertford-shire. To spruce up things, young Brock—he was only twenty at the time—brought in the Brothers Ridolini, along with acrobats from Paris's Cirque Napoléon, as well as the Rocky Mountain Wonders. Special trains were organized to get people to this somewhat out-of-the-way place. The occasion must have been a success (unfortunately there is no record in the Brock archives of either who won the competition or what the Brothers Ridolini did, much less the activities or identity of the "Rocky Mountain Wonders") because two years later Charles Brock put on another "Grand Competition of Pyrotechnists." This time it was held at Sydenham where in 1854 the Crystal Palace had been re-erected from its original site in Hyde Park. In this case, there *is* a record of the competition's winner—none other than William Brock, the young entrepreneur's father.

One of Felix Grucci's fears when the invitation came in from Monte Carlo was that his company had no experience in such European competitions. His people would not know what to expect. He had discovered that over the years two American fireworks concerns had gone to Monte Carlo and had done badly. His two sons, Jimmy and Butch, were much more sanguine; their information was that the European companies still ignited their shells with flares; they had not yet perfected electrical-firing procedures. Electrical firing, which meant that the entire show could be carefully choreographed beforehand, and sent up with split-second precision by throwing switches on a firing box console, would give the Gruccis a tremendous advantage.

Thus, in Bellport, the decision was made to go. They planned an extraordinarily extravagant display—fourteen hundred aerial shells, ranging from four to eight inches in diameter to be fired electrically; color-coordinated, the show was to open with a mammoth U.S.A. sign flanked by two American flags with red, white, and blue shells bursting overhead. The display would include gold comet shells arching over the harbor. Matching large Niagara Falls were to cascade down the façade of each breakwater at the harbor entrance while the Gruccis' great split comet shells performed overhead. The finale was to cap things—an effect the Gruccis named "Grucci in the Sky with Diamonds"—which involved a total of over two thousand shells: three levels of seven hundred aerial shells with "patriotic" colors on level one, spider shells at the next level up, and, above it all, multiple-break shells to provide an umbrella effect. Ho-hum, they thought. They imagined they would sit up above the harbor with feet up on the balustrade and click a few switches on the electric panel.

I flew to Monte Carlo to watch the Gruccis' big night. I arrived to find complete confusion. A third of the show, including part of the finale, and all the Gruccis' split comets, their most famous shells, had not arrived. They were

Jimmy Grucci of the Bellport fireworks family connects the fusing of a finale, or what the French call a bouquet. Each shell, the majority of them of the three-inch variety, is connected to the next by a rapidly burning fuse, so that the shells, often in multiple rows of mortars, go off in rapid succession, building in volume to a climactic fusillade. (Photo © Ken Clark, 1978)

still either en route to France or in storage at the Charles de Gaulle Airport in Paris. Worse, most of the mortars collected from various European countries to provide the enormous number needed to fire a show electrically (a mortar in an electrically fired show is only loaded and used once) turned out to be the wrong size—a few millimeters too small so that the American shells would not quite fit into them. Jimmy Grucci had sent his men to buy up every jar of Vaseline in Monte Carlo to coat the shells in the hope that some of them could be squeezed into the mortars available. The Monte Carlo authorities, watching all this frantic activity, were spending their time trying to get the Gruccis to sign an indemnification bond that would have them pay the city a substantial sum if the show did not go on as scheduled.

Shouting matches were being carried on in a number of tongues, most of them with a hysterical Frenchman, a Monsieur Quiry, who was the entrepreneur responsible to the Principality of Monaco for the fireworks competition. Having failed to produce about three thousand of the four thousand mortars the Gruccis had requested, and most of them the wrong size, he took it out on the Americans for the enormous size of the show. He threw up his hands and said he had never *heard* of so many fireworks. The fact that the Gruccis were still missing a considerable portion of their display only increased his astonishment. "Here in Monte Carlo we ask for a fireworks show, not a *cataclysme!*" I heard him exclaim on one occasion.

He was of little help in trying to find the errant crates of fireworks. Eventually, through a series of phone calls, they were tracked down in the air cargo area of the Charles de Gaulle Airport. A member of the Grucci contin-

---

Chinese firecracker-carton labels. These were used to decorate the boxes in which fireworks were shipped and sold throughout China from the mid nineteenth century to 1910. The larger labels were pressed from gold leaf with hand-carved wooden blocks and then hand-painted in unusual combinations of vivid colors to attract the notice of customers. Trees and bushes were painted in bright orange with multicolored leaves. A favorite color was a deep Chinese red—symbolizing happiness and strength. It is still the predominant color in fireworks packaging. A wide variety of subjects turn up on the labels—many of them with little apparent connection with the fireworks themselves. Some show religious gods surrounded by animals and flowers; others depict such myths as the creation of the Moon Goddess. Many labels include the three "happiness gods" that often appear in Chinese religious art: the God of Wealth (a large figure usually sheltered by an umbrella of ten thousand people), the God of Longevity (an elderly man with a curiously elongated forehead who is holding a peach), and the God of Fecundity (holding a child). Other common symbols on the labels are the white crane (also a symbol of longevity), tree peonies (representing wealth and honor), the unicorn (for perfect harmony), the phoenix (for creation), five bats (for good luck), and the deer (for success in academic study—perhaps the most farfetched choice for a fireworks label). The labels range in size from five inches for individual firecracker packages to those twenty inches across which were placed on packing cases. The most sought-after are those pressed from gold leaf, which can sell for upward of five hundred dollars each. Most of these labels come from the Canton region, especially from Fatshan (also known as Fo-shan), which was a center not only for fireworks but also for religious prints, papercuts and charms. Assembly-line techniques were used to prepare the labels. Sometimes the faces in the designs are left incomplete, as if before that final step could be completed there was a need to meet a shipment deadline. (From the collections of John Enns and of Orville Carlisle, Norfolk, Nebraska)

OVERLEAF *A display on the Seine put on by the famous Ruggieri family to celebrate the overthrow of Charles X in 1830 in favor of the "citizen king" Louis Philippe. The shells glow above a machine built on the Pont Royal. Original gouache by Lefevre, 1836. (From the Collection of Ruggieri, France. Photo by Jean-Loup Charmet)*

gent flew up to Paris. Trucks were arranged to bring them down to Monte Carlo.

When it was clear that some sort of show was going to be put on, the municipal authorities of Monte Carlo, even M. Quiry, became far more pleasant. We were invited to a number of functions. A lunch was given in our honor. One of the judges took me aside and said that he had strolled down the pier that morning to see what we were up to; he had been startled by the minuscule size of our American flag set piece. "Don't fire your flag tomorrow night," he whispered to me. "It's much too small. It'll lose votes. The Danes had a flag which was fifty meters long. It took up one entire side of a breakwater. Yours is a *blague,* a joke."

I thanked him, wondering vaguely if the information he had given me called for some sort of under-the-table compensation. I informed the Gruccis. "We've got to scrub that flag," I said.

Felix was upset. It seemed another indication that we were doomed in the competition, a reinforcement of his absolute conviction that the Italians were going to win.

The judge I had met was one of six officials who would be sitting up on a hotel balcony distinguished by a pale blue canopy overlooking the harbor front. On score sheets a competing country would be marked in a number of categories. Among these were brilliance of individual shells, the performance of the set pieces, the overall choreography of the show, and the strength and effect of the finale. Timing was also an important element. At seven-thirty in the evening, we were told, the municipal lights of Monte Carlo would dim. The national anthem of the competing country would be played over a loudspeaker system strung out along the length of the harbor-front quais. It was required, then, that six salutes would be sent aloft—like the twitch of a curtain before the show itself was unveiled. After that, the display was supposed to last exactly twenty minutes.

There could hardly be a prospect more spectacular than Monte Carlo for a fireworks extravaganza. The city rises up on the steep hills that curve around the small harbor so that those aboard yachts coming through the narrow entrance between the two breakwaters imagine themselves floating into a great amphitheater. The fireworks are shot off the length of both breakwaters; the crowds gather on the quais around the curve of the harbor. I was told that the curve of hills and buildings contained the sound, so that the concussion of shells echoed and reverberated long after they had performed in the night sky— just the kind of prospect of great advantage to the Gruccis with their dependence on noise.

The harbor began to fill with yachts gathering to watch the show—a couple of them fancy enough to have helicopter pads on the sterns. The largest yacht in port was *La Belle Simone,* which belonged to William Levitt, the housing-

---

A nineteenth-century Japanese woodcut by Hiroshige, "Fireworks over Ryogoku Bridge." Fireworks sparkle above the Sumida River while in the foreground a single rocket performs in the annual display, which goes back three hundred years and continues to be one of the great pyrotechnic sights of a Japanese summer. (Freer Gallery of Art, Smithsonian Institution)

development tycoon. The yacht is named after the latest of his wives. It has a swimming pool in the stern, which somehow in a private yacht seems far more impressive than a helicopter pad. The afternoon before the display we were invited on board. Our host took us down a circular stairwell of inlaid marble—it curled around a huge globe of the world illuminated from within—to show us the master stateroom. Low-ceilinged and resplendent in warm yellow-gold colors, it was dominated by a vast bed. Mr. Levitt pointed out a console by the bedside table. "Watch this," he said.

He pushed an ivory-tipped button. First, a glass paneling on the side of the room slid apart, and then with a soft hydraulic groan the wall itself pushed out from the ship. The harbor came into view. Sunlight flooded into the stateroom. A ladder swung out automatically and snapped down into position with its bottom step submerged. We could hear the children shouting on the quais, the splash of oars. We went and stared at the water three feet below the lip of the stateroom carpeting. People on the dock opposite stared in. Mr. Levitt was saying that the installation was for the benefit of his wife, Simone, so that she could step out of bed and, in less than a dozen steps, could be taking her morning swim without the bother of going above deck to her swimming pool. *La Belle Simone* had been leased to a film company for the making of a film named *The Great Tycoon*. The stateroom had been the scene of an extraordinary line I remember, delivered by the actress Jacqueline Bisset. Playing the part of the tycoon's wife, seated on the edge of the great bed, she had cried out in anguish, "I can't take this life anymore."

The next morning, Tuesday, the day of the Grucci show, we started work at first light. Out on the piers a colony of young people were sleeping on blankets or sleeping bags set out on great, flat concrete slabs on the seaward side of the breakwaters. The sun rose above a gray sea. A lovely girl, naked, skinned herself out of a sleeping bag, as if emerging from a cocoon, and stood poised for an instant on the edge of a rock before arching into the quiet sea, breaking the surface with hardly a sound and into water so clear that the bubbles streamed off her as she let her momentum carry her down.

That morning, it was pleasant enough to leave the mortar racks and the wiring of the finale shells and lean against the concrete balustrade to have a smoke, looking out across the Mediterranean and then down, almost awkwardly, at the people sunning themselves on the rocks. Many were blondes.

"I think they're Swedes," I told Jimmy Grucci.

He said, "If the mortars aren't set right and the show goes off sideways, we can blame it on the Swedes."

At midday the shells arrived from Paris. Each shell had to have its electric squib with its wires removed and replaced with a three-foot length of fuse, secured properly, so that the shell could be fired manually by putting a flare to a fuse. The lack of sufficient mortars to fire the show electrically meant that each shell would have to be hand-loaded. The advantage the Gruccis thought they had with electrical firing was gone. They rounded up a half dozen people who had never touched a firework before, and at long tables set up in a deserted slaughterhouse perched high on the rocks above the Mediterranean, we worked desperately to prepare the shells.

The finale racks on one of the breakwaters flanking the entrance to the harbor of Monte Carlo. At right is the column of the small lighthouse that marks the harbor entrance. The author stalks about in the background. The nudes mentioned in the text are disporting themselves on the near side of the breakwater. (Photo by Hubert Le Campion/People Weekly, © 1979 Time Inc.)

The professionals worked down on the piers setting up the larger mortars and the finale racks. Jimmy Grucci believed that one hope of impressing the judges lay with doing reasonably well in the category in which individual shells were judged for beauty and sharpness of color. Firing the show manually, with flares, and without the electrical firing, there was no chance of impressing them with choreographic precision. The shells would be going up helter-skelter, with no plan except to get as many in the air as possible. One could only pray for impressive random combinations.

Their best chance lay with the finale—a Grucci specialty. Its increasing roll of thunder and color might sway the judges and make them forget the haphazard quality of what had preceded. It was certainly an impressive preparation to watch—literally hundreds of three-inch mortars in rows, interspersed with dozens of four- and six-inch mortars—mortar lines that doubled, then tripled, snaking back and forth so that the breakwater piers seemed to have sprouted a surface of mortar mouths . . . like a thick cluster of pipe coral.

That evening I decided to watch the show from the parapet high above the harbor entrance—a command post from which Jimmy Grucci would be directing things through a walkie-talkie. We looked directly down on the piers. It had taken a long time to work our way through the traffic around the perimeter of the harbor. The crowds were vast.

I looked down at the bathers' rocks; judiciously their occupants had moved. It crossed my mind that actually it would have been an interesting place to watch from, almost under the mortars; in the spark showers those lovely girls could have rolled off into the warm sea to escape, treading water, and looking up at the shell bursts.

I heard Jimmy click on his walkie-talkie and ask Phil Butler, his brother-in-law, who was in charge of the mortar lines on the near breakwater. "How're things going?"

Phil's voice came back, scratchy over the walkie-talkie, but astonishingly calm considering what he had to say. "My partner's not here," he told Jimmy. "I'm here alone on the pier. Looks like I'm going to have to shoot this whole side myself. And I guess I could do that, except I haven't got anything to fire the show with—not even a book of matches."

There it was, the ultimate horror, competing for the championship of the world, the fireworks set in their mortars, the crowds gazing up into the sky, two minutes to go, and absolutely nothing for Phil to do but squat there on the stones of the breakwater, chin cupped in the palms of his hands, and wait for the hands to start the rhythmic clapping that would drift across the dark harbor to indicate the multitudes on the harbor-front quais were getting bored and restive.

I walked away from Jimmy down the cobblestone street. I could hear him shouting incredulously into the walkie-talkie, but my own despair was such that momentarily I could not bear to be part of the proceedings. I felt slightly nauseated. I walked by the elder Gruccis, who were not aware of what had happened, and I wondered how Felix would take it and whether he could *survive* his son explaining, "Hell, Pop, we just didn't happen to have any flares out there on that breakwater."

I stood leaning against the balustrade looking down at the harbor below. The distant quais around the curve of the harbor seemed to shimmer from the mass of spectators packed there. Then the municipal lights—the street-lamps and the building illuminations—dimmed and went out.

I walked stiffly back to Jimmy. He was listening to his walkie-talkie. Phil was telling him that he had spotted a small dinghy rowing across the harbor mouth from the opposite breakwater. In it (I saw Jimmy's cheeks puff out with an exhalation of relief) were the two French *tireurs* assigned to Phil's breakwater, one of them holding up a flare to show Phil that he was supplied.

"How's the other pier?" I asked.

"They're in place," Jimmy replied.

We could see the men from the dinghy clamber up and hurry down the pier to their stations by the shell bins. In the great façade of buildings against the dark hills the lights continued to wink off. A rather tinny version of "Home on the Range" drifted out across the water. When it was done, there was a long pause. We could hear the murmur of the huge crowd along the water-front.

I asked Jimmy, "Do you think that's their idea of the national anthem?"

Jimmy shrugged. "You've lived in this part of the world," he said. "What do you think?"

"I'd begin the show," I said.

Jimmy spoke quickly into his walkie-talkie. Just then, the first shell went up—not the first of six maroons as required, but a lone, rather insignificant shell that popped open with a small umbrella of blue lights high above the harbor. It could have been a flare fired from one of the yachts in the harbor.

"Good God!" Jimmy shouted, "what was that?"

Apparently one of the French *tireurs,* perhaps unhinged by the silence that had descended on the harbor after "Home on the Range," had reached for-ward with his flare to get things going.

It was at this stage that we had the six obligatory salutes, soon followed by the steady barrage of shells that constituted the main part of the show. To those of us who had visualized what the sky would have looked like had the careful choreography been possible with electrical firing, the haphazard thrust of shells seemed confused and artless, like paint being thrown amok. Yet it was impressive enough. Some of the shells soared to extraordinary heights, farther than I had ever seen shells fly. Over the uproar, Jimmy explained that these were the "Vaseline shells" squeezed into pipes too small for them, so that their propellants shot them out as if from the snug confines of rifle bar-rels. Others, especially the big six-inch shells, were too loosely confined in their mortars and thus burst low so that the breakwaters were alive with star-bursts, through which one could spot the *tireurs* scampering like firemen es-caping the showery collapse of a burning building. We could hear the distant applause when some of the Gruccis' special shells went off—especially the great eight-inch split comet shells, which produce thick, furry tail-like appendages,

69

like long golden boas, which then, at their ends, suddenly split into a triad of miniature comets. At times I was reminded of the arbitrariness of a Jean Tinguely sculpture with its abrupt kinky twists of effect and sensation. On one of the breakwaters the little American flag the judge had urged us to scratch suddenly blossomed; it had probably been ignited by a wayward spark. A pinwheel suddenly started to turn; and then its partner on the other pier, many minutes later, began to spin busily. A Niagara went off unexpectedly. Some of the bales of hay which were to act as protective barriers caught fire and began to burn briskly along the breakwaters, as if the Gruccis in a desperate attempt to beef up their display had resorted to the most primitive of pyrotechnical effects: the bonfire.

One could not help wondering what was passing through the minds of the six judges sitting under the blue canopy with their scorecards in front of them.

A show which is without design begins to pall after a while. Eventually I said to Jimmy, "What do you think? Don't you think we'd better unleash the finale on them?"

I heard Jimmy call into the walkie-talkie to tell his people to stop the single-shell firing and light the finale racks. We heard the rapid thump of the three-inch finale shells begin arching up.

The Grucci formula for their finales is usually to start with various color combinations—the sky ablaze with red, white, then blue, with a constant rumble of noise to go with it, but then the colors begin to give way to the salutes and the *saettine* and titanium bursts, so that finally the sky is alive with nothing but barrage—the white searing explosions pounding at one's eyes. The lines of mortars sending this material up are doubled, then tripled, so that when it seems impossible to increase the noise level, yet another decibel level is reached so that finally the gut begins to feel it; mouths drop ajar to relieve the pressure on the ears and often one shouts soundlessly into the racket, carried away by the outrageousness of the noise.

Monte Carlo turned out to be a perfect sounding board for the Grucci finale. Not only did the explosions ricochet sharply off the building fronts but they were gathered by the surrounding hills and flung back out over the dark harbor as if from the throat of a vast horn—so that one seemed to be buffeted in a vortex of sound. In the casino the play stopped at the tables—the only time anyone could remember such a thing—and the players ran out into the streets to catch a glimpse of the show, or at the very least to find out what was going on.

Usually a Grucci finale—typical of the Italians—ends with an enormous, single eight-inch report—a stunning kind of punctuation mark to the show. Echoing and reverberating, this monstrous cacophonous sound usually gives way to the faint wails of children crying as the general public catches its breath.

In Monte Carlo the Gruccis decided to use a color effect to end the finale. From each breakwater a pair of eight-inch shells went up. They had been adapted from a Chinese shell called Silvery Lights, which pops open into a slowly descending cluster of fluttery stars. The Gruccis had a bit of luck. Just

Prizewinning fireworks by the Gruccis light up the harbor of Monaco during the World Fireworks Competition of 1979. (Photo by Hubert Le Campion/People Weekly, © 1979 Time Inc.)

as the last thundering echoes of their finale died away, absolutely simultaneously these four shells opened up high above the harbor—such a shift of pyrotechnical effect from concussion to beauty that I turned to Jimmy, his own face turned up, his mouth ajar with wonder, and I said, "My God, Jimmy, that might do it!"

Then we heard an extraordinary sound. At first I thought it was an echo of the Grucci finale that somehow had got caught in the warrens and alleys of the back streets of Monte Carlo, entrapped in there for a while, and was now only just emerging—a confused blat of sound, full of an odd dissonance that I had not heard before—and then I realized that what we were hearing was the honk and wail and hoot of horns throughout the area in tribute to what had just been seen and heard—every horn in the place, from the cars in the traffic snarls along the waterfront to the deep-throated bellowing from the yachts in the harbor—one immensely deep horn I had to assume from our friend *La Belle Simone*. The din lasted for ten minutes. Witnesses said that it lasted longer than any salute given a show over the eleven years of the competition.

What I particularly remember, during that great cacophony of horns rising up to the balustrade where we were standing, was looking over at Felix Grucci. He was visibly moved. When I went over to shake his hand, he kept saying about the horns, "They're for us. They're for us," and his wife told me that it was the first time in thirty-five years that she had ever seen tears in his eyes.

Afterward, we gathered in the Loews Hotel. As each *tireur* walked into the room, applause broke out and we gazed at them; their faces were caked with soot, as if they had returned from the most dangerous section of a battlefront. Claude, one of the French *tireurs*, showed me blisters on his hands that he said had come not from sparks but from dropping flat against the rough surface of the concrete breakwater, and then pushing himself up to tend to another mortar. Phil Butler said to me: "That's the most chaotic show I've ever been involved in. I've shot in worse conditions, I've been huddled in the corner of a steel barge in Boston Harbor with the wind strong, and the air around me just alive with sparks and noise, but here"—he shook his head—"lighting those big shells . . . I kept saying to myself, 'This is the last time . . . I'll never do it again.' You get pushed around by the concussions, buffeted. It's like being roughed up by four or five muggers pushing you from one to the other, real hard."

I asked Phil what it was like standing on his pier at seven-thirty, alone, the lights dimming along the waterfront, and finding himself without the means to light a fuse. He grinned. "That was when I suddenly saw the little dinghy coming over from the other pier. It was a tiny one. When you sit in the stern the bow goes almost straight up. There were three people in it. It just *crept* across the water. The guy who was rowing got the others to promise him seventy-five dollars to get them across. Every time he put an oar in the water it was five dollars' worth of francs."

The Gruccis stayed around Monte Carlo for a week to watch the Italian display on the final Tuesday of the competition and to stay for the awards ceremony that night. We heard a lot of rumors about the Italians. "You watch them," Felix kept telling us. "They know the secret." We heard their team had arrived in six great vans; forty workmen had clambered down to unload them; their mortars were painted red and green, the national colors; there were even rumors of an electric panel.

I went down to the piers a couple of times to check. Nothing out of the ordinary seemed to be going on. The Swedish girls still baked on the great stone slabs on the seaward side of the breakwaters. I saw two or three Italian workmen. Squat, heavily browned men, they wore skimpy black bikini-like bathing suits and black silk stockings that reached to the knee. They smoked, I noticed. They leaned against the balustrade and gazed at the Swedes.

I reported all this to Felix. He was not in the least mollified. "They are going to rock the mountains," he told me.

The night of the Italian show we sat on the balustrade wall at the inland end of the harbor—a long line of Gruccis drumming their heels against the old stones. In front of us a huge crowd meandered along the waterfront. *La Belle Simone* had gone. I felt a quick surge of relief that her immense horn would not be added to the tribute the Italian show was bound to receive.

The show was delayed. A small schooner under power, her skipper apparently unaware of the scheduled festivities, picked that particular moment to enter the harbor. What could he have made of it—to come in past the little lighthouse and from the cockpit to look out from under the boom at thousands of people packed along the waterfront, many of them shouting at him angrily. He found out soon enough: the lights of Monte Carlo dimmed—which must have increased his bewilderment—the Italian national anthem sounded weakly over the public-address system, and behind him the first shells of the display roared up into the night. Throughout the show—I kept an occasional eye on him—he moved his yacht aimlessly around the harbor, trying to settle in somewhere but getting precious little help from any of the harbor masters, whose eyes were doubtless looking heavenward.

The feature of the Italian show was the magnificence and performance of their big shells. They erupted from the mortars with tremendous concussions that seemed to shiver the surface of the dark water in front of us. What was wondrous about them—to my startled eyes—was that the shells began to break on the way up, throwing off branch-like effects—comets, color clusters, whizbangs—until, far up, they blossomed and produced their main display. The upward thrust of the fireworks caused a quite novel sensation, one almost of exhilaration, a soaring of spirits, as opposed to the faint, lovely sadness of watching fireworks wink out and expire on the way down.

The crowd was excited, gasping at the violent concussion of the propellant charge and exclaiming at the various outcroppings as the shells boomed up. The whole show lasted only eighteen minutes. Their finale was more subdued than ours, pretty rather than concussive, but beautifully paced, and

The author displays the dragon trophy symbolizing the Grucci victory at the fireworks competition in Monte Carlo in 1979. The trophy is not an official award; it was, in fact, purchased by the author in Cannes for the Gruccis in his excitement at their triumph. (Photo by Hubert Le Campion/People Weekly, © 1979 Time Inc.)

at the end the harbor echoed with a tribute of horns. Our only chance for winning the championship rested, I thought, with the Italian show being nowhere as massive as ours; it had been so surprisingly short, and· we wondered if that would not affect the judges' voting. And of course there were the other contestants, whose displays we had not seen—the French, the Danes, and the Spanish.

The officials had their awards party at the Loews Hotel. We met the Italian team. Felix congratulated them. He was convinced they had won. He said that if anyone had to win, he was pleased that it was the Italians. After all, were not the Gruccis from Italy originally, from Bari on the Adriatic? It was important that the great tradition of fireworks-making be kept in the national family. Now if the Danes had won . . . !

Jimmy had been staring at the judges. They had not returned his glances, thus he tended to agree with his father. It was just like a jury. If they looked at you and smiled, that meant you were exonerated.

The mayor stood up on a dais and called for the crowd to quiet down. He had the winners to announce. He did his presentation with a flair for suspense, announcing first that the Danes had come in third; then after a long pause, as if he were having trouble reading the card in front of his nose, surmounted with pince-nez glasses, he informed us that the *Spanish* firm was second, an announcement that made my heart sink because it was hard to imagine that the Italian show we had seen that night would not place in the top three. I was about to get angry that the Gruccis had placed fourth when the mayor looked out at us and announced: *"Première classe: Les États-Unis"*—the United States—*"sous le direction de Félix Grucci."*

We tried to be nonchalant about it, but it was difficult. There was a short cheer and tears appeared once again in Felix Grucci's eyes. He tried to tell the Italian pyrotechnician that *he* should have won; he could not seem to rid himself of his belief in Italian supremacy.

After the party the Gruccis called Bellport to tell Felix (Butch), Jr., the news. He had stayed at home to mind the shop. By turns they took the phone and yelled at him happily. When they had done, they put me on the line. I called out: "What's the biggest shell you got in the shop? A twelve-incher? Shoot it up over Bellport. You've won. You're the champions of the world. You might as well let Bellport know." Mrs. Grucci at my side said: "Tell him to shoot the big salute."

"Your mother says, 'Shoot the big salute!' "

Mrs. Grucci announced to everyone in the room: "Butch's going to shoot the big salute. Hey, everybody, the big salute."

A champagne cork popped. A few of the Gruccis jumped involuntarily, thinking, I guess, of the big salute over Bellport and the noise it would make. I have noticed that about fireworks people. They tend to jump at sudden noises.

On August 21, 1956, a huge firework rose high above Tokyo Bay and at three thousand feet burst into the lovely chrysanthemum pattern typical of Oriental aerial shells. Its maker, the Marutamaya Ogatsu Fireworks Co., Ltd., had named their shell the Bouquet of Chrysanthemums. Its cost was in the neighborhood of two million yen—about eighty-five hundred dollars—and it had taken almost four months for a subcontractor—a man named Kose who specializes in such devices—to finish the shell. Ball-shaped, the shell weighed over two hundred pounds; it emerged from a mortar thirty-nine and a half inches in diameter. Later the *Guinness Book of World Records* gave these dimensions and it listed the Bouquet of Chrysanthemums as the "world's largest firework."

Fireworks people have a rather ambivalent attitude about huge shells such as the Bouquet of Chrysanthemums. In a pyrotechnical display a firework of that size is not of much practical value. Its effect in the sky can be duplicated by shooting up a dozen or so smaller shells simultaneously—by electrical firing—and at considerably less cost. The main virtue of the *tama*—as the Japanese refer to this oversize shell—rests almost entirely with its publicity value as a curiosity. During the day, spectators can gawk at the huge mortar from which it will be fired that night. Photographs of the shell, and the mortar, and very often someone standing alongside to indicate the scale, appear in the local newspaper together with a few paragraphs describing the device and saying that its performance in the sky will climax the evening's festivities.

Up until the Japanese began making their *tamas,* the largest aerial shells on record were English-made. In 1886, two such shells were made at Brocks' South Norwood plant. Twenty-five inches in diameter, weighing two and a quarter hundredweight (252 pounds), they were designed to go up a thousand feet, with the debris of their bursts covering well over a quarter of a mile. The first was sent off that same year over Lisbon's River Tagus on the occasion of the marriage of the Crown Prince of Portugal, the Duke of Braganza.

The entire display involved thirteen men-of-war, troopships, and barges. Five hundred and eighty mortars were required and more than eighty tons of fireworks material were used as a curtain-raiser for the big shell's performance. Two years later, at the same location, the second shell was fired to celebrate the visit of King Oscar II and Queen Sophia of Sweden and Norway.

I have seen a photograph of one of the shells and its attendant mortar—the latter about seven feet high and outfitted with an enormous pair of wheels over four feet in height, and a shaft so that the apparatus could be pulled into position by a horse or a mule. A man with a heavy beard and a bowler hat is standing alongside in the photo, looking very pleased with himself.

The last of the English outsized shells was sent up during the World War II victory celebration on June 8, 1946. It was reported to be the largest fireworks shell to that date—at least according to accounts in *News of the World*. A somewhat worried reporter for that journal wrote of the shell: "We are looking forward with some trepidation to the Big Bomb, which is to go up not far from Big Ben (on the south side). It is the largest firework ever discharged—25 inches in diameter. It is to fill 700 feet of sky with golden rain and who knows what!"

The shell, which was fired off a barge lying between Lambeth and Charing Cross Bridge—a traditional stretch on the Thames River for fireworks shows dating back to the time of Henry VII—apparently went up to its designed height in the night sky, filled the sky with "who knows what," and performed without a hitch.

These days in the United States the largest shell commercially available is a Japanese model twenty-four inches in diameter and weighing approximately a hundred pounds, about half the size of the Ogatsu record-sized Bouquet of Chrysanthemums. It is a special item in the repertory of a California fireworks firm known as Pyro-Spectaculars which imports on the average three of these monsters a year. One of them was fired on the occasion of the London Bridge's "opening" at its new location on Lake Havasu, Arizona. The shell fits into a special mortar which is transported to the firing site in two sections and is then bolted together with binders like barrel staves. The shell is usually ignited electrically. From a considerable distance an employee throws a switch, and a squib, connected with wires from the firing box, explodes inside a lifting charge under the shell in the mortar, setting it off so that the shell, with its time fuse now lit, is propelled up into the sky. On one occasion in 1976 in Boston Harbor, a Grucci employee, an Englishman named Bernie Wells, used a railroad flare to light the fuse of what his fellow employees often refer to as "the thing." He and "the thing" were alone together on a barge from which, whatever the process of ignition, there was no escape, short of a dive into the water.

"What always fascinated me about 'the thing' going up," Wells told me, "is how little sound it makes coming out of the mortar. It makes a small *harrumph,* a sort of clearing of the throat. But then the launching site—whether it's a barge or a field—*trembles,* which is quite enough to remind one of the forces involved."

78

In this instance, "the thing" made up for the weak murmur of its departure by prematurely exploding only fifty feet above the barge, so that Wells, crouched face-down in the scuppers, felt as if he were suddenly in the crucible of a blast furnace. He escaped with a few singe holes in his clothing, but on the next occasion of being asked to ignite a *tama* in Boston Harbor, he stood off from the barge in a motorboat and touched his flare to an extra-length fuse strung through a long coil of garden hose supported by a series of buoys. The notion was that as the flame moved toward "the thing" through the hose, Bernie Wells would be moving in the opposite direction at considerable speed in his motorboat. On this occasion, the shell performed admirably, spreading its lovely umbrella of stars high above the harbor as, below, Bernie Wells, staring straight ahead, his shoulders hunched forward, spanked across the dark water in his motorboat with its throttle wide open.

Though, occasionally, these large Oriental shells are fired in an aerial fireworks show in the United States, there has been very little concern with bettering the Ogatsu record in the *Guinness Book of World Records*. Fireworks people know of the great shell—the Ogatsu company has been a major supplier of fireworks to this country since the war—but the need and the wherewithal to construct such a device, much less the interest, has never been apparent.

Then, in 1976, an interested party emerged from a curious source—Harvard University's undergraduate humor magazine, the *Harvard Lampoon*. That year, the publication was celebrating its hundredth anniversary. Proud to point out that it is the oldest undergraduate humor magazine in the country, the *Lampoon* was financially very well suited to celebrate this event in considerable style. A few years before, it had sold the right to use its name to the *National Lampoon* for a percentage of the latter's gross profits; because of the *National Lampoon*'s unexpected and enormous success, the *Harvard Lampoon* found itself with an annual income of over $100,000. Its young editors, who in the past ran the magazine from the meager assets derived from initiation fees, a few pages of advertising, and the profits from an occasional parody issue, behaved in a very lively fashion indeed with this windfall. Among other things, $20,000 was set aside to be bestowed on the "funniest professor of the decade." To go along with the cash prize was an $11,000 Cadillac El Dorado, painted purple (the *Lampoon*'s colors) and with an ornamental ibis (the *Lampoon*'s symbol) for the radiator cap. The editors decided that the recipient should be John Kenneth Galbraith, the economist. He was to receive the awards during a February weekend featuring numerous celebratory functions, including a mammoth dinner in the vast reaches of Cambridge's Memorial Hall. A large percentage of the windfall was set aside for this. Liveried footmen were to be hired to stand behind each chair at the banquet.

It was very much in the spirit of this haywire excessiveness that when asked—as a former editor of the *Lampoon*—if I could think of something appropriate for the February celebrations, I raised the possibility of building the world's largest firework to set off above the city of Cambridge at an appropriate moment. I told the *Lampoon*'s editors about the record in the *Guinness*

Book of World Records, and how the event would be immortalized in that volume if it were carried off successfully, or, very likely, even if it weren't.

The *Lampoon* thought it was a splendid concept, or, as they wrote me, "quite an appropriate and phun-philled idea" (the *Lampoon* editors in their communications traditionally substitute *ph* for *f* as in "don't be phoolish"), and immediately two thousand dollars of their funds were apportioned to build such a device. The *Lampoon* expressed the hope that a "phrightphully big bang" could be programmed into the firework so that people asleep in their beds in Cambridge who might miss the bright flash of the aerial stars would be abruptly jarred by the concussion into an awareness of the *Lampoon* centennial. That was important.

All of this, I knew, was very much in the *Lampoon*'s tradition of keeping the populace on edge. Indeed, much of one's time as an undergraduate on the *Harvard Lampoon* was devoted to thinking up "stunts"—public events whose purpose was invariably *pour épater le bourgeois.* Among the more famous stunts in the *Lampoon*'s history had been the "lifting" of the "Sacred Cod" in April 1933, the stuffed fish that had hung on display in the State House in Boston untouched by human hands for thirty-eight years. There was quite a furor when it was discovered missing. Who had taken, much less *wanted,* such a thing?

The Cod was eventually returned along with a copy of the *Lampoon* to give a hint to the authorities as to who might have been responsible. A similar flap had been caused in Washington, D.C., where, on May 7, 1936, the *Lampoon* had raised the Communist Hammer and Sickle over the U.S. Supreme Court, so skillfully fixing it in place (three *Lampoon* editors in the early dawn had avoided the guards to get up on the cupola) that the flag had to be burned off by a workman perched on a length of extension ladder. Here again, a copy of the magazine was left on the premises.

One of the more recent *Lampoon* escapades occurred in the spring of 1982. It involved a confrontation with a Russian fishing trawler coming into Boston Harbor off the Grand Banks. The *Lampoon* editors had "lifted" an ancient cannon, mounted it in the bow of a launch, and had gone out to confront the Russian trawler. Moving along in its lee, they had shouted and pleaded through megaphones at the bewildered Russian crew for the immediate release and repatriation of "American fish."

The Moguls were enchanted by fireworks. Women often entertained each other with fireworks in their private gardens. This eighteenth-century Indian miniature illustrates not only a private celebration, but also a more elaborate display, visible in the background. (The Trustees of the British Museum)

OVERLEAF *Fireworks were once traditionally part of an annual celebration at the Castel Sant' Angelo in Rome. Joseph Wright of Derby, an English artist, witnessed one of these spectacles in 1774 while on a tour of Italy. He painted this scene from memory. Some years later, fireworks at Castel Sant' Angelo were discontinued when cracks were discovered in the castle walls. Today, fireworks are shot from barges on the Tiber to prevent further damage to historic buildings. (By permission of the Birmingham Museum and Art Gallery)*

Stunts of this sort, however sophomoric to a general audience, would inevitably delight past *Lampoon* members, especially ex-*Lampoon*-presidents, who would dash off congratulatory notes, usually with the words "very phunny indeed" tucked away in the text.

So it was with considerable relish, and the anticipation of constructing the biggest onslaught yet on the public sensibility, not to mention the chance of supplanting the Ogatsu mark in the *Guinness Book of World Records,* that when the two thousand dollars arrived from the *Lampoon,* I got to work on the shell.

The pyrotechnical firm I found to build what the *Lampoon* began to refer to in its correspondence as the Fat Man (or, rather, Phat Man)—the nickname of the atomic weapon that destroyed Nagasaki—was, of course, the Gruccis. When I went out to Bellport to talk to them about Fat Man, the two sons, Felix, Jr. (Butch), and Jimmy, turned out to be far more entranced by the idea of designing and building the world's largest shell than their father. To someone of the older generation like Mr. Grucci—so sensible and practical—the project was difficult to explain, especially the involvement of the *Harvard Lampoon.* When I told him about the *Lampoon* attempt to repatriate "American fish," he shook his head solemnly. "Who are these people?" he asked, a question he was to put to me on a number of subsequent occasions.

Work on the shell started a couple of months before the *Lampoon*'s February party date. The Ogatsu *tama* had been fashioned in the round-ball shape that is typical of Oriental shells. American-made shells have invariably copied the cylinder-like European models, and it was in these proportions—what was described as a great "vat-like shape"—that the Fat Man slowly began to take form in Shed No. 16 in the Grucci compound. To break the Ogatsu record, the shell was designed to be forty and a half inches in diameter, one inch more than the Japanese shell (the diameter is the criterion required by the *Guinness Book of World Records*), but its height was somewhat arbitrarily set at three feet by the Grucci brothers, which meant that when it was filled with pyrotechnical material the shell would be tremendously in excess of the *tama*'s weight of two-hundred-odd pounds. It was estimated that the American shell would weigh well over seven hundred pounds. Felix Grucci, Sr., could never understand this. "You tell me," he remarked, "why that thing out there in Shed

---

A colored aquatint of a spectacular fireworks display in Paris on the Place de la Grève given for Napoleon and Josephine by the City of Paris to celebrate the Emperor's self-coronation on December 16, 1804. The set piece shows the Great St. Bernard Pass through which Napoleon passed in 1800 on his way to military victories in Italy. An extraordinary incident took place on the occasion of this display. The show ended with the ascent of a vast hydrogen balloon (barely visible, top left). Unmanned (un ballon perdu), it was built by Jacques Garnerin and carried a huge golden crown hung with three thousand colored lights. A freak storm carried the balloon all the way to Rome by the morning of the second day, where it finally came to earth, the crown breaking up against the ruins of Nero's tomb—of all places—and what was left tumbled into Lake Bracciano. The newly crowned Emperor, a very suspicious man, and short-tempered as well, became extremely upset by the incident—to the point of firing the balloon maker, Jacques Garnerin, and thereafter forbidding all mention of this odd occurrence. (Print Collection. The New York Public Library. Astor, Lenox and Tilden Foundation)

16 is so big. The Japanese bomb is two hundred pounds. Our bomb"—fireworks people invariably refer to shells as "bombs"—"is almost eight hundred pounds. Why are we making a bomb *four* times as big as the Jap bomb? If we want the record, which we do, and so do those crazy guys up in Boston, why not build one two hundred and one pounds? You answer me that."

I never could, although I liked the idea of the great size of our shell—if one were to beat the record it seemed appropriate to do so in a quantum leap—and he would shake his head and, in his sweet, gravelly voice, complain that none of his thirty-five relatives listened to him anymore, except perhaps his grandchildren, though he wasn't too sure about them either—they were growing up too fast.

Two shells were built out in Shed 16: Fat Man I for a test shot to make sure the device worked properly and Fat Man II for the actual ceremonial shoot in Cambridge. Many of the discussions out at the Bellport compound concerned how much propellant charge should be placed under the Fat Man in order to push the shell up the projected thousand feet in the air. The pyrotechnist's rule-of-thumb with large shells is that one tenth of the weight of a shell is the proper propellant charge. In the case of Fat Man, this meant that eighty pounds of 2F (FFA blasting) black powder (a coarse-grained commercial grade used for propelling charges) would be set in the bottom of the mortar—such a mammoth portion that the Gruccis were worried that it would shatter the steel walls of the mortar and disintegrate the shell itself. After a lot of hassling, the figure of thirty-four pounds of propellant was chosen. No one was sure if this was enough, or too much. There was even talk of dispensing with a propellant entirely by dumping the shell out of an airplane—simply lighting the fuse and shoving the Fat Man out. At this, there was a startled demurrer from the oldest Grucci son, Jimmy, who is so frightened of air flight that he has never been in a plane. He told us that the thought of helping to heave an eight-hundred-pound firework, its time fuse sputtering, out of the open door of a Cessna, four or five thousand feet above the dark countryside, the people on the plane with their shoulders to the Fat Man ("One-two-three-HEAVE!"), was enough to make him quite ill.

"I wouldn't know what to be the most scared of," he told us, "the bomb or the airplane." Sometimes he would shiver involuntarily and we knew he was thinking of the night of the "drop," and what it would be like up there with the pilot looking back over his shoulder and saying, "Well, we're closing in on the drop zone, fellas . . . You can start thinking about lighting her up."

Once the idea of an airplane was dismissed, with the Gruccis still not sure of their calculations about the propellant, it seemed prudent to ask for another opinion. I picked the most exalted authority I could find—the U.S. Army Research and Development Center, more commonly known as the Picitinny Arsenal. A considerable facility situated in Dover, New Jersey, its primary function is to design and develop military projectiles. The specialist I reached there was Sid Bernstein, who worked in a department announced by anyone who answered the phone as "Propulsion!" After some bureaucratic finagling—including a letter of authorization from Washington, D.C.—Mr. Bernstein was allowed to give our problem his attention.

First, he told me, he was going to take the figures I had given him (the size of the projectile, the length of the mortar, the type of powder in the propellant, and so forth) and run what he called an analogue-digital hybrid computer program. The readout would tell him what would have to happen inside the mortar—the interior ballistics—in order for the firework (or the "bullet" as he referred to it) to achieve the proper speed to meet "exterior velocity requirements"—namely, to get one thousand feet up in the air. He told me that it would not be particularly easy. The properties of black powder were difficult to verify exactly. In fact, Bernstein told me over the phone, with mild disgust, that a certain amount of rule-of-thumb reckoning was going to be necessary in the calculations about the Fat Man—rare indeed in a military facility involved in the deadly science of placing a "bullet" exactly on target.

For me, it was exhilarating to think of all this attention being given to Fat Man by the U.S. Army. I had the feeling that the Picitinny people were delighted to be working on the project. To begin with, the Fat Man was a peaceful projectile—surely a divertissement for a staff working in a somewhat grim environment devoted almost entirely to destruction. Moreover, the Fat Man, somewhat to my surprise, was exciting to them by the very nature of its bulk. Nothing at Picitinny even approached its dimensions. "The size of the bullet is very unusual," Mr. Bernstein told me. He said that the largest shell in the Arsenal was a mere two-hundred-pound specimen made for an eight-inch howitzer. The dimension that particularly impressed Bernstein was the diameter of the Fat Man's mortar—40½ inches—far outmeasuring even the enormous fifteenth-century bombards which still rank among the largest pieces of artillery ever built. For example, Edinburgh Castle's famous "Mons Meg," made around 1500, while it weighed five tons and could fire an iron ball nearly a mile, only had a bore diameter of 19½ inches. The huge thirteen-ton bombard of Ghent, known as "Dulle Griete," fired a two-hundred-pound stone from a barrel that was a mere 25 inches across. The largest of them all, the "Great Mortar of Moscow," also known as the "Tsar Puckka" (King of Cannons), which could fire a stone ball weighing well over a ton (or was supposed to: it was never actually fired) only had a 36¼-inch bore, quite a bit smaller than Fat Man's. Even in contemporary weaponry, the largest mortar—a weapon ordered by the U.S. Army in World War II—measured exactly the same bore dimensions as the Russian piece built over four centuries before. "Little David" (as the only one built was named) was designed for the U.S. Army to destroy underground fortifications with a projectile weighing thirty-seven hundred pounds. Again, like its Russian counterpart, it was never used.

I did quite a lot of research to see if any mortar (much less the firework it was to fire) could equal ours. I even checked out a large mortar I had read about as a child in Philip Gosse's *History of Piracy*. Large enough in the mouth to contain a man, it indeed had one in there; the illustration in the book showed a man stuffed in up to his shoulders. He was (as one read with eyes popping)

A curious use of a very large mortar. The caption under the illustration from The History of Piracy *by Philip Gosse reads "The Algerines firing off the French consul from a mortar at the French fleet." The lifting charge, of unknown quantity, would be resting in the bottom of the weapon, underneath the consul. (From* The History of Piracy *by Philip Gosse. © Tudor Publishing Company, 1934. Courtesy of The New York Society Library)*

the French consul in Algiers who in the Pirate Wars of 1830 was captured by the pirates and, in an act of horrid derision, fired at the French fleet. For years the mortar graced the walls of Algiers (it is now in the Musée de la Marine in Paris) and in honor of the man who was fired out of it was named as only the French would have the flare to do: La Consulière. I was able to discover that the diameter of La Consulière was 650 millimeters, or about 25 inches.

Sadly, my research did turn up one bombard that slightly exceeded the diameter measurements of Fat Man's mortar. The Turks had a bombard with a caliber of 42 inches which they used against the walls of Constantinople in the springtime of 1453. They were able to get seven shots a day out of the monster, which had a barrel twenty-six feet long. It was hauled into position by sixty oxen and two hundred men and the missile it fired, a stone cannonball, weighed twelve hundred pounds. I was sorely tempted to call Felix Grucci and request that we increase the diameter of our shell.

"Not much, Felix. Just two inches."

"Why?"

"Well, the *Turks,* Felix. They dropped a stone ball on Constantinople in 1453 just a bit wider than what you've got out there in Shed 16."

"The Turks?"

"So if we're going to beat the Japanese, we might as well go all the way and beat the Turks too."

I never did call him, of course. Felix was puzzled enough as it was, by not only the "guys from Boston" but also the problems and unanswered questions that kept coming up about the device in Shed 16.

Certainly one of his greatest surprises (as indeed it was for all of us) was Sid Bernstein's report from the Picitinny Arsenal on how much propellant would be necessary to get Fat Man up a thousand feet. It was an astonishingly small amount: a little over four pounds.

"Four pounds!"

Out in Bellport this figure was greeted with hoots of disbelief. The consensus among the Gruccis was that the Fat Man wouldn't even budge from the mortar with such a minuscule amount of propellant; the top of the canister might show at the mortar's muzzle, but then it would slide back down.

"But surely these people know what they're doing," I said. "After all, they're in the business of throwing a shell thirty miles. You don't hear of their shells dribbling out of the muzzles, like something falling off a shelf . . . it's all been checked by a computer."

I telephoned to ask Mr. Bernstein how far up the shell would go if the Gruccis fired it out with thirty-four pounds of propellant.

"The mortar and the canister would not survive the shock," Mr. Bernstein said. "If conceivably everything held together, the bullet would go up, oh, about eight miles."

"Eight miles!"

"Slightly more, I would guess," Mr. Bernstein said, "than what you had in mind. That's a long way up for a firework."

Finally, it was decided to test-fire a dummy Fat Man to see if the Picitinny calculations were correct. To do this, the Gruccis fashioned a solid block of wood of the exact weight and shaped to the proportions of the Fat Man. Arrangements were made to send up what was referred to as "the log" from the grounds of the Westhampton Municipal Maintenance Yard. A couple of miles from Bellport, it was a wasteland of dunes and sand heaps, bordered by scrub pines—a desolate area, especially on the day of the test shot which turned out to be cold and rainy.

Quite a crowd, including Mr. Bernstein from Picitinny, arrived for the test, bundled up against the cold and stomping their feet to keep warm. The mortar arrived on a flatbed trailer truck—a tube of two tons of rolled steel, ten feet long, ¾ inch thick, with its diameter wide enough to accept the 40½-inch Fat Man series. We stared at it in awe. It had been donated by Paragon Steel of Detroit, whose president, Philip T. Warren, though not a *Lampoon* man, had heard about the project and offered his services. A crane on caterpillar tracks lifted the mortar with a cradle of heavy chains and dropped it into a vast hole scooped out earlier that day by a diesel shovel. Here it was steadied by sand loads dropped in around its circumference by the diesel shovel; the mortar, pointing straight up, was buried just about to its lip. The four pounds of 2F powder, poured into a small cellophane bag, was set down on the mortar's base plate—very harmless-looking, rather like a discarded junk-food wrapper—indeed, so insignificant, sitting forlornly in the bottom of the mortar, that I truly began to wonder if the Picitinny computer machines had not left a zero off their final computations.

The ignition was done electrically. Stuck in the lifting charge in its cellophane package was what pyrotechnicians call a "squib"—a little firing cap, perhaps an inch in length, attached with a long length of wire leading back to a source of electrical power, in this case a car battery. Often the wire is attached to a kind of box-like plunger device, familiar from films where the train robbers push down on the handle to blow up a section of track. When the electric power pulses through the wires, it explodes the squib, which spits out a flame in a tiny detonation sufficient to set off the charge in which it is embedded.

We stood staring at the mortar lip, three hundred yards or so across the field. Jimmy Grucci touched the leads from the wire to his car battery. Out of the mouth of the mortar came a small puff of what looked like steam. There was a mild thump, rather like the short belch of a tuba. To my astonishment, the dark shape of the Fat Man replica emerged, quite slowly, but it kept rising inexorably, almost as if the log were being drawn up into the sky by an invisible fishing line, tumbling up until it was just a dot above us in the gray sky before starting down. It had been in the air about twelve seconds before it thumped heavily in the sand on the far side of the mortar. The Gruccis looked stunned. I ran over to congratulate Sid Bernstein. He told me that according to his azimuth reading the log had gone up 995 feet, just five feet short of being right on target.

That evening I telephoned the *Lampoon* to tell them of the day's success. There was a certain amount of confusion at the other end. I could hear the hubbub of a party going on in the background. "A log?" I was asked. I heard the voice reporting to the others: "Trees, they're shooting up trees over Long Island . . ."

Perhaps not surprisingly, no one from the *Lampoon* turned up for the live test shot. Once again, the day was cold and dank. The Fat Man had emerged from Shed 16; it now hung from the arm of the crane, swaying back and forth above the muzzle of its mortar. The canister had been lacquered, so its surface glowed a dullish orange through the mist. Within the Fat Man were three hundred pounds of sawdust packing, four hundred pounds of magnesium stars, ten pounds of a pyrotechnic substance known as flitter stars, and one hundred pounds of black powder at the center of the shell to burst it apart at the apogee of its flight and ignite the contents. If everything went well, the stars would perform in a vast umbrella of silver; the flitter would appear to hang in the sky like a golden dust cloud, and the sawdust would sift down and lazy off in the winds.

Since the Fat Man was going up in the afternoon so that we would be better able to monitor its performance, it would be difficult, of course, watching

OPPOSITE: *The author standing beside the ten-ton mortar used in the Fat Man series.*   LEFT *A log replica of the Fat Man has just been fired from the mortar mouth in an experiment to determine the size of the lifting charge to be placed under the real thing.   Fat Man I detonates in the ground, thus committing itself to the* Guinness Book of World Records *as the "world's lowest firework." (Grucci Collection)*

the test shot, to assess what the effect would be like in the night skies over Cambridge. Still, the crowd was twice what it had been for the flight of the log. Sid Bernstein brought his wife up from Picitinny Arsenal. I stood with them as we watched the Fat Man being guided down into the mortar at the end of its length of chain. Under the shell the Gruccis had at the last moment added two more pounds of 2F powder for the lifting charge—"just to be on the safe side," I was told. I worried about this, but Sid Bernstein assured me that it was of small consequence. The mortar was strong enough to contain the additional explosive thrust; the "bullet" would simply go a bit higher.

The procedure for sending up the Fat Man was the same we had used with the log replica—that is, by touching the two wire leads to a car battery. When this was done, though we were standing three hundred yards away from the firing site, all of us flinched in expectation of a considerable and quick reaction.

Nothing happened. Then I noticed a faint plume of white smoke drifting out of the mouth of the mortar.

"What's that?" I asked.

Jimmy Grucci, standing next to me, grabbed my arm, and pulled me down. It seemed ludicrous to be forced into a crouch, staring out across that quiet landscape at the distant mound of dirt heaped around the mortar's lip. But Jimmy knew what had happened—that of the two fuses on the device (one led to the propellant and the other to the charge inside the shell to burst it apart at its apex) only the bursting-charge fuse was lit. Apparently the other fuse, which ran down the inner side of the mortar to the propellant charge, had been sheared away during the loading of the shell. The fuse that was burning, sending up its little trail of white smoke, was timed to reach the bursting charge in ten seconds, performing just as it should with the canister in flight. But because the propellant had not gone off, inevitably, the whole thing, sitting stoutly in the mortar, was going to blow. We watched the smoke drift idly out of the mortar's mouth.

Then, abruptly, as if a huge naval gun buried to its muzzle and tilted vertically at the sky had erupted, the whole caboodle exploded—an enormous billow of dirty white smoke mushrooming until it seemed to loom over us. We could see great shards of the mortar, ripped apart by the explosion, whirling off through the smoke toward the scrub pines bordering the field. The concussive sound seemed to hang around us, shivering the air, and for almost a minute we could hear the patter of dirt drifting down into the distant pines that bordered the field. Sirens at the adjacent airfield began to blow. We walked gloomily over and stared into the enormous crater that Fat Man had left. It was about twenty feet deep, still smoking at the bottom, and at least fifty feet across. Sid Bernstein climbed down into the pit and began scratching around in the dirt. He had placed a number of pressure gauges in the bottom of the mortar. These, of course, with everything else had disappeared. There was no evidence of what had caused the crater; it might as well have been spooned out of the earth by a monster steam shovel.

A portion of the ten-ton mortar splintered by the premature blast of Fat Man I and thrown a quarter of a mile across the pine barrens of Bellport, Long Island. (Grucci Collection)

The failure of Fat Man resulted in a number of repercussions. The shock wave, spreading out like a ripple from the detonation, caused, among other things, crockery to topple off distant shelves; a quarter of a mile away a man reported to the local newspaper that sitting idly reading a magazine he had been knocked off his sofa; we were told that considerable consternation at the air base had been caused because a huge canoe-shaped part of the mortar had materialized on the runway, clanging down, and rocking briefly back and forth.

The *Lampoon* was not overly concerned about the news of the failure. They were especially delighted to hear about the man who had been knocked off the sofa. "Great phun!" they wrote me in a letter. It was all very much in the *Lampoon* tradition—a true-life example of *pour épater le bourgeois,* this business of knocking people around with shock waves.

And besides, there was Fat Man II. They asked me up to Cambridge to try to persuade the Fire Commissioner that the remaining firework could be used for the centennial celebration despite its sibling's failure. I could tell the Commissioner that certain "kinks" had been worked out after the test failure of the first device, and now Fat Man II was not only safe but would simply *dazzle* the citizens of Cambridge with a vast silvery umbrella of soft comet-tail-like brilliance that could be admired not only for its beauty but as a credit to the *Lampoon* for thinking of such a display and *especially* to the Fire Commissioner for allowing it to be done.

The Commissioner would have none of it. He had found out what had happened at Bellport. In Cambridge all of us walked down to the varsity baseball diamond off a corner of the Harvard Stadium, a relatively forlorn spot, with the nearest habitation four or five hundred yards away—quite legal by all civic regulations I had heard of. I told the Commissioner that we could sink the mortar right about where third base was. "The shell," I said, gazing aloft and waving my arms like a yachtsman admiring the shape and pull of his spinnaker, "would pop open just about there"—pointing— "and the chrysanthemum-like spread—"

"If that thing," the Commissioner interrupted abruptly, "turns up here, much less across the borders into the Commonwealth of Massachusetts, you people are *in* for it."

The *Lampoon* crowd was all for going ahead with Fat Man II anyway. They spoke of midnight activities—trucks they could hire and steam shovels to excavate instant trenches into which to lay the Fat Man and a covering of wintery-looking grass like the camouflaged cover of an intercontinental missile to be removed at firing time. "The community will never know what hit them," they said. "We'll clear the evidence out before the Commissioner has taken his eyes off the sky."

The *Lampoon* centennial dinner which was to have featured the huge shell was held in mid February. The Gruccis put on a considerable fireworks show on the banks of the Charles River without, of course, Fat Man II who, despite the *Lampoon* entreaties, remained in Bellport. The night was bitterly cold and clear, moonless, which allowed the shell bursts to etch themselves brilliantly against the darkness. The spectators stamped their feet to keep warm and they cheered loudly at some of the pyrotechnic effects. The Cambridge community must have been puzzled by the timing of the show—a dead-winter display—but many came down along the banks of the Charles to watch. After the show the *Lampoon* had a fleet of limousines on hand to deposit its members and graduates at Memorial Hall, where the dinner was held. For an undergraduate organization it was an astonishingly opulent affair. Those who were not in black tie were in various costumes, most of them, as I recall, medieval. A contingent of liveried footmen had indeed been hired. They stood awkwardly behind the high-backed banquet chairs. Almost invariably they changed plates and served the food from the wrong side. The *Lampoon* janitor, a man named Elmer Green, was carried into the banquet on a sedan chair. John Updike, who had been an undergraduate president of the magazine, rose and made some mild remarks about the extensiveness of the occasion and wondering if the magazine was using its windfall from the *National Lampoon* in the most responsible manner. These remarks were greeted with a murmur of disapproval from the undergraduates. A few hard rolls were lobbed up at the dais from the darkness, and butter pats, catapulted with astonishing speed off the spring of a table knife, slapped wetly up against the wall behind us. Dave McCord got up to speak. A distinguished member of the *Lampoon* in 1921, the author of *What Cheer?* among other books, he had written a long ode celebrating the magazine's centennial. When the undergraduates realized that he was going to treat his subject at considerable length, once again hard rolls began to whistle up at the dais from the distant tables. There was a sharp cry of "Louder and funnier!" Those of us seated along the length of the dais stared bleakly out into the darkness, weak with embarrassment at the rudeness of our fellows. It was then my turn to speak. I tried to explain the failure of Fat Man I. I heard cries of "Shame! Shame!" A voice shouted out of the darkness, "Hoist him on his own petard!" and I could hear the crack of bakery products on the wall behind me.

I finished my remarks by saying that the reserve Fat Man was available. I hoped that a suitable occasion could be found on which the device—which, after all, belonged to the *Lampoon*—could be sent aloft.

Sometime after the *Lampoon* festivities, a friend of mine called to ask if I had seen the new edition of the *Guinness Book of World Records.* "You'll be interested," he said. "You're in it." Somehow the editors had got word of Fat Man's failure. Could it have been from the man toppled off his sofa by the shock wave? There, in the new edition, under the designation "Largest Fireworks," it continued to list the 36-inch Bouquet of Chrysanthemums from the Marutamaya Ogatsu people, but then the passage went on to describe the world's *lowest* firework, specifically that it was "George Plimpton's 40½-inch 720-lb. Roman candle 'Fat Man' which was supposed to break the record over Long Island, N.Y. in February, 1976. Instead, it sizzled, hissed and exploded, leaving a crater 10 feet deep."

I did not relish having my name attached to the firework. Had not the Gruccis constructed it? Nor did it help my frame of mind to have the Guinness authorities refer to the Fat Man as a "Roman candle," and, what's more, to minimize the size of its crater. But then again, perhaps matters could be rectified with Fat Man II. After all, the great device was sitting, ready to go, in Shed No. 16 in Bellport. The steel company in Detroit had provided another mortar. It was simply a question of finding a fitting occasion and a site from which to launch the device.

I kept in touch with the *Lampoon* people. Not surprisingly, its editors had a number of startling suggestions as to launching possibilities. Some were what were considered "pragmatic" ideas—such as firing off the device next to Trinity Church in Boston to see how its steeple would handle the shock wave; or the Hancock Building to discover if its windows—which were famous for tumbling out—were truly finally in place. Among other possible sites was the deck of *Old Ironsides* in Boston Harbor from which the Fat Man was to be lobbed "in the general direction of the Boston suburb of Somer-ville." Another, far less "pragmatic" notion involved firing the Fat Man down the chimney of the *Harvard Crimson,* the undergraduate newspaper and long-standing rival of the *Lampoon.* Yale University was not forgotten. One rec-ommended launch was to fire the Fat Man out of the garden of Yale's secret society, the Skull and Bones, to be followed by a phone call to the *Yale Daily News* from a "Bones" representative stating that the society with this sym-bolic blast was letting everyone in New Haven know that it had decided to "go public" and open a restaurant on the premises.

While these wildly impractical ideas were being offered (most of them in notes addressed to me, for some reason, "Dear Charles . . ."), a curious fig-ure appeared on the scene. He was a Florida-based car dealer named Remar "Bubba" Sutton—a tall, bald-domed man of enormous energy whose special ability was to galvanize people into undertakings that under normal circum-stances they would not dream of doing. I had first heard of him in football circles for having persuaded the Players' Association of the National Football League to become involved in an exhibition game in Paris, France. Appar-ently, the promotion had not been much of a success. The players were out of shape (the game was played in May); *Le Monde* in its review of the pro-ceedings reported that the Americans were "clearly in precarious physical condition." Since the plays were programmed beforehand at a meeting in a hotel ballroom (". . . then Bob Hayes will go around end for thirty-five yards," etc.), the French got very little sense of the contact aspects of the game once the contest was underway. *L'Équipe,* the French equivalent of *The Sporting News,* was especially scathing. The lead read: "Relax, Frenchmen, our na-tional game is not in jeopardy."

When I was introduced to Bubba Sutton, I mentioned in the course of our conversation that I too had been involved in an unsuccessful public event. I told him about the Fat Man and the ignominy of being responsible for a very large hole in the vicinity of Bellport, Long Island, notice of which had been published in the *Guinness Book of World Records.*

"The *Guinness Book of World Records* . . . what an extraordinary coinci-dence!"

Sutton was particularly excited to hear there was a second Fat Man.

"You mean to say you've got *another* one—just sitting there waiting to go up?"

I nodded.

"Titusville!" he exclaimed. "We'll send it up off Titusville during the Guinness Record week!"

I must have looked puzzled. Sutton hurried on to explain that Titusville is the community immediately inland from the Kennedy Space Center on Cape Canaveral. Brevard County—Titusville is the county seat—happened to be in the middle of a promotion campaign of which he—Bubba Sutton—was in charge. He explained that since the decline of the NASA space program, Bre-vard County had itself slid into a despondent state with vacancy signs turning up in profusion along the coastal Route A1A. He had persuaded the county leaders to let him attract national attention to Brevard, and thus spur tourist interest once again, by mounting what he referred to as a huge "assault" on the *Guinness Book of World Records*. That was his intent: to use Brevard County as a kind of vast stage on which various people with specialized skills could come and try to get themselves into the renowned record book. He had not realized that "fireworks" was a category. What could be more fitting! What a coincidence! He saw the performance of Fat Man II as a climax to the festivities of the Brevard County promotion, the vast umbrella of Fat Man in the sky as a kind of punctuation to the promotion.

I got caught up in Sutton's enthusiasm. I tried to pass it on to the undergraduates at the *Lampoon*. They did not find Brevard County as exciting as some of their other sites. "Dear Charles," they wrote, "we are vague about Brevard County." They had just come up with Niagara Falls as a possibility, the burst of Fat Man—as they imagined it—timed to go off while the members of the magazine partied aboard the *Maid of the Mist* below. Nonetheless, I was able to get them to agree that there was a certain nicety about the world's largest firework being sent aloft from the Space Center. Finally, they agreed; they promised that they would send down two representatives to attend the event ("to watch the phun").

The assault on the *Guinness Book of World Records* began in the fall of that year. The Gruccis brought the Fat Man down from Bellport by truck. I arrived in time to watch almost the entire week's events. I kept notes on some of the record-breaking attempts. I actually saw only one record established— that by a tireless and frisky six-year-old whippet named Pogo. He was on hand to try to break the Guinness record for a broad jump by a dog—which stood at thirty feet, set by a greyhound in Gloucestershire, England, in 1849. Down on the beach Pogo did so, racing after a Frisbee hurled by his owner, Mike McLaughlin, for a leap that was measured out at thirty feet, six inches.

Certainly the most poignant of the would-be record-breakers was a man Sutton had persuaded to come to Brevard County to try to break the world's oyster-shucking record. He failed, but only just barely. I did not watch this valiant struggle between man and bivalve, but I did meet the shucker afterward, a Mr. Roland Hill. He had missed the record—one hundred oysters in three minutes, one second—by only three seconds, or, in concrete terms, by an oyster and three quarters. He explained to me, "It's early in the Florida oyster season. I'm out of practice." He seemed very woebegone.

I put in my notes that there is nothing as vacant and despairing as the hunched posture of a man who has missed the Guinness oyster-shucking record by a bit more than one oyster. He told me gloomily that it might be six months before he could work himself into a proper state to give it another try.

There was one odd event cooked up by Sutton which was remembered by everyone who participated in it. It was called "The Reach on the Beach." Sutton's idea was to get the population of the county to walk out on the beach and hold hands in a long line. His hope was to construct an unbroken chain of people holding hands that would stretch for forty-eight miles of the county's length along the Atlantic coastline from Cape Canaveral to Sebastian Inlet. A "love chain," he referred to it. Why, if it ever could be done, Sutton thought that the *Guinness Book of World Records* would rush to get this category into their pages I have no idea. It rained on the day of the "Reach on the Beach," but there had been so much publicity that an estimated sixty thousand people heeded the Sutton appeal and wandered out onto the oceanfront to hold hands at the designated time. I did it too. It was a curious and quite memorable experience—to grasp an absolute stranger's hand (in my case, on one side a small, bright-eyed girl wearing a damp straw hat, and on the other a rather crusty gentleman wearing gloves who wasn't quite sure why in "tarnation" he was out there and a bit miffed about it) and to see the weave of people like us, stretching out, up and down the coast, all the way to either horizon.

Throughout the week the Gruccis worked on their preparations for sending up the Fat Man. Sutton had tried to get permission to shoot the "firecracker"—despite my entreaties, he would not refer to it as a firework—off from the grounds of the Space Center itself. It seemed appropriate enough. A letter was written to the proper authorities. The reply came back quoting the Air Force legal department's opinion that if the Fat Man happened to veer off course on an errant flight pattern, it was capable of causing $100,000,000 worth of damage to high-technology buildings and equipment at the Center. Because of this, Sutton's request was denied.

He could not let this pass. He telephoned the Air Force authorities—the Public Information Service at the nearby Patrick Airforce Base—and told me that he had the following conversation with an officer there:

"Do you mean to tell me that this firecracker of ours is capable of destroying the VAB?"—referring to the assembly building for moon and space rocketry, indeed one of the largest buildings in the world—"Could it do that?"

"Yes sir," the officer replied. "That's what I understand."

After a pause, Bubba asked: "Well, is there any chance that the Air Force might consider adding the Fat Man firecracker to our weapons inventory?"

"I beg your pardon."

"I mean, if the Fat Man can do that much damage and only cost a couple of thousand dollars to build," Sutton went on, "it might be a good idea."

The officer hesitated. "Well, sir, I don't know . . ."

Sutton persisted. "Could it be, let's say, *considered* by the military?"

The officer demurred, but finally he admitted, "Well, yessir, anything is possible, I guess."

It was a mistake. Sutton passed on the story to a reporter friend of his, Hubert Griggs, from the Orlando *Sentinel,* who published a story in the paper whose headline read: AIR FORCE SAYS FAT MAN IS A HUNDRED MILLION DOLLAR BOMB. In the article was his prognostication that the device might possibly be added to "America's arsenal of weapons."

At this point, the director of the Chamber of Commerce offered the Fat Man contingent the use of a small, forlorn sandspit in the middle of the Indian River. It was an appropriate site—just across from the riverfront of Titusville, and behind it, the great ghostly gantries of Cape Canaveral shimmering in the distance through the heat waves.

The Fat Man's mortar was transported in a thirty-ton crane-barge out to what by this time was referred to as Fat Man's Spit, swung off with the crane and set down on the island, where it was propped up with a great mound of sand. Then the Fat Man itself, dangling from the barge crane, was slowly carried out to the island, where it was guided into the interior of the mortar.

The firing was scheduled for nine o'clock.

We went back out to the island by motor launch about an hour before. The means of ignition this time, rather than electrical, was with the use of a long, old-fashioned fuse. It hung over the lip of the mortar and stretched down the sand mound thirty yards, almost to the water's edge. The fuse was timed to burn for five minutes—an elapse that would give us plenty of time to evacuate the islet and move by motor launch far upriver before the shell went up.

A few minutes before nine o'clock, those who had come out to Fat Man's Spit—about a dozen—waded back out through the shallows and clambered aboard the launch. I was left alone on the island with the device. The bulk of the mortar was huge against the sky. The river was black and very calm. Amid the distant lights of the Titusville shore, thin beams of light stretched across at us from the headlights of cars and trailers still jockeying for position. The vans and the campers had begun to arrive that morning—veterans of space shots, I took them to be, settling into beach chairs and gazing out at Fat Man's Spit from under their long-billed fishing caps.

I bent to the fuse and removed the protective paper tubing at its tip. "Is everybody ready?" I called out, my voice as high as a coloratura's. I spun the wheel of a Zippo lighter and applied the flame to the fuse. It sparked immediately. I rose and stepped away, trying to effect a nonchalance, but then I suddenly broke into a trot, the warm river water splashing up as I tore through the shallows and was hauled over the stern of the launch. My unease was infectious.

"Gun it! Gun it!" I heard Jimmy Grucci yell. The propeller bit at the muck of the river. Amid cries of alarm ("Everyone move forward! Get the weight out of the *stern!*") the launch strained ahead, then suddenly, with a lurch, we were free. We tore upriver at full throttle. Fat Man Spit with its great, dark cone-like configuration housing the mortar receded until it disappeared in the darkness. The lights of Titusville went by to port and began to dim in the distance. After a while Jimmy Grucci called out, "One minute to go." We kept hastening up the river until finally, perhaps two miles from the launching site, the skipper cut the engine. We drifted softly onto a sandbar; the grit of sand scraped against the bows. We stood staring downriver. The time for ignition had come and gone. One of the Gruccis began murmuring petulantly, "Oh God!" I knew what he was thinking—that, like Hemingway's Francis Macomber having to go back into the bush to look for his wounded lion, we would eventually have to return to the islet . . . with the Fat Man waiting, perhaps nurturing a tiny spark in its mortar, one that could spring it into violent life just as our bows touched shore.

Just then, a large orange fireball materialized downriver—the sort of boil of flame that appears when a gas tank explodes. It hung briefly in the sky, emitting a few jagged shards of what looked like flaming debris, and then it

The world's largest firework being lifted by a crane to a waiting barge to be transported out to Fat Man's Spit. (Grucci Collection. Photo by Bill Kilborn, 1977)

Fat Man II rises from Fat Man's Spit opposite Titusville, Florida, on the Indian River, October 22, 1977. (Grucci Collection)

winked out abruptly. A few seconds later, a shock wave reached us in the darkness—a palpable shift in the atmospheric pressure that stirred the cigarette smoke, a soft odd caress—and then a thundering blast of sound, deep and concussive, went by us and rolled and meandered up the river.

"Jesus, what was that?" Jimmy Grucci asked, his voice cracking with surprise. What we had seen, after all, was so utterly unexpected. Rather than a chrysanthemum spread high in the sky, we had been given a curiously artless jumble low to the horizon. The first reaction was that what had happened was not of our doing. Somebody else had got into the act with a rival device.

But from Felix Grucci's vantage point on the Titusville shore, the sight was far more impressive. Standing at the end of a dock, much closer to Fat Man's Spit, Felix had first seen the running lights of our launch as it sped northward; he kept watching until eventually the lights disappeared in the distance. He was wondering vaguely where we were going when suddenly the Fat Man rose out of the mortar across the water directly in front of him and almost immediately went off.

What he remembered especially about its abrupt performance was the impression of heat—as if a vast oven door had been opened. The shock wave was much firmer than what we remembered upriver on the launch—indeed, strong enough, he said, to move a cigarette on a smoker's lip. A gasp had gone up from the crowd on the dock—many of them sucking back from the blast as, briefly, the river glowed orange from the fireball. The stars that had been ignited by the bursting charge soared helter-skelter over the water—like a huge flock of outraged birds, as one witness on the dock remembered them. The flitter hung for an instant, and then was gone. The noise was not as heavy and reverberating as we experienced it upriver. The visual effects simply overpowered everything else. Felix told me that the sound he would always remember was the faint ringing of a number of burglar alarms set off by the shock wave behind them in the town. Not only were over fifty burglar alarms set off, but a large front window of a furniture store dropped out of its supports with a roar. In perhaps the most bizarre occurrence, the back window of a car being driven down U.S. A1A simply disintegrated. There were the normal episodes—the sudden snapping-up of window shades, the shiver of glasses in the cupboard, the mysterious soft bellying of gauze curtains, the occasional tilt of a ceremonial plate jarred from its position on the fireplace mantel, and, of course, the Titusville switchboard lit up with inquiries: what *force* was it that had passed through town?

There were postmortems as to why the Fat Man had behaved so unlike a typical aerial firework. The general consensus was that the Gruccis had put too large a bursting charge inside the canister—that is to say, the hundred pounds of black powder which was supposed to break the shell apart and ignite the hundreds of stars had actually detonated some of them and blown the rest far out over the river, producing thus a fat, angry boil of flames, with the few tendrils of those burning stars hurrying away from the blast as if horrified.

Still, the shell *had* actually come out of the mortar—if not very far—and functioned. Indeed, as the celebrations that evening wore on, the height at which the Fat Man had exploded seemed to increase. until by the time the party was breaking up one had the impression that its performance had been an outstanding success.

"How far did you think it went up?" Jimmy Grucci asked me.

I kept sticking to fifty feet or so. "Maybe sixty or seventy," I said, to be kind.

"We were too far up the river," he said. "We weren't in a position to appreciate its . . . ah . . . effect."

I telephoned the *Lampoon* the next day to report on the Fat Man's performance. After a while someone answered the phone. I announced, "The Fat Man has flown!"

After a pause, the voice said, "What's that again?"

"The Fat Man went up at nine p.m. last night . . . not very far, but up."

"Who is this?"

I told him that I was calling from Titusville, Florida. "It's where the Fat Man—"

"Do you want to speak to someone on the business board?" I was asked. "Actually there's nobody here. Is this about a subscription, or something?"

Subsequently, I sent a short report to the *Lampoon* people. Perhaps it was read out at one of their regular meetings. It would not have surprised me if it had not been. A new board had taken over. Perhaps they knew nothing of the great firework. The organization tended to develop its own spheres of enthusiasm. Indeed, I never heard from the *Lampoon* again about the Fat Man.

Not long after Fat Man's somewhat marginal performance over the Indian River, the Japanese pyrotechnic firm Marutamaya Ogatsu decided to fire another huge *tama* to try to eclipse its own mark in the *Guinness Book of World Records*. The ball-shaped shell was only slightly larger in diameter than the original—just under forty inches—but it weighed much more—564 pounds. It was planned to be fired out of a three-ton mortar thirteen feet high. In his home province of Niigata, an artisan the Japanese refer to as a "fire-flower master" worked for almost a year on the huge shell. The device—another Bouquet of Chrysanthemums—had a descriptive designation almost as impressive as its dimensions: *Ascending with Small Flower Brocade, first Silver, then Red-illuminated, with Configuration of Small Motives in Relief.*

The firing site where the mortar was settled into place by a derrick was a peninsula in Tokyo Bay near the community of Futtsu in Chiba prefecture. The mortar was buttressed by an enormous mound of sand that rose half its height—indeed, very much as we had supported the mortar on Fat Man's Spit in Florida. There was a lot of publicity about the shoot; on October 16, 1980, over thirty thousand people turned up in Futtsu Park. The Fuji TV Co. was on hand to televise the event live. Four helicopters maneuvered overhead to get pictures from a bird's-eye vantage. Thirty "fire-flower masters" arrived from around Japan to lend assistance.

The ignition was done electrically from almost a thousand yards away. According to Ogatsu's written account, the shell performed exactly as it was supposed to. It rose from the mortar with a "terrible thudding sound . . . as if caused by terrestrial trembling . . . during its ascent small flowers neatly scattered from the ball . . . at the summit the ball exploded and blossomed out as planned and expected. At the same time I felt heavy gaseous pressure from above which was caused by the explosion . . . the floral petal formed a circumference of two thousand feet, extending an umbrella above me, far beyond where I was standing."

Ogatsu went on to report: "Suddenly and unexpectedly the roar of 'Banzai! Banzai!' rose from the staff workers. Then the flower vanished and was submerged into the darkness of the night sky. Gradually the reverberations of the audience's amazement came from afar."

What was especially pleasing to Ogatsu was the performance of his shell. In his report on the huge *tama* he wrote: "The size of a firework may be worth competing over, but to my mind height of ascent and size are matters of secondary importance. No matter how large a flower may open, if its shape is warped or disintegrating, that flower is valueless. If one of a thousand of stars fails to appear, one missing star is a shame to the 'fire-flower master.' All the flowers have to open at once. In this respect, the largest ball ever of the world successfully accomplished a metamorphosis into the most beautiful flower of the world."

In 1981, the new edition of the *Guinness Book of World Records* came out. Perhaps if Ogatsu had had the chance to read the proofs he would have had his "fire-flower master" in Niigata increase the circumference of the shell by three or four inches. To my astonishment, and certainly to the surprise of the Gruccis and very likely the Ogatsu organization, the people at the World Records had got word of Fat Man II's brief ascent. In the *Guinness Book of World Records* the pertinent paragraph reads: "The largest firework ever produced was Fat Man II, made by N.Y. Pyrotechnics Products, Inc., fired near Titusville, Fla., Oct. 22, 1977. The 720-lb. shell was 40½ in. in diameter." Neither of Ogatsu's fireworks is mentioned. The offending paragraph about "George Plimpton's lowest firework" had disappeared completely.

I called up the Gruccis in Bellport. "I have some great news," I told them. "The Fat Man has been recognized."

"What's that?" It was Felix Grucci on the other end.

"The *Guinness Book of World Records* got word of the Titusville shoot," I went on. "It's in their newest edition. The world's largest firework!"

Felix was silent for a moment. "Well, it *was* the biggest," he said. He seemed almost petulant about it.

"You should celebrate," I said. "Send up a salute or two tonight to let the people of Bellport know." I did not mention Mr. Ogatsu's dictate that one missing star was a shame to the firemaster.

I could hear Felix calling out the news. "The big bomb's been recognized," he was saying. Then, as ever, he refused to refer to the firework as the Fat Man.

After I had hung up, I telephoned the *Lampoon*. No answer. I thumbed through the new edition of the *Guinness Book* to see if any of Bubba Sutton's other "assaults" had made it. There was no mention of the Reach on the Beach. The whippet, Pogo, did not make it for some reason. There was no word in there about the world's second-best oyster-shucker either.

Today, the Fat Man's mortar, unearthed from Fat Man's Spit, stands amid some scruffy vegetation just off U.S. A1A at the eastern end of Titusville's Birdwatchers Park. A Howard Johnson's does a brisk business just up the road. About a half mile away, across the slow flow of the Indian River, is the low hump of the Fat Man's Spit, its little beach glistening above the gray, flat water. Occasionally a porpoise rolls between the two points of land. Once, at the mortar's base was a plaque describing what had come out of it that warm October night—the world's greatest firework—but it has disappeared. Someone though—could it have been Bubba Sutton?—has written in chalk high on the tube: *The Fat Man lived here until he came out and performed on Oct. 22, 1977.*

There are two nationwide official organizations of fireworks people in the United States. First, there is the American Pyrotechnics Association (APA), made up largely of professionals—displayers, importers, retailers, and a few manufacturers. Second, there is the Pyrotechnics Guild International (PGI), which is largely composed of amateurs who make or collect fireworks or fireworks artifacts, such as firecracker labels, as a hobby and are often jocularly referred to by the professionals as "basement bombers."

The two organizations hold each other in mild disregard. The amateurs don't believe the professionals have very much in the way of aesthetic regard for fireworks, or care about their history, and in most cases don't even *make* fireworks. The most common jibe is that less than five percent of the APA can actually construct an aerial shell by themselves. "Bunch of importers!"

The professionals tend to think of the amateurs as rather dangerous fanatics who tinker around too much in an area which should not be treated as a hobby, and who often give fireworks a bad name—especially when on occasion a "basement bomber" is catapulted through a roof by a detonation.

Actually, very few professional pyrotechnicians are trained chemists. I once asked Felix Grucci about the need for a knowledge of chemistry and whether he had ever purchased a chemistry set for his children. He said, in that high querulous voice, "What would we want with a chemistry set?" and waved his hand at the mixing sheds in the compound. "We got enough chemicals around here already."

Thus Jimmy and Butch Grucci learned their craft in the Bellport complex almost by osmosis, picking up information practically in the course of running errands for their father. He never sat down and taught them. It was not until Jimmy was twenty-one that he made his first aerial shell—a four-inch shell-and-report which, he recounts, "worked, but just barely." He had not taken any chemistry courses in high school. His best subject was biology. His brother, Butch, told me that *his* best subject was "biography."

Neither of the Grucci brothers thought much of having chemists around a fireworks compound. "They're more hazardous to work with than someone who doesn't know anything," Jimmy once told me. "They're always fooling around with their little bottles, trying a little of this, a little of that, usually trying for a better color or a faster burning effect, and suddenly they haven't got any hands."

Butch agreed. "I can't talk chemistry, but I can talk pyrotechnics," he said. "That's better than the other way around. I may not know what is going to happen chemically, but I sure know what will detonate."

Both fireworks organizations have annual conventions. The professionals tend to put on a fairly traditional event—one would be hard pressed to distinguish their gathering from a convention of clothing manufacturers. At the one I attended in Las Vegas, the convention bulletin boards urged members to sign up for various athletic events. Everyone wore identification badges in their lapels that announced *Hello My Name Is* and, below, had a blank space to be filled in. In the hotel lobbies and in the hospitality suites there was talk of the headliner shows not to be missed on the Strip, and how one had done the evening before on the gambling tables. The official business of the APA— talks and discussion groups were arranged throughout the day—concentrated on various aspects of merchandising, and, in particular, on the legal restrictions and lobbying pressures that the fireworks industry traditionally faces from organizations like the National Fire Protection Association and the National Society for the Prevention of Blindness, and especially its running confrontation with such authoritative bodies as the Consumer Product Safety Commission and the Bureau of Alcohol, Tobacco, and Firearms. The year I went, one of the discussions centered on insurance requirements for trucks carrying explosives.

Very technical stuff. But in the evening, in the hospitality suites after the supper shows, the fireworks people would gather to drink and they'd start reminiscing about the old days and some of the legendary figures of the industry.

One of their particular heroes was Thomas Gabriel "Ray" Hitt, who established Hitt Bros. in 1905 in Seattle's Rainier Valley. He played the French horn in the Elks and Shriners bands and his hobby was experimenting with perfumes. His greatest passion was fireworks. When they were banned after World War I he had said, memorably, "They've taken independence out of Independence Day."

I was told that a Ray Hitt label on a firework was a special collector's find. So were the fireworks themselves. His procedure was to adapt and label fireworks from Macao—reworking them with such care that even after three quarters of a century the fireworks—mostly Roman candles and missiles of various sorts—performed admirably. "They don't improve as wine does," someone said, "but they show how great Ray Hitt made them back then."

Not that he couldn't make a mistake. The story was told of a display Hitt had arranged for the opening of the Exhibition Fair in Vancouver. The Canadian Governor-General was to push a button to send up a barrage of fireworks among which a large canister shell was to pop open into clusters of Canadian flags. What suddenly appeared and self-inflated in the sky was a large Uncle Sam. Apparently someone had mislabeled the container. Fortunately for Ray Hitt, a hard wind sailed the Uncle Sam balloon figure off toward the horizon before anyone in the crowd could truly make out what it was. "Did you see that?"

Jerry Elrod, a fireworks man from Portland, Oregon, stirred his drink noisily with his finger, as if to gain attention with the clinking of the ice cubes, and said he was reminded of a large display he'd fired in Seattle to which he had brought a friend who had fired shows there with Ray Hitt and knew a lot about fireworks, and so forth. Everything went smoothly until after the final barrage. Discovering he had an unfired shell left, Elrod decided he'd fire it rather than carry it back home. Up the shell went. A piece of paper—as often happens—fluttered toward the barge's surface, burning, and Elrod's friend took one horrified look and somehow got it into his head that it was the shell itself coming back down. Elrod heard these five steps, *boom, boom, boom, boom, boom,* reverberating against the iron flooring of the barge, and then a loud splash. The friend was eventually fished out of the Seattle harbor by a tugboat skipper.

When the laughter had died down, the conversation turned to the odd places fireworks were fired from—barges, rafts, swamps, wharfs, the tops of skyscrapers, the sides of mountains. A pyrotechnician wearing a lapel card which identified him as Ray Stout, from Arizona, said he was probably the only fireworks man there who had ever set off a fireworks display in a nudist colony.

I asked him if he himself had been asked to perform nude while shooting the show, and he said, "Certainly not." He said it was a chilly night anyway, and that the spectators, from afar, at any rate, seemed no different than any other crowd.

He asked me if I had ever fired a display before as unlikely a crowd—thinking I was a *bona fide* fireworks man, which pleased me no end—and I said that no I had not, but that I had *heard* that at one of William Randolph Hearst's wilder evening gatherings at San Simeon he had shot off a barrage of rockets *inside* the Great Hall, which went roaring and ricocheting and exploding among the rafters and the great heraldic banners. I said that I would have been nervous at *that* party and would have asked if I could watch the proceedings from the outside, staring in through the windows.

"Yes, give me the nudists anytime," said Stout.

The Grucci family was not at the Las Vegas APA convention, but they wanted to be filled in when I got back East. I told them about my impressions, and said, to compare notes, that I was planning to go to the amateurs' PGI convention in Rochester, Minnesota, in a few weeks' time.

"That'll be interesting," Jimmy said. "They've got some strange cats in that organization." He described a PGI convention at Spring Lake, Michigan, where he had been invited to judge the amateur fireworks competition. He remembered one amateur working on a grooved shell designed to spin like a bullet as it emerged from its mortar and thus bore through the air and go a lot higher. Another contestant had a salute on the bottom of his shell intended to act as a propellant charge. Jimmy said he spent a lot of time walking around saying, "No, no, you can't do that." But then he smiled ruefully. Apparently, at a display on the last night of the convention the woods caught fire on the island where the fireworks were being set off. The fire reached the bomb boxes, which went up with a huge roar, followed by a great flurry of different devices whisking and scurrying about as if to escape the spark that had ignited them. Ironically, the mishap was caused not by amateurs, but by a professional concern putting on a show for the amateurs.

At the meeting I went to in Rochester nearly two hundred members of the PGI organization turned up. In the lobby of the Ramada Inn, the other hotel patrons stared curiously at the T-shirts imprinted with colorful fireworks company emblems and slogans ("Fireworks make people happy"). I heard one man at the next table at breakfast say that he would rather be at a convention of snake-farm operatives than in a hotel full of fireworks people.

To me, the PGI membership seemed composed largely of young, rather intense people, many of them bearded—the overall effect that of the enrollment of a graduate psychology course. Their wives were with them in many cases, sitting alongside at the meetings, listening to the lectures, an arm over the other's shoulder; in the back corner of the conference rooms small children slept in strollers or curled up on the carpet.

Actually, the range of their normal professions turned out to be wide—from Kent Orwoll, a professional skater on tour with the *Ice Follies,* to Bruce Snowdon, a very hefty man from a small town in New Hampshire who, when in need of income, "puts on the feed-bag," as someone said of him, and balloons himself upward to 650 pounds so he can hire himself out as a circus Fat Man at seven hundred dollars a week!

A president of the Guild for a while was a Lutheran minister, the Reverend Brian Bergin, referred to by the Guild members as the "blaster pastor." I was delighted to discover that the Reverend combines his hobby with his clerical work—that is, at a wedding, he will give a short sermon on the theme "The Coming of Light in a Dark World" and then at the wedding party itself that evening he will put on a sixteen-shell display of his own design to illustrate what he had said earlier. Around the Minnesota area he is especially welcome at services, I was told, since his fireworks display is often longer than his sermons!

"Do you ever use fireworks *during* a sermon?" I asked him.

He nodded. "Well, not *in* the church, but during an outdoor sermon I might say, '. . . and thus is the way of the Lord.' *Boom!*"

"You light a salute?"

"Oh, absolutely. I think fireworks should be available for just about everything."

From the outset I was struck by this kind of crusading attitude in the PGI. In fact, its members feel strongly that whatever advances are to be made in fireworks and techniques lie only in their hands—that the professional companies have little interest in experimenting with new effects or even improving the performance of their own shows. "They're too busy eking out a living to experiment," one member told me. "They do the same thing over and over again."

Guild members admit that they have a number of advantages over their commercial brethren in the APA—the chief one being that cost and time are not of particular importance. No commercial maker, for instance, is interested in making the ball-shaped chrysanthemums, since it is so much easier to order such shells in bulk from the Orient. The amateurs, however, have the luxury of being able to fashion such things. Larry Homan from Fresno, California, has a reputation among PGI members of being able to match the very best round shells that Japan and China can produce.

The goal among the shell-makers in the Guild was to make a flawless shell, not only in its eventual performance, but as an object in itself. The shells were handled as if they were ship models, turned in their hands as if even in the smooth sheer of the shell's surface there were things to be admired. To my unpracticed eye there was very little to be exclaimed over—each canister was as similar to another as a pair of artillery shells—but each was a thing of beauty to the experts. A shell's "integrity" was constantly mentioned. "Wow! What integrity!" would be announced as the shell, especially if it was of considerable length, was hefted, studied, and prodded. The term denoted the desirable conformity of strength and delicacy—the equivalent in yachting circles of what used to be called the "yare" of a yacht.

In Rochester I was introduced to some of the prime movers of the PGI. One of them was Max P. Vander Horck, the founder of the organization and the editor of the *American Pyrotechnist,* which refers to itself as an "educational and informational journal for all fireworks enthusiasts." Vander Horck started the *American Pyrotechnist* in 1968. A monthly publication, printed on the same color stock as Kraft fireworks paper, it continued on a reasonably steady basis until 1981. Its cover bore a logo of a hand holding a lit match which if held that way in real life would eventually ignite the fingers. The journal was always very chatty and personal. Vander Horck kept his readers informed about not only the present state of fireworks, but also the health of his own family dogs (a series of them—Corky, Hobie, Scamp, et al.—appear and die off in its pages) as well as those of fellow members (". . . saddened by a call from Orv Carlisle informing us that his and Mary's longtime pet, Jacques Pierre, whom you may have seen at various conventions, had died of a heart attack"). There was often mention of Vander Horck's wife, known as "super chick." In reference to the medieval symbol of the fireworks figure known as the Green Man, she was also described as the Chief Green Lady.

When Vander Horck finally ceased publication of his pamphlet in 1981, immediately a new house journal—this one entitled *American Fireworks News*—sprang up with Vander Horck as its contributing editor. The slogan of the new publication is: "He who hath once smelt the smoke is ne'er agin free."

Vander Horck published a number of guest columns in the *American Pyrotechnist.* The most outspoken, by Chuck Tenge, entitled "Chuck's Choice

PGI group portrait from the 1981 convention. (Courtesy of Robert M. Winokur)

Comments," was full of words like "rip-off," "junk," and "fast-buck artist," inevitably followed by an exclamation point. Tenge wrote in one column that he had been driven to drink to "vent my aggravation" when an ill-made shell performed poorly at one of his displays.

On occasion a poem appeared. One I noted—in free verse—extolled the bygone pleasures of throwing a cherry bomb under the tuba player as the band marched by the courthouse square on the Fourth of July.

Also published for fireworks aficionados—and available at the convention—was a far more sober and reflective magazine with the elegant title *Pyrotechnica*. Edited by Robert Cardwell, it was beautifully produced, with slick paper, color reproductions, graphs, various tables of enormous complexity—at least to my eyes—along with learned essays on various aspects of fireworks-making. One of its staff editors, Robert M. Winokur, was in attendance in Rochester. He is a professor of zoology at the University of Nevada, and his particular interest in fireworks involves what is called "glitter"—the star-dusty, after-effect phenomenon that accompanies certain shell-bursts. It is also called "flitter," and by the old-time Italians, *"tremolante."* Winokur spent two years experimenting and data-collecting, and of the result—a paper entitled "The Pyrotechnic Phenomenon of Glitter"—Robert Cardwell, his publisher, was moved to write: "Its greatness speaks for itself."

I went to one of Winokur's seminars at the convention. Pleasant-faced and much younger than I would have expected, he was giving a talk on the sensitivity of chemicals. When I walked in and sat down in the back of the room, he was saying that a mixture could be so unstable that the composition could change. "You mix on Monday," he said, "and on Tuesday it no longer functions in the same way."

His talk was full of warnings. He said that just because a mixture *seemed* stable, that was no reason to assume it was all right to continue with it. "It's like cheating on the Internal Revenue Service," Winokur said. "If you don't get caught, that doesn't make it okay."

He drew on a pair of gloves and a set of welder's goggles. After setting a laboratory mortar in front of him on the table, he sprinkled in slight portions of various chemicals. Then he picked up a pestle to show us in miniaturization what would happen if the combinations were unstable and put to a stress. The first demonstration was red arsenic—a common ingredient in the early days of fireworks-making. After some hefty grinding on Winokur's part, suddenly a sharp crack and flash from the mortar made everyone jump. Cries of "More! More!" erupted from the seats. A small child began to murmur in the back corner of the room; a mother rose to attend to it. "Whew," someone next to me said, "it's no wonder so many Italians went up through the roof."

Winokur showed us a number of mixtures. The biggest flash and report he got with his pestles and mortars was from a combination of perchlorate and dark aluminum, which surprised me because I had always understood that the perchlorates, which are used extensively in making fireworks, were safe, and a vast improvement on the more unstable chlorates. Before he ground it, Winokur poured some of the powder out, saying there was a bit much of it in the mortar—which produced mock cries of dismay from his audience who made it clear at any opportunity, even in jest, that it preferred good, solid concussions. Even so, there was enough of a flash and sound produced by the perchlorate and aluminum to promote some exclamations of satisfaction ("Ah! Ah!"), and some applause.

Some of the experiments did not work. Winokur ground away at a mixture of barium chlorate and hexamine, which makes a beautiful green, but which is not on his "safe" list, and he could not get any sort of reaction. "Bang it!" someone called from the back of the room. He finally gave up. He said the atmosphere was a little damp, which was probably responsible for making the mixture less sensitive than it normally was.

He concluded the lecture with some safety tips about chemicals. He urged his listeners to use plastic bottles with press-on lids in which to keep them; he held up a glass lid to the microphone and we heard the grinding of particles as he screwed it onto a jar. "The slightest *sput* from this sort of thing can put your garage into orbit," he told us graphically.

Over the course of the convention I attended a number of the panel sessions. Most of them, despite being on technical subjects which I didn't understand, were entertaining enough because almost every topic had its firm proponents and opponents. Often members of the audience stood up and involved themselves. There were intense disagreements about such items as "flashbags"—a kind of bursting-charge device—or the efficacies of different types of fuses. Someone who innocently praised the use of bran as a bulking agent was roundly taken to task by a critic who hooted at him that "bran" shells had to be fired almost immediately because, if left on a shelf, beetles and bugs tended to get into the bran and lay eggs, whose larvae would eat through the walls of the shell, leaving holes through which fire could pass and ignite the contents prematurely.

One of the most intense of the panelists was Chuck Tenge, the author of "Chuck's Choice Comments." Wearing a garish Silver Jet T-shirt, he would lean forward, almost belligerently, at his audience and insist: "*Scrape* your comets, for heaven's sake. *Rough* them up. *Brush* them with homemade black powder. They *must* be primed, for heaven's sake!"—his voice as outraged as an evangelist's.

Given the intensity of all this, I was not at all surprised to be asked if I had entered a shell in the amateurs' competition to be held on the last day of the convention, and if not, why not? I said that I had not brought any fireworks with me, and indeed had none at home from which to pick a display. I had never even made a firework.

"It's about time you did," I was told, "especially if you're in the journalistic practice of trying other people's professions."

I agreed, but I protested that I didn't even know how to *start*.

They insisted. They would provide the materials, and, of course, someone to help. Jim Freeman would be just the person. He was a local resident and had a manufacturer's license. He was a great enthusiast and expert— "Knocks the socks off the best of the Japanese," as an admirer said of him.

An unusual medium for an artist depicting fireworks: a crystal bowl designed by Edward Hald for Orrefors of Sweden in 1923. (Nationalmuseum, Stockholm, © Mrs. Edward Hald)

The Guild's favorite story about him was that he had become so engrossed in making a shell that he had been an hour late to his own wedding.

At first glance Freeman's garage seemed the usual suburban clutter of garden hoses, rakes, hoes, and lawnmowers. But in the corner he had a workbench and the paraphernalia of shell-making—awls, mallets, scissors, casting forms, glue, and various containers of stars. Jim told me that he had been making fireworks practically since his childhood in Stillwater, Minnesota—shown how by his father, who was a commercial painter. The charcoal came from the fireplace, and the saltpeter and sulfur from the local drugstore. Saltpeter was in popular use then as a diuretic; sulfur was apparently the regional remedy for dandruff problems. The pharmacist was astonished at the amount of the last two ingredients the Freeman family seemed to be in need of.

I had hoped we could make a mammoth shell—oh, perhaps one of eight inches in diameter, which would have placed it among the largest entries in the competition; but Jim Freeman, grinning slightly, said that he thought it would be wiser to make something less grandiose, namely a *three*-inch shell, which was the smallest size, mainly because of the limited amount of time we had.

"There are other reasons," he said. "The smaller the lifting charge, the less chance there is of the shell itself breaking apart in the pipe from the shock."

"We mustn't overburden the integrity of the shell," I said.

We spent some time deciding what kind of shell it would be. I hoped to program in a noise, something that would hum and shriek in the sky, and Jim Freeman said he had just the thing—what he called "wild jobs" or "buzzers." "Some people think they sound like Bronx cheers . . . a sort of fart sound."

"Oh," I said. "Well, I'm not quite sure that's what I had in mind."

"It's a *hornet* sound, really—that's what most people take it for," Jim reassured me.

"Excellent," I said.

The first step in making a shell is to fashion the container. This is done by cutting off a length of sixty-pound Kraft paper two or three inches wider than the eventual length of the shell and long enough to roll six or seven times around a wooden form just under three inches across which looks exactly like an old-fashioned rolling pin for kneading bread. The last turn of the paper is pinned down with tape and glued with a squeeze of Elmer's Glue (Elmer's Glue is as staple an ingredient in the pyrotechnical craft as measures of 2F gunpowder). The protruding ends are tucked in against the bottom of the rolling pin, fastened, and then the rolling pin is pulled out, leaving a hollow container ready to receive the ingredients of the shell.

First, down the middle of the empty container we placed a metal tube called the cannula (pronounced "can-yuhluh"), which would be in position temporarily, in which to pack the bursting charge and around which would be placed the stars, and, in the case of my shell, the "buzzers," or what Jim

HIRAYAMA IMPERIAL JAPANESE DAY FIREWORKS

One of the greatest fireworks novelties ever offered. These goods are fireworks in the day time. The finest article in the fireworks line to delight a crowd in the day time.

Assorted Effects Including American Flags, Figures, Animals, Birds, etc.

2 inch diameter, packed ½ dozen in box, **with Mortar** .... per box, $ 6.00

3 inch diameter, packed ½ dozen in box, **with Mortar** .... per box, 10.00

4 inch diameter, packed single, Mortar loaned .... each, 3.50

6 inch diameter, packed single, Mortar loaned .... each, 5.50

We loan Mortars to fire 4 and 6 inch sizes.

The Unexcelled Fireworks firm advertised these "Japanese Day Fireworks" to its American customers as "one of the greatest fireworks novelties ever offered." (Courtesy, Hagley Museum and Library, Wilmington, Delaware)

Freeman kept referring to as "wild jobs." He had already made them—small two-inch-long fused tubes which looked something like M-80s. There was enough room in the container to place seven of the buzzers in a circle, their fuses sticking inward toward the cannula. Then we put in the stars—irregularly shaped small black clumps of barium chlorate and red gum which would provide the green balls in the sky through which the hornets would perform. We sprinkled them in among the buzzers, up to the top of the container, and tamped them down. I felt slightly nervous pounding on the barium chlorate stars and did so with tentative pushes since the word "chlorate" without a "per" in front of it has a tendency to produce the same sense of discomfiture as the word "cobra" without a "dead" as its preceding descriptive. But Jim Freeman kept assuring me that barium chlorate composition was a perfectly stable compound, especially in the chunky form we had put in the canister.

"Besides," he said, "it is important to pack everything down so that the shell has—"

"Integrity," I said.

"Exactly."

We filled the cannula with a homemade gunpowder mixture called polverone, tamped *it* down, and then carefully pulled out the metal cannula, leaving the canister with its interior column of the polverone, which would burst the shell apart at the height of its climb and ignite the outer circle of stars and buzzers. After sprinkling on a topping of 2F gunpowder (to facilitate ignition of the mixture) we then sealed the container with a fitted cardboard disk which had a hole punched through it with an awl for the fuse—a two-inch-long Japanese time fuse (Hosoya brand, which is considered the best) with one end inserted through the disk. The bottom end of the fuse had a one-inch-long fuse stuck in it crossways—a process called "cross-matching" to make sure that the bursting charge ignited.

Jim referred to the match which went down the side of the shell from the fuse at the top to the lifting charge at the bottom as the *passafuoco,* and the paper pipe in which the match was contained as the *mapolle.* The fireworks jargon there in the garage included a number of Italian words, which the PGI tended to use rather than their English equivalents. It was as if the historical background of shell-making had to be preserved. Indeed, I heard far more Italian terminology in Jim Freeman's garage than I remembered from the Gruccis' compound in Bellport. The bunched paper at the top of the shell which contained the firing appurtenances was referred to as the *bochetta.* And, of course, the *passafuoca.* I found *myself* using the term: it is one thing to say "match" and quite another to be talking grandly about a *passafuoca.*

As we worked on the final process of finishing the little shell—adding a lifting charge at its base along with its *mapolle,* strengthening the casing with a crisscross pattern of Italian twine, and so forth—various members of the Guild stopped by to see how we were getting along. One of them was Bill Hoyt, the secretary-treasurer of the PGI, slim, red-bearded, wearing faded overalls and a plaid woodman's shirt; he was carrying a four-inch shell about

The American Fire Works issued this poster in 1872 to advertise their wares. The symbolic set pieces of the American eagle and a Statue of Liberty are bordered with pictures of a full range of offerings, including "flowerpots, grasshoppers, volcanoes, flying pigeons, rosettes, pinwheels and serpents." (The Bettmann Archive, Inc.)

thirty inches in length which he said he had worked on for three days. We stood admiring it—a tall firm column that he told us contained a series of six breaks, each of them featuring serpents and buzzers.

I exclaimed, "You've got buzzers in yours too?"

"Fifteen serpents per break," Bill Hoyt was saying. "So that means this one shell will produce, in its series, some ninety serpents and buzzers."

"Beautifully finished," Jim Freeman commented, prodding the shell with his fingers to test the resistance of the surface.

The *most* number of breaks incorporated into a single shell Bill said he'd ever heard of was twenty-two! The shell itself was four feet, four inches tall and was shot out of a ten-foot pipe that was set on a railroad tie deep in the earth to stabilize the mortar and give the shell a more rigid base to kick off from. The recoil had apparently broken the tie in two. What integrity *that* shell must have had! The timing devices were set to begin the breaks almost as soon as the shell left the mortar's mouth—eleven on the way up and eleven on the way down.

That afternoon we finished my shell in time to visit the PGI auction, which was conducted by a spirited Guild member named Rob Berk. Over half the items auctioned off were packages or "bricks" of firecrackers, wrapped—most of them—in fire-engine-red (which is the Chinese color that symbolizes "happiness") wax paper and colorfully decorated with distinctive brand-name labels. Some of the bricks were bid for what seemed to me astonishingly high prices. A brick of four-inch "Bo-Peep" firecrackers, the package itself about the dimensions of a thin paperback novel, went for thirty dollars! Every time Berk held up a brick of firecrackers, the aficionados stirred in their seats. The Chinese manufacturing names were whispered back and forth—Yick Loong (Duck Brand), Wang Yick (Camel Brand), Kwan Yick (Cock Brand). Originally, I was told, the firecrackers imported from China up until the First World War were called "mandarin crackers." They came in plain wrappers and were not distinguished by colorful labels or brand names. Nor were they particularly popular in the United States, whose Fourth of July celebrants at that time preferred the awesome concussion of what were practically dynamite sticks— the various varieties of "cannon crackers." The "mandarin crackers" were very small potatoes in comparison.

Then in 1916 the Hitt Fireworks Co. of Seattle gave the Chinese some new formulas—most of them from experiments with photographer's flash powder. The Chinese incorporated what they learned into a new series of firecrackers, distinguished by a brilliant flash of silver in addition to a big report. The labels identified them as "flashlight crackers," "silverfish salutes," "thunder firecrackers." They began giving their products brand names (often wonderfully misspelled—my favorites include Best Tire Crackers, Firecrad Ker, and a fireworks packet commemorating Wah Shing Ton) and decorating their firecracker packages or "bricks" with brilliantly colorful and distinctive labels. The brands were mostly named for animals—Polar Bear, Swallow, Tiger, Giraffe.

Fireworks artifacts, such as this trade catalogue cover, circa 1910, from the Lloyd's Jubilee Fireworks Manufacturing Co., would attract high bids from collectors among the membership of the PGI. (Courtesy, Hagley Museum and Library, Wilmington, Delaware)

Then in the 1920s the "animal" series was extended to cater to the more particular tastes of the importing countries—or at least what the Chinese thought would be popular—brands with such names as Jester, Samson, Bo-Peep, Captain Kidd, Homerun, Lone Eagle, Pagoda. The great exporters were Fat Shan and Im Po, both from Canton Province. Always, their labels were beautiful and sylvan, almost as if to belie the racket of the product within the red

Fireworks memorabilia being auctioned off at the PGI meeting in 1979. (Courtesy of Robert M. Winokur)

wrappings of the brick—artfully painted birds, animals, temples, bridges, flower maidens, invariably settled in among lush vegetation—a strong Art Deco quality, rather as if Maxfield Parrish had put in a long stint in the art shops of Canton.

These days the label designers have shifted their emphasis—much to the dismay of the purists—to reflect more accurately the contents of the fire-

This random selection from Orville Carlisle's fireworks museum in Norfolk, Nebraska, illustrates the variety and range of fireworks devices. Among them are a representative group of die-cut cardboard novelty items, all of which after varying performances (the elephant shoots sparks from its trunk, the boat and the white mule whistle, the fire engine scoots along the ground emitting smoke) self-destruct, blowing themselves into a shower of paper shards. The outhouse (at top, right center) contained a strip of paper on which were attached numerous pellets of a cap-pistol-type composition which caused the structure, after a burst of smoke from its half-moon ventilator, to destroy itself in a series of explosions. The Animal Crackers (lower right), much sought after by collectors, were patented and made by the National Fireworks Co. in the 1930s. The curious item next to the Animal Crackers box is a "Utility Fireworks" manufactured by the Hitt Fireworks Co. in Seattle, Washington. According to the information on the device it was a mailman's "Scare Away Salute," thus its inspired brandname "Doggone." One cannot help wondering how often it was used for what it was designed to do; it is hard to rid one's mind of the mental image of a mailman fishing in his pockets for a "Doggone" and something to light it with while a bulldog is fastened to his ankle. The mock rocket (top center) is actually an ordinary fireworks mortar tube with a detachable cover over its mouth. Its manufacturer (Tipp Fireworks Co.) can redesign the cover to suit the times and the public enthusiasms. Heroes from Buck Rogers to Luke Skywalker have had their days on these slip-ons. This one, in bright colors, shows an early space vehicle, complete with astronauts in a reclining position in the nose cone. The rest of the items in the grouping are now outlawed. These include a row of Hitt's Flashcrackas (bottom center)—the odd spelling because the company could not get the more appropriate word "flashcracker" copyrighted. It must have rankled Thomas Hitt; he revolutionized the fireworks industry in 1918 with patents for a "safe" flash powder and a way of using it in noisemakers. The Hitt Flashcrackas were made in lengths from two to five inches, the larger items (far left, center) known as "Salutes." All of them contained a charge of flash powder enclosed in a paper bag located in the middle of the tube. Because flash powder burned with such speed (it is essentially the same substance on an early photographer's tray that went poof!) it was not necessary to use a heavy case or close in the end with any sort of crimp or hard plug. The air space at either end of the tube was compressed so fast by the gases generated by the burning flash powder that the force of the explosion was greatly increased, accompanied, due to the aluminum in the powder, by a brilliant flash of light. The three devices in a row under the "Doggone" are the most popular and thus the most infamous of the noisemakers. At the left is the forebear of the M-80, introduced in the 1920s and referred to in the industry as a Side-fused Tubular Flash Salute. The other two are Globe Flash salutes, which arrived on the market in the late 1920s, smaller versions of which came to be called cherry bombs. The cases were made of rock-hard sawdust and glue which often did not disintegrate in the explosion and were thus capable of injuring anyone in the area. (Collection of Orville Carlisle, Norfolk, Nebraska)

cracker packages; the beautiful birds and flower maidens have been sup-
planted by military rockets and bombs. Rather than the beguiling choice of
Bo-Peep, the brand names are now called Mini-Bomb or Grenade Bomb, and
one doubts that many of the contemporary labels, so bland and conventional,
will have very much value, at least aesthetically, to the collectors of the future.

I asked my neighbors if American-made firecrackers had as much market
value as the Chinese products and was assured that they did. Of particular
value were the Ray Hitts, of course, and Gangster Brand and the Superman
Brand made by a legendary figure named Larry Lomaz—he sells fireworks by
mail (Buckeye Fireworks)—who over the years had been a large supplier of
firecrackers to the Chinatown sections of San Francisco and New York.

Over the course of the afternoon other items which were auctioned off
by Rob Berk included a "no smoking" poster (which raised a laugh), a set of
polished steer horns, an exploding cigar made by United Fireworks ($6), an
empty Du Pont dynamite box made of wood ($15), ten pounds of barium
sulfate, a red cap pistol dating back to 1909, a Buckeye Fireworks wind-
breaker, a half gross of antique cherry bombs, a "popping cane" that exploded a cap when hit sharply against the ground, a pair of small brass cannon, a single small Spanish plastic shell only three inches in diameter, which,
after spirited bidding, went to a Guild member named Al Colantino for $51
(he told me he was going to take it apart and analyze it—it was a beautiful
shell and not many of them were around), wooden tamping mallets, a painting of Mickey Mouse carrying a large firecracker ($105), an antique carbine
machine gun ($75), a gross of Rozzi's Silver Jets (". . . bring them back in
ten years when fireworks are completely banned," Rob Berk shouted from
the podium, "and they'll be worth a million!"), a bag of sulfur, a book on
explosives by a man named T. L. Davis (*The Chemistry of Powder and Explosives,* 1943) which went to Tom DeWille for $151!, a six-pack of Coors beer
(which is not available in Minnesota), garish fireworks posters, assorted firecracker decals, a large empty box with "Agricultural Use Only" stenciled on
its side ($105), a large colored photo of Bruce Snowdon at his 650-pound hef-
tiest ("a lot of people pin this on the outside of their refrigerator door," Berk
told us), various tubes, for use as two-inch finale rockets, or "perhaps" (Berk
suggested) in "uh-uh-uhs," by which he meant—I was informed—large illegal firecrackers.

The last offer of the evening went for the privilege of lighting the Superstring—a length of firecrackers, fifty feet or so long, and including a quarter
of a million firecrackers, which was to be set off at the Fair Grounds as the
climax of the night's festivities. Since the first day of the convention, Guild
members had been working on the Superstring, its enormous length laid out
on the floor of a barracks-like shed at the Fair Grounds. It would eventually
be rolled up like a great carpet and taken out to the Grounds to be fired. A
PGI member named Chuck Gardas won the right to do so. He bid $275. The
year before he had also won the bidding. As an anniversary present, he had
let his wife touch off the Superstring. This year he could not resist. He would
do it himself.

Orville Carlisle, from whose large collection these firecracker pack labels have been selected, has provided the following observations: Navy Brand (top left) and Hitt's Stars and Stripes (top right) are two of the first Chinese-type firecrackers, prepared with Hitt's patented flash powder, made in China and imported by the Hitt Co. ca. 1920. The two Yan Kee (sic) Boy labels (top, ca. 1920; bottom, ca. 1950) show how the label designers catered to the Western importers—the boy in dress and looks in the 1950 label being completely westernized. Carlisle writes of the Black Cat label (lower right): "Trademark registration 1952, in use before that date. This early Black Cat label shows a mean, wild-looking cat with the mange, even rabies! Later issues of this label depict a more domesticated, well-fed, brushed and vaccinated, domesticated house cat!!" The item on the right showing a youngster being startled by a bursting firecracker is not actually a label, but rather an example of the Fourth of July greeting cards, whose subject matter varied from crude humor to beautifully embossed works of art with patriotic themes. The exchanging of such cards was a popular custom from the late 1800s to World War I. Such well-known contemporary popular artists as Tuck, Clapsaddle, and Corbett contributed to the series, examples in mint condition being highly prized by collectors. The most valuable items shown, according to Carlisle, are the earlier of the two Yan Kee labels, the Black Cat, and the Captain Kidd label (trademark registration 1938), any one of which would fetch twenty-five dollars or more on the market. (Collection of Orville Carlisle, Norfolk, Nebraska)

The Fair Grounds were in Kasson, a small town about fifteen miles from Rochester, which announced itself on billboards as the "Tree City"—a somewhat odd and wistful appellation, I remember thinking, since the terrain was empty, rolling farmland with only an occasional small clump of big trees sheltering a farmhouse or a water trough with a horse or two standing alongside in the summer heat. Nor was Kasson easy to classify as a "city." We were through it in no time at all. We could hear the spit of firecracker strings as we drove into the Fair Grounds. A small concrete grandstand overlooked the tumbled ruts of a car-racing track. The fireworks displays were to be set off at the far end of its infield, out against a distant backdrop of cottonwoods. Jim Freeman said that the grandstand would be jammed with people. The PGI convention was a big event in Tree City.

The earlier part of the evening was reserved for members who wanted to fire off Class C fireworks. One end of the track was set aside for those who preferred to shoot aerial stuff. The opposite end was for the firecracker people, the *noise* enthusiasts. The faint, acrid tar-smell of a Fourth of July drifted over the field. There was something curiously appealing about this aspect of the PGI gathering—that its members, who built extraordinary shells in their workshops, were out there in the mud of the car tracks, bent over, firing off five-cent bottle rockets and firecracker strings. It was as if Grand Prix drivers were down on their knees on the carpet moving miniature model cars around between thumb and forefinger and making car-engine noises with their lips.

"Oh, no," Bob Winokur told me, "it's not a childish activity at all. Don't forget, many of the PGI members come from states where Class C stuff is against the law. So this is a great occasion for them—the chance to do legally what they cannot do at home."

The stands began to fill up—many parents carrying small children already asleep on their shoulders. The teenagers came wheeling in on their bicycles, balancing them against the wire-mesh restraining fence and looking up into the stands for others of their kind—blond, bare-legged. Cries for someone named Judy drifted through the evening.

The Class C fireworks continued to whirl up into the stiff breeze, shredded by the wind but increasingly brilliant as the light faded. Sometimes a cluster of rockets going up together produced applause from the stands, and a buzz of anticipation for the big stuff that would be going up later.

The wind began to die down. It was still chilly. I noticed a small child wander by in a bunny suit. Over the loudspeaker set up on a pole in the infield a phonograph record began to play "God Bless America." The crowd stirred uneasily—wondering if it should stand. The recording stopped in midperformance. A version of "The Monster Man" came on.

That evening my "shell" opened the competition. I walked across the infield to where the firing lines were set at the far end of the track and let the shell down into the mortar. I heard my name mentioned over the loudspeaker system. I was handed a flare. I lit the fuse, took a few steps back, and, hearing the *thunk* of the propellant shooting the canister up into the darkness, I looked up for the burst. That was unusual in itself. Usually the pyrotechnician's attention is rooted to the ground—to concentrating on the bomb box, the mortars, the business of loading and firing, and rarely until he touches off the finale, and has no more to do, does he get a chance to look up and watch the result of his labors.

I am not sure what my expectations were—confident, I guess, since Jim Freeman had helped me with the shell, though it would not have surprised me if the sky had remained comfortably dark, unrent by even a spark until the last conceivable chance of ignition for the burst had gone by, and then, inevitably, to hear the humiliating *thump* in nearby weeds of the unexploded canister coming back down. So it was with a combination of relief and awe that the shell immediately above me suddenly began its little performance. The serpents, all eight of them, buzzed merrily against the background of green stars.

"Damn!"

Once again I was struck by the aesthetic pleasure fireworks provide to those who set them off—that the act of touching a small flame to a fuse, as insignificant as the tap of a conductor's baton on the shelf of his music stand, initiates the splendor above. I heard the patter of applause from the stands.

"Damn!" I said again.

Bill Hoyt touched my shoulder. I turned in the rose glare of the flare and I could see his shy grin. He said nothing, but it was clear that he knew what pleasure the small, busy confection above us had given me.

The shell was, of course, utterly overshadowed by the displays that followed. The competitions included *novice, advanced,* and *limited* in various categories—rocketry, aerial shells, ground pieces, and fountains or gerbes. There were a number of multiple winners. My friend, Jim Freeman, won in six different categories.

One memorable big eight-inch shell made by Kent Orwoll—he was the Ice Follies skater—pushed its mortar into the mud as it was fired—the mortar base fetching up against so little that was solid that the shell was able to gain very little altitude. It burst only about fifty feet up. Most of its breaks worked busily on the ground, including a large, glittering spider-web effect that hopped and danced its sparks in the grass. Kent put the best possible face on the situation. He described the shell's performance to me as "very nice and really interesting. Didn't look quite like what I expected." He eventually won second prize with the shell.

I congratulated him. I asked him how many entries there had been in his category.

"Two," he said.

"Oh, I see."

Certainly the most imaginative entry was Orville Carlisle's. It consisted entirely of Class C fireworks—mostly bottle rockets and flying saucers of different kinds—choreographed to go off in quick succession. Above his display area the sky buzzed and whistled busily; a storm of disks suddenly rose, trailing thick tails like sea anemones. Everything performed about fifty feet up.

The famous "Superstring" from the 1979 PGI Convention is seen here. (Courtesy of Robert M. Winokur)

All of it lasted just about a minute; there were shouts of delight at each different effect.

"Goll-*ee*," someone in the stands behind me said. "Shows what you can do with fifty milligrams"—in reference to the maximum amount of flash powder allowed in Class C fireworks. "The man is a genius."

Carlisle is a native of Norfolk, Nebraska, where in the back of his shoe store he has a fireworks museum. Out front he makes custom-made shoes (the model is called Foot-so-Port Supreme) which many members of the Guild wear, but he is perhaps best known for being the inventor of the prototype of the model rocket engine. It sits on display in the Smithsonian Institution. His particular specialty is miniature fireworks—one of them a minuscule shell that comes out of a tiny pipe, rises thirty feet, and performs with three breaks and then a minuscule report, a little click of sound, like a pebble hitting the sidewalk.

Afterward Orv told me what he had done to make such a whirligig of color and noise. He had mounted 124 tubes, none more than an inch and a half in diameter, in four rows on two-by-four boards and loaded them with every kind of glitter comet, whistling projectiles, reports, hummers, screamers, and a device that makes a loud Bronx cheer. Connected with quarry cord—which burns about one foot per second—the battery was arranged so that the display started with the whistles, then the glitter, then a build-up into what Carlisle referred to with a grin as that "humming blamming racket."

The climactic event of the convention was the ritualistic firing of the gigantic string of firecrackers. It had always been a great tradition of the meetings. Each year the intent was to make the Superstring longer and its effect more cacophonous.

I had watched it being constructed—Guild members on their knees fusing together the bright red packets, most of them Chinese brands. The Superstring was arranged in successively packed tiers so that at the end of the string, when the fuses had reached that point, literally thousands of firecrackers would be going off almost simultaneously. One Guild member had figured out that if the string was unrolled and stretched out, packet after packet, it would end up five *miles* out into the countryside.

"You won't believe the sound," I was told.

The Superstring was borne through the crowd from the shed to the Fair Grounds preceded by cries of "Put out your cigars! No cigars!" In the darkness, as its bearers came through the gate in the wire-mesh fence out onto the track, the bulk of it, undulating and slipping, with the men struggling to keep it aloft, resembled a listless serpent of vast proportions. It was hefted up and suspended from a pole out in the infield of the track. Chuck Gardas, the man who had won the privilege of lighting the Superstring, stepped forward, a dim figure in the distance, and touched it off.

It was an extraordinary sound, a ripping concussion, and, without any attendant beauty of aerial work or set pieces, it was violent and angry. When it was done, after about ten minutes of ear-splitting noise, thousands of firecrackers knocked off the string by the explosions crackled and continued to go off in the grass around the pole.

During its performance, oddly, I found my mind wandering, thinking back on the pleasure of setting off the little shell that had opened the evening's proceedings. I did not really envy Chuck Gardas the privilege of lighting the Superstring. Truly.

On Thanksgiving Day, 1982, at two in the morning, Bill Hoyt's small home in Beaver Falls, Pennsylvania, blew up and he and his wife, Sue, were killed. Apparently, it was as if a terrible hammer had come down on the house. His grandmother was the nearest neighbor. She heard the concussion and called the fire department. I read about the tragedy in the *American Fireworks News*.

I remembered the pair from my PGI visit in Rochester: Sue, a tall, striking girl inevitably in blue jeans—bare-stomached—and a man's shirt with its tails tied up around her waist, and Bill, thin, red-bearded and quite reserved, so that I always felt a bit awkward talking to him. My enthusiasm for fireworks—so unfocused and unprofessional—was in such variance to the technical and profound absorption that Hoyt enjoyed about the craft of fireworks-making. With him I felt rather like someone who loves music but who himself sings loudly off-key in church or who isn't quite sure whether the music pouring out of the car radio is Beethoven or Brahms.

I telephoned Chuck Tenge. He told me he had heard the news within hours. The voice from the other end of the phone had said, "Sit down. I have something to tell you." Tenge had gone up to the site in Beaver Falls the next morning. The blast had knocked the house absolutely flat. It was possible to walk straight across its rubble.

"What do you suppose happened?" I asked.

Tenge said, "Bill was using a green aluminum for making green electric stars. That's not easy stuff—it contains barium chlorate—and it can be affected by heat and humidity. You should always make the stars in winter, or where it's cool. What they reckon is that Bill must have brought the stuff inside to keep it out of the rain, and down there in the cellar, in its warmth, it must have started cooking. Of course, this is guessing. Bill would have been aware—the smell, maybe, the sound—and hurried down to put it out. But other things were down there—black powder, chemicals, a big case of dynamite caps (Bill had a blasting license) and it all went up, detonated, blowing the walls out laterally so that the roof fell into the basement."

I thought of Sue lying in her bed. Tenge was saying, "Bill must have had a lot of copper sulfate down there. Because I was told that the ground all around burned blue."

After a pause, Tenge began talking about how important the Hoyts had been to the PGI. He was the secretary-treasurer. They took care of all the paperwork and records of the organization—all of which had gone up in the explosion. Sue was just as enthusiastic about fireworks as her husband. She sat in the car as close as she could get to his shows and watched him at work. Tenge stayed around after the funeral and purchased a number of Bill's stars from the estate. "Bill made wonderful zinc stars," he told me, "and always great blues and greens. His gold flitter wasn't that good, and his charcoal stars weren't any good at all. But then who *does* make great charcoal stars?"

6

Nobody is quite sure on what occasion the greatest pyrotechnics display ever fired was given. The Brocks fireworks family in England has always singled out the enormous extravaganza of July 19, 1919, put on to celebrate the signing of the Treaty of Versailles; they say it's the largest show ever fired, at least by their company. Certainly the prints and engravings of the time— showing the entire length of Hyde Park alive with rocketry and aerial bombs, including hundreds of curlicue serpent shells—would seem to support their claim. The finale alone had an effect with two thousand rockets in the air at the same instant!

For sheer geographical scope, Queen Victoria's Diamond Jubilee in 1897 has surely never been surpassed. Crated fireworks displays with directions for using were sent out to the remotest parts of the empire—perhaps the most far-flung outpost being Blantyre, three hundred miles up the Zambezi River in Africa, where the "kit" (which included a scaffolding of the head of the Queen outlined in lances) had to be carried in by porters. It was eventually set off before a crowd of startled natives who had probably never seen a firework before, much less the enormous head of a mysterious woman outlined in fire.

According to Brock's records, the distinction of giving the most elaborate and costly *private* fireworks display belongs to the Earl of Sheffield who, in 1893, gave a party to honor, of all things, the arrival of the Australian cricket team!

Up until the Bicentennial celebrations in 1976, the largest display of fireworks on the American continent was back in 1908 when the tercentenary of the founding of Quebec by Samuel de Champlain was celebrated. The show was fired from the banks of the St. Lawrence River. It included huge lance portraits of those identified with the river's history, including Jacques Cartier, its first explorer, 1534–35, and the two generals, Montcalm and Wolfe, who opposed each other and were both mortally wounded in 1759 during the battle of the Heights of Abraham overlooking the river.

Certainly in contemporary times the most massive concentration of fireworks shot up in a single night is a display fired off a Japanese golf course
every August 2. The event, which is reputed to cost in the neighborhood of
a million dollars (compared to approximately $150,000 for the largest U.S.
shows, such as the Brooklyn Bridge Centennial and Chicago's Venetian Night),
is staged by a religious organization known as Perfect Liberty. The order's
headquarters and a number of facilities, including the golf course, are settled
in a huge compound called the Sacred Precincts in the small town of Tondabayashi, not far from Osaka in the southern part of Japan. The display is
watched by over a million people.

The founder of Perfect Liberty, who is buried in the compound under a
massive heap of smoothed earth (a scholarly friend of mine was reminded of
the great Scythian kurgans of Siberia), was a priest named Miki Tokuharu-
Hijiri, the latter part of his name meaning the Enlightened One. Founded in
1935, the order, which has a couple of million members, has as its main thrust
the perpetuation of peace. Its principal tenet is "Life is Art," and theologically
and for its rituals it borrows variously from Catholicism, Buddhism, and,
oddly, from the Quakers. The order practices a number of secular activities—
tea ceremony classes, flower arrangement seminars, various youth activities;
on the grounds of the Sacred Precincts is a hospital and a considerable research facility. As mentioned, golf is available for members of PL at Tondabayashi; since the game is so extremely popular in Japan, and golf-course
memberships so coveted, I wondered if perhaps some of the members joined
PL because they equated "Life is Art" with "Life is Golf."

No matter. When Miki Tokuharu-Hijiri died on the second of August,
1936, reputedly his last words to the followers grouped around his bed were,
in so many words, "Fire *hanabi* (fireworks) for peace! Let *hanabi* shine for peace
in the world!" In his will the Enlightened One was more specific: he felt that
his death would mean the propagation of his teachings about peace, and that
therefore it should be "celebrated and rejoiced in after I am gone"—namely
with fireworks. It followed that as a symbol for peace the use of explosive
material for beauty and to promote peace rather than destruction was most
appropriate.

The worthies gathered around him—including his son who succeeded him
as head of the order—took him at his word. The firework is practically as
much a symbol of the Perfect Liberty organization as the Cross is of Christianity. Every August 2, the Perfect Liberty *hanabi* show is put on not as a
mere "summer entertainment" (as the official program literature on the event
explains) but as a "gigantic bouquet offered to the soul of the patriarch who
joined the community of the immortals while praying for world peace."

The PL display—as it is popularly known—is obviously a place of pilgrimage for fireworks people. Thus a trip I took to China in 1980 with Jim
and Gary Souza, members of a California fireworks clan, and a fireworks buyer,
Jerry Elrod, from Portland, Oregon, was scheduled to end in Tondabayashi
so we could watch the show before returning to the United States.

Even landing at the Osaka airport, which is the nearest major city to

Tondabayashi, one gets a quick sense of the importance the Japanese as a nation attach to fireworks. As the plane touched down we could see the distant thistle-like bursts of large chrysanthemums going off at a number of locations around the perimeter of the evening horizon. I pointed them out to the Souzas. Both of them rubbed their hands in pleasure. "Pyro heaven!" Gary said.

Others were not as enthusiastic. While waiting for the luggage at the Osaka airport baggage claim, I met a young American who had been on a camping trip through Japan. He had long hair tied in a bun resting on the back of his neck. He was traveling alone. Solitude was what he was looking for—silent, unroiled Japanese lakes, like black mirrors, to set his sleeping bag beside—but he told me fireworks had plagued him wherever he went. "I had some insect repellant, man, but it wasn't bugs that bothered me. It was fireworks! They're pretty to see across the water," he said, "but not all night long. I couldn't sleep worth a damn."

In Osaka we stayed at the Royal of Osaka—a very snazzy hotel indeed, which just about everything in town is. The city was almost completely razed by bombs during the war, but, oddly, there are no scars to be seen. Everything has been put together again in contemporary styles—modern, neat. In the hotel room the television set was murmuring in the background. It was showing one of the five baseball games available on the various channels. We watched a manager shout from the dugout through a little yellow megaphone and then rush out and verbally abuse an umpire from closer range, and finally *shove* at him. Gary Souza mentioned how mild-mannered Billy Martin, the baseball manager so volatile by U.S. standards, would seem in a Japanese stadium.

Our hosts for the stay were the Ogatsu family—the major owners of the Marutamaya fireworks firm, well known to us, of course, for being the makers of the great *tama* fireworks which the Gruccis and the *Harvard Lampoon* had challenged with the Fat Man series.

The Ogatsu family has been a particularly influential fixture in international fireworks circles since the end of World War II. Toshio Ogatsu, heading a company 250 years old (his eleventh forefather provided fireworks for the feudal lords in the eighteenth century), came to the United States just after the war to offer his products and expertise. He created quite a stir. First of all, he referred to himself as an "artist"—a startling nomenclature for the average American pyrotechnist to hear—and he took pains to show them how he was inspired by the aesthetics of waterfalls, flights of birds, and the movement of fish in an aquarium (one of his aerial extravaganzas was called "Tropical Pool").

First he painted his concepts on canvas, and then with meticulous care tried to emulate his designs in the night sky. All of this was relatively new to American pyrotechnists. His reputation and the beauty of the Japanese shells he brought with him made a considerable impact, as they did elsewhere. Ogatsu became world-known, and highly praised except, perhaps, in the Soviet Union, where he made the mistake of concluding a show on the Moscow River with a huge fiery replica of Mount Fuji. It completely dwarfed the penultimate dis-

play, which had been a rather tacky representation of the Kremlin towers. Ogatsu was not asked back. "Insensitive," he said tartly of the Russians.

In the United States, Ogatsu was most famous for his New York City fireworks displays during the late 1950s and '60s, an annual Fourth of July show sponsored by Macy's Department Store and shot off a string of barges in the Hudson River held taut against the quick currents by tugboats at both ends. Ogatsu oversaw sending almost two tons of fireworks into the sky. A million people lined the New Jersey and Manhattan shores to watch the show.

John Serpico, my old friend from the International Fireworks Company, fired the displays for Ogatsu. Ogatsu's English was nonexistent, and most of his communicating with Serpico's technicians was done by sign language and by imitating the sound effects of the aerial bombs he wanted loaded and fired in the program. Serpico described to me Ogatsu's pops and cheek-bulging hisses and whistles, his eyes widening with effort, as he tried to explain what he wanted—a fireworks show in itself. John told me, "People thought he was auditioning to be a one-man band."

Out on the barges, Ogatsu wore a special ceremonial jacket and a bandana covered with Japanese characters. Just before the first aerial reports went up in the early evening sky—the maroons that traditionally open a big show— Ogatsu would go off to a corner of the barge and pray.

One warm summer night in 1953 Ogatsu was not on board the barges. "He never came out," Serpico said.

"Why not?" I had asked.

"I don't know," Serpico said. "Maybe he *felt* something. We certainly could have used his prayers that night."

Halfway through the program, on the first barge, a big Japanese shell burst prematurely, just a few feet above the muzzle of its mortar, and its spray of stars ignited the entire deckload of fireworks beneath. The concussion knocked two of Serpico's men off the barge; they drowned. "Cases of shells just kept on going up, on and on," John described it. "It lasted for an eternity."

From the shore what was happening almost seemed to be part of the show. The barge bloomed like a thick multi-petaled flower, long pistils of color arching out of it. Along the riverbanks the faces of the crowd shone in the magnesium glare and applause broke out in admiration. Perhaps only Ogatsu, standing in the crowd, knew that something awry and awful was going on out there in the middle of the river.

His younger brother, Kyosuke, is now the present head of the firm. Apparently shy, and very solemn, in a competitive business where the social amenities toward a potential customer such as the Souzas are crucial, he cared startlingly little about such things. Jerry Elrod remembered being introduced to Kyosuke Ogatsu and being asked what the weather was like in San Francisco where he had just come from. "Quite seasonal," Jerry replied, and was about to continue when the interpreter interrupted him to say, "Mr. Ogatsu has said that is enough talk of social affairs; now he wishes to get down to business."

OPPOSITE AND PREVIOUS PAGES *One of the world's largest firework shows was the display at the Brooklyn Bridge Centennial Celebration, May 24, 1983. (Photos © Diego Goldberg, 1983/SYGMA)*

Jerry said that the Ogatsu offices had two girls and four men crowded into a somewhat confined space, and that all of them—to his surprise since the Japanese are very concerned with their dress—were quite scruffy. Mr. Ogatsu's tie was hanging askew, and his shirttail was out. Jerry remembered only one occasion when Mr. Ogatsu picked up a check in Tokyo. It was for three Coca-Colas. When Jerry told me the cost of three drinks totaled the astonishing amount—at least in these times—of fifteen dollars, it struck me how practical it was for the senior Ogatsu to be inhospitable.

For our visit to the PL show, Mr. Ogatsu sent his nephew, Toshio, named after his uncle, to represent the Ogatsu family. The nephew turned out, quite unlike his uncle, to be a most hospitable and friendly host, nodding enthusiastically in the affirmative to every question, even those—because of his somewhat stumbling English—he did not understand ("What is the largest shell we'll see tomorrow at the PL?" "Yes, yes, yes."). The only Ogatsu trait that was typical was his rather shabby appearance. When he turned up at the Royal of Osaka he was dressed in the scruffy white overalls he would be wearing the next day on the golf course for the display.

Toshio told us something about the show we would be seeing. Four fireworks companies would be involved, each firing from their respective sites. The Marutamaya firm had been given two firing points. Toshio had a little kit with him which he unpacked to show us what he, and everybody else on the golf course working on the show, would be wearing: a little pyrotechnician's apron, not unlike a carpenter's waistbelt, a ceremonial robe which he would put on just before the show began, and a miner's helmet with a light on it to help guide himself around in the flickering Verdun of the firing lines. The robe is called a *shirushi banten* or "happy coat"—a dark-blue jacket, usually with the manufacturer's trademark on the back. Practically nothing in the PL display was fired electrically. The tremendous flights we would see were connected and fired with quick match. He described the firing procedures with individual shells—which was that the shells, the largest of them, the twelve-inchers, weighing as much as forty or fifty pounds, were hefted from the bomb boxes, carried across and dropped into the mortar pipe, at the base of which was a red-hot coil. The ball-shaped shell had a cardboard tube sticking out the top to keep it from turning as it went down the pipe, so that the propellant charge at the bottom of the shell would fetch up properly against the coil. When this happened, the propellant was ignited and the shell emerged almost simultaneously. From time to time the firemaster would reach into the pipe with a stick with a hook on the end and remove the cooling coil to replace it with another, a fresh one which had been cooking to white heat on a brazier set off from the firing line. Toshio told us that a coil would last for about two minutes, or about long enough to ignite thirty shells and send them up on their way.

He began talking about his favorite shells. There was one called the Silver Crown—a big willow. Another was a chrysanthemum whose stars changed eight times as the bloom of the shell expanded. To do those he explained that the husk of the star—usually a rice seed—was rolled in eight different chemical mixtures which burned off in succession as the star—hundreds in a single large shell—ignited, and was exploded out into its final flight by the bursting charge.

"Will we see some of these?" Gary Souza asked, excited as a child.

"Yes, yes, yes," Toshio said, which meant that either we would or we wouldn't.

The next morning we took a train out to Tondabayashi. The first sight we caught of the PL complex was from the station platform—a number of large balloons in primary colors moored against the distant sky; sticking up among them was a monstrous structure like a pointing gray finger, as huge as the superstructure of a battleship. Built as an interreligious memorial to the war dead of all nations, it is known as the PL Peace Tower. Open to visitors, it has an observation lookout tower at its summit with a diadem of arched bay windows, not unlike the brow of the Statue of Liberty. The view looks out on the grounds of the PL complex, the "Sacred Precincts."

Ogatsu had reserved seats for us on the porch of the clubhouse—a fine vantage point since the structure was built on the side of a hill looking out over the golf course. Directly in front of us was a campanile, softly chiming, and in the distance, at the far end of the course, we could spot the outlines of a marble-hued structure, not unlike the Jefferson Memorial in proportions, which was referred to as the Shrine and where we were told various ceremonials involving the PL order would be taking place. Clusters of red and white balloons, so huge that they barely seemed to move in the breeze, were moored at various sites on the golf course, and we could see the long, sweeping curve of the cable that supported the Niagara—a waterfall of colored fire that was scheduled in the show—suspended between two cranes. We estimated its length to be well over a kilometer.

We spotted Toshio Ogatsu toiling up the walk toward us from the golf course below. With him was his uncle, who was the president of the Japanese pyrotechnics association and the chief "engineer"—as he was introduced—of the Marutamaya team. With them they had a detailed program of the evening's show, page after page meticulously indicating the order and number of shells that would be rising off the golf course.

Toshio had hoped to show us around the golf course, but the officials would not allow it. From the clubhouse veranda he pointed out the firing sites in the distance. We could see a glimmer of silver—a protective material called "oee"—covering the mouths of the long lines of preloaded mortars from which the various barrages would rise. In the United States the Souzas used a polyethylene material, either black or transparent, named visquine. The pyrotechnicians do not bother removing the coverings when the display starts; the shells simply punch up through the material.

The big individual shells, Toshio told us, were kept in cartons with cardboard covers, these in turn covered with a canvas tarpaulin. Next to each mortar is a kind of rattan shield which the igniter can duck behind if he has a mind to—which is very much the case when he has dropped a shell down a pipe that is a ten-inch monster or larger.

The show is under the direction of a PL official who sits in an observation post overlooking the golf course and is in radio communication with the various firing sites. One of his functions, we were told, was to hold up the show if he felt that smoke from the explosions was obscuring things. The carillon would play music until the winds had cleared the night air, then the official would once again give the command to get the next segment started.

I thought how unlike American procedures, where if there is any pause in the shooting of a big civic display, it is assumed that something has gone wrong. There is a general *uneasiness* that one may have driven all that way, set out the picnic basket, and so forth, only to be shortchanged.

Toshio Ogatsu bowed and said he had to return to his people out on the golf course. He said that we had a long stretch of entertainment ahead. Indeed, soon after he left, at noontime, introduced by a concussive eight-inch salute rolling its thunder across the golf course, a show of daytime fireworks began. Every half hour thereafter the displays came on again, increasing in volume and effect as the afternoon wore on. The best by far were the "Dragon Shells," which seemed to unwind swiftly in the sky like the colored paper streamers thrown in ballrooms on New Year's Eve. The shells came in a variety of colors: red, green, blue, purple, and black (which was very effective with the others), curlicuing down in corkscrews of smoke that hung in the still afternoon air, slowly thickening, until the colors merged like a painter's palette as they drifted away.

Music drifted over the golf course from the carillon, varying from the thin lute-strains of Oriental music to the sort of romantic Muzak one might expect in a Las Vegas marriage chapel. I recognized "Sunrise, Sunset." On occasion the sound of bells—the three-note xylophone chimes on Pullman trains to announce that the dining car was open—would introduce a priest's voice. That would drone for a while (apparently on some aspect of Perfect Liberty's history and theology) and then another stretch of music would come on. In a temple-like structure on the far side of the golf course we could see a ceremony in progress. The robes of hundreds of priests were barely visible; then, as the darkness fell, we could see that they were carrying torches.

By this time the crowd of spectators was enormous. Leaning far over the balustrade of the clubhouse porch, we could see people packed in against the golf-course boundaries a hundred deep; presumably the line stretched around the perimeter of the entire golf course—a circling ribbon that must have numbered a million-odd spectators. In the earlier heat of the afternoon, the quick whisking back and forth of fans had made the ribbon shiver in pale light as if it were being shaken; now the myriad firefly glow of thousands of cigarettes marked where the spectators were standing.

It was not at all like an American audience . . . none of the codicillic little displays that sprout on the outskirts of any U.S. professional show as the darkness falls . . . the rise and pop of bottle rockets, the rattle of firecrackers, the occasional big bang of an illegal M-80, perhaps the puffball of a Roman candle or a fountain going up . . . none of this at all . . . simply that huge, respectful crowd waiting up against the mesh-wire barricades. Nothing moved on the golf course in front of us, no hint of what was to come.

A small flight of herons flew over—a familiar evening sight—their wing-beats slow and steady as they pumped serenely along above the thousands of mortar mouths pointing up. One could not help but to urge them quickly through the airspace, soft and cool now as the evening darkness came on, but which within minutes would be subjected to the most violent of changes. I leaned across from my veranda chair and told the Souzas about an owl I had seen at the perimeter of a giant Japanese peony bursting over a Long Island beach, pale in the light, flustered and tossed about like a leaf.

At seven-forty, just at the appointed moment our program said things would get underway, a girl's voice sang out from the carillon tower: "And now the act of *hanabi* begins!" An organ fanfare pealed forth, and then abruptly a solid curtain of star mines rose into the sky in front of the Jeffersonian structure—the Shrine—at the far end of the golf course. In remarkable contrast to the civilized sounds of the organ notes, a crackling, explosive roar swept toward us—as if an animal sound had overwhelmed the murmur of human communication. In the curtain's garish light we could see a throng of priests streaming across the square in front of the monument—almost as if in panic at that upward sweep of blood-red fire.

I was told that all of this had been unleashed by the upward sweep of the high priest's arms—the signal to begin—which alerted the official in the observation tower to lean forward and announce into his communication system the Japanese word for "Fire!"—*Ten ka!*—which means literally "Unite fire." It was hard to imagine that in the arts any human gesture, even an orchestral move such as the downbeat of a baton, has ever produced such an awesome reaction. How Leonard Bernstein would have envied this high priest!

According to my notes, forty-four hundred shells were fired in this first barrage—going up in great tiers from thousands of mortars (some of them five inches in diameter) all connected with quick match. The star mines rose with great tails, which enhanced the concept of a great curtain rising into the sky. A huge smoke cloud drifted off the golf course—produced by the enormous convulsion of star mines—and assumed the shape of a mushroom cloud. One of the Japanese gentlemen down the line turned and called up to us "Hiroshima!" with a big grin. Our little group was somewhat stunned, not knowing quite how to respond, especially since the Japanese gentleman seemed so pleased with the reference. Gary Souza finally replied, "Pearl Harbor!" for lack of anything else to say, and that produced a hearty round of appreciative head-nods and gigglings.

Toshio Ogatsu had outlined the plan of the show for us. We could look down at our notes and see what was coming next. The display was divided into various coordinated effects, each usually lasting from three to five minutes, followed by seven minutes of single-shot shells of very heavy caliber fired from the five locations, leading in turn to another series of effects, then seven more minutes of huge aerial shells, followed by another segment, moving along in that progression up to the finale, which would start at eight twenty-five—exactly forty minutes after the opening command of *"Ten ka!"*

The effects were almost invariably composed of flights of the same kind of shells. One of the first series of the evening was a sky full of an extraordinary shell called the *kamuro* (the Japanese word for a boy's haircut) which produces a great willow spray with tendrils that reach almost to the ground before the stars—trailing the gold behind them as they come down—wink off after one last sudden color change to red. These shells went up in volleys, the largest of them twelve-inchers, for over five minutes, and when the concussion of the last bursting charge from the last shell had died away, the thousand tendrils from it and other *kamuros* seemed to hang in the utter silence as if a fixture had been added to the night skies of Tondabayashi.

The coordinator in his tower waited until all of this and the smoke had drifted away toward the town—not only to clear the sky, it seemed to me, but also to allow us to relish what we had just seen.

I made notes on what some of the other effects were—a long barrage of Saturn shells, shaped exactly like the planet, ring shells, perfect hoops of stars, the great puffy-tailed palm trees, huge, busy configurations of serpents, what the Japanese call *polo loka,* butterfly shells shaped like huge bow ties. There were, of course, great flights of different-hued chrysanthemums and peonies, the most familiar of the Japanese fireworks, along with strobe shells, comets, Silver Clouds, an endless variety. Many of the segments ended with a great rush of star mines into the sky, as if the shells in an American finale went up all at once rather than in succession. There was even one segment devoted entirely to reports—twelve-inch shells some of them, we were told—which produces such a concussive gut-pounding sound that it seemed to us more a weapon than a firework. How the Italians would have enjoyed that!

The silver cascade, or what Americans call a Niagara, appeared, quickly, the long suspension of cases hung between the two huge cranes opening up along its length like a spinnaker breaking out of its stops, until the expanse of glimmering falls stretched for over a mile. At its base thousands of Roman candles began to puff up their stars, adding to the effect of a vast curtain being established across the breadth of the golf course.

In one of the most startling aerial segments, the shell bursts literally spelled out characters and letters in the sky. I had always heard about "letter shells," but never quite believed they could do such things. I had been told that during the Algerian crisis Ruggieri had been approached by Arab nationalists who wanted to learn the shell-making trade so they could spell out anti-French slogans in the skies over Paris. Ruggieri said it couldn't be done. When people spoke of remembering letters in the sky from fireworks shows they had seen in the past, what they were usually recalling were set pieces spelling out product names or messages such as "good night."

But there they were! Apparently Ruggieri could have done it had he wished! Shells high in the sky burst out in the calligraphic designs of Japanese characters, and along the line on the porch heads nodded and people leaned to each other and spoke the names which they had read *off the sky*. We were told the names were of leaders in the religious order. I could not get over it! It was as if one looked at a fireworks shell bursting high over Yankee Stadium and read *George Steinbrenner III*. The only characters in English I noted over the golf course were PL—sometimes askew in the sky so that one had to twist one's neck to make them out. The pyrotechnicians had no way of lining up the stars in the shell so that at the burst they would automatically read right-side up.

The finale was simply awesome—so concussive and sudden that I thought for an instant that there had been a terrible mistake and the entire golf course was going up. Uncontrolled, unbridled, furious, a tall wall of white magnesium rose in front of us, solid finally, so that a horrifying feature seemed to have materialized in the landscape in front of us—the silver-bright façade of a thousand-foot glacier cliff it might have been except for the wave of heat that came off it, a hot breath that backed us up against the wall of the clubhouse. Its noise was a long, violent, tearing sound, curiously high and liquid, those thousands of shells *splitting* rather than reverberating so that the sound was rather like the grinding screech of ice under terrible strain—that odd image once again of a towering glacier wall. It beat on us. Our mouths dropped open to relieve the pressure. What we were seeing and hearing did not seem related to fireworks, but rather to some chain reaction over which human control had been utterly lost. The golf course shone in its awful light like a moon.

It only lasted for twelve seconds. Ogatsu had given us a list of what was to be included in the finale: 2,000 four-inch shells, 4,000 fives, 1,060 sixes, 200 eights, and 180 twelves, but we had assumed that this mammoth complement—its total value we estimated at $200,000, a larger sum than any ever paid for an *entire* display shot in the United States—would be shot off over the course of fifteen minutes or so, rising to a splendid climax like every great fireworks show we had ever seen.

Instead, a concussive wallop, just one, this long shriek; as if an orchestra, rather than finishing with a long roll of kettledrums and the brasses joining in with a series of rotund chords, simply concluded things by firing a row of cannons at the audience.

We continued to gasp. The golf course began to burn in places in front of us. We could see distant figures scurrying to put out the fires. The soft wind began to dissipate the huge roil of smoke clouds; it carried us the soft, tinkling chimes from the bell tower, as if to remind us that there were still gentle things in the world. The Japanese crowd began to stir. The Souza brothers were beside themselves. "Long live *hanabi!*" one of them shouted, and the Japanese smiled and nodded.

Inside the clubhouse a large number of them collected to watch the end of a baseball game on television. A few of them had been in there the entire evening, baseball having such an extraordinary hold on the Japanese that one even wondered if they had glanced up through the plate-glass window to watch the holocaust of the finale.

It took a long time for that immense crowd to disperse by the various

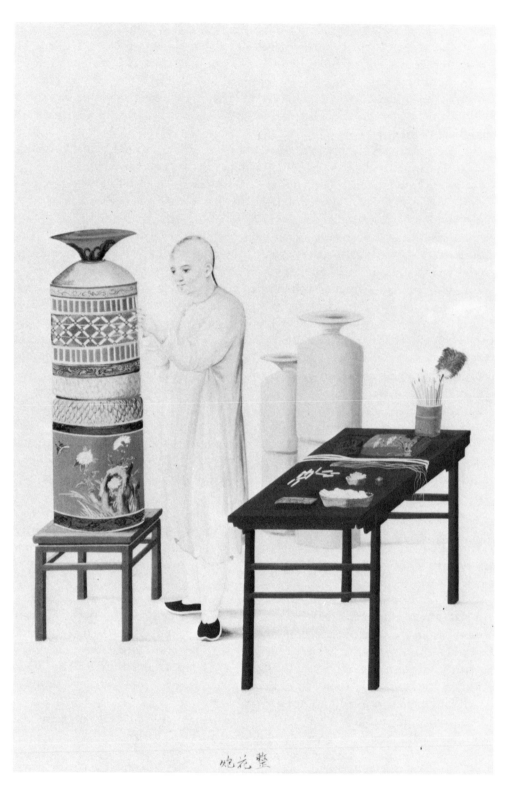

炮花整

A nineteenth-century Chinese fireworks maker puts the finishing touches on a large vase which he will fill with the accouterments of his trade, an assortment of which lies on a nearby worktable. Exterior decoration of the artifacts of fireworks—such as the Chinese fireworks labels—are almost as important to the craftsman as the contents. (The Trustees of the British Museum/Photo, Courtesy, American Heritage Publishing Co.)

routes out of Tondabayashi. Our little group went down to the station to take the railroad back to Osaka. We walked through the streets littered with an astonishing amount of detritus left by the spectators—cans, wrappers, paper boxes, bottles, wax containers—so that the bus convoys moving from town crunched their way out past us with little sharp snaps and pops that seemed to mimic the mammoth show we had just seen. The bus windows framed people looking out and waving; their mood reminded us of people exhilarated by a great musical extravaganza—many still celebrating as the exuberance wore off, with others lost now in reflection, until in the quiet of the long lines waiting to move through the turnstiles onto the railroad platforms it was as if there had been a sobering essence to that vast tumult of color and sound we had all been witness to. My ears still hummed. When I closed my eyes, vague configurations of light were still etched on the retina. It was very easy to recall the various components of the show. They would stay with us for a long time.

Shuffling slowly forward, I began wondering if it was a simple business to join the Perfect Liberty. I wondered how one did so. An application blank? I told the Souzas. "Guess what. I'm thinking of joining the order," I said. "Maybe even becoming a monk—a Perfect Liberty monk."

They did not seem the slightest bit surprised.

"The monks certainly get the best view of the fireworks," Jim Souza said.

"It beats being a Unitarian," I said.

This painting by James Abbott McNeill Whistler titled Nocturne in Black and Gold: The Falling Rocket *shows a fireworks display in London's Cremorne Gardens, an amusement park where Whistler would often take an evening stroll. The painting was the cause of a celebrated lawsuit. The art critic John Ruskin accused Whistler of "throwing a pot of paint in the public's face." Whistler brought a lawsuit against Ruskin and, although he won, the legal fees left him destitute. (The Dexter M. Ferry Fund. Courtesy of The Detroit Institute of Arts)*

OVERLEAF *Watercolor by Joseph Mallord William Turner:* Santa Maria della Salute, Venice, 1835. *(The Trustees of the British Museum)*

THE GRAND DISPLAY OF FIREWORKS AND ILLUMINATIONS

AT THE OPENING OF THE **GREAT SUSPENSION BRIDGE** BETWEEN NEW YORK AND BROOKLYN

ON THE EVENING OF MAY 24th, 1883.

VIEW FROM NEW YORK, LOOKING TOWARDS BROOKLYN.

The Bridge crosses the river by a single span of 1,595 ft. suspended by four cables, 15¾ inches in diameter, each composed of 5,434 parallel steel wires. Strength of each cable, 12,000 tons. Length of each land span, 930 ft. New York approach, 1,562½ ft. Brooklyn approach, 971 ft. Total length of Bridge and approaches, 5,988 ft. 6 ins. Height of Towers, 278 ft.

Height of Roadway above high-water, at towers, 119 ft. 3 ins., at centre of span, 135 ft. Width, 85 ft. with tracks for cars, roadway for carriages, and walks for passengers. The Bridge is lighted by the United States Illuminating Co. with 70 Electric lights, of 2,000 candle power each. Construction commenced, January, 1870. Completed, May, 1883. Estimated total cost, $15,000,000.

EPILOGUE

I knew something was wrong as soon as I walked into the house. It was Saturday of the Thanksgiving weekend, 1983. I had driven out from New York. It was early in the afternoon, the sun bright but low over the Long Island potato fields. My son, Taylor, wanted to play football out on the lawn, but my wife took me aside. "There have been phone calls," she said. "Something terrible has happened down in Bellport. The Gruccis' plant has blown up." She could hardly tell me. "The radio reports say six people are dead. Jimmy Grucci is missing."

I tried phoning the Grucci number at the factory. A busy signal came on.

"I don't think there's anyone, or even any *thing* at the other end," she said. "They say the place is flat."

Our home is an hour farther out on Long Island than Bellport. Eventually, I reached a member of the family and later that day I drove down to see what I could do. Over the car radio the reports kept coming in. Debris from the blast was reported to be drifting down in townships ten miles away. The shock had been felt for twenty miles. There had been panic along Maple Avenue, which runs parallel to the Grucci compound. The radio said babies had been tossed out of windows by people who thought their houses were collapsing around their ears. One report described an area near the Grucci compound of trees festooned with hundreds of little American flags, presumably from crates of novelty shells that had gone off in the explosions.

Watercolor and white gouache on white paper by Winslow Homer: Sailboat and Fourth of July Fireworks, Gloucester, *1880. (Courtesy of the Fogg Art Museum, Harvard University. Bequest of Grenville L. Winthrop)*

Nineteenth-century chromolithograph by Currier & Ives: The Grand Display of Fireworks and Illuminations at the Opening of the Great Suspension Bridge between New York and Brooklyn on the Evening of May 24th, 1883. *Thirteen tons of fireworks were involved. The centennial was celebrated in 1983, with many of the effects—such as a Niagara—duplicated from a century before. Considered one of the country's greatest fireworks displays, it was watched by over two million people thronging the shores of the East River. (The Metropolitan Museum of Art. The Edward W. C. Arnold Collection of New York Prints, Maps and Pictures, Bequest of Edward W. C. Arnold, 1954)*

Inevitably, the radio reports described the huge cloud that had boiled up from the compound. It crossed my mind that the cloud was actually composed of a multitude of aerial shells beautiful to see individually, and graced with such flowery names: Red Silk, Flower-Scattering Maiden, Gardens on a Mountain, Silvery Fish, Monkey Child, Red Peony . . . the thin tracery of the gold of the split comets, the small balls of blue, orange ring shells—as if an agency was working busily but fruitlessly to suggest a sense of order in all that chaos.

Suddenly a voice came on the radio and verified two deaths. Jimmy Grucci and his cousin Donna Gruber, nineteen years old, had been killed. I remembered Donna from the shop—a pretty, dark-haired girl who was Jimmy's special assistant and worked with him on the big shells he loved to make. She had been on board the charter boat we had taken out to watch the Brooklyn Bridge Centennial fireworks show, which the Gruccis had fired just six months before. I had watched her sitting up on top of the pilothouse with two of her co-workers—three young girls in a row—and on occasion one of them would exclaim happily as the shells went up, "Look, there goes one of mine!"

The family had gathered at Felix, Sr.'s house on Station Road. I had to talk my way past a number of police barricades to get there. The houses along the street were dark. Cars were parked out in front of the Grucci house. It was small and unpretentious, with a glass-screened porch in front and a couple of steps that led up to it. The door squeaked when pulled open.

Inside, family members were sitting quietly, some standing for lack of chairs, many of them staring at the framed tinted photographs of the Grucci children and grandchildren hanging on the wall. The screen door squeaked and Felix Grucci, Sr., was led in. His hair, usually sleek, was disheveled and stood up like a cockatoo's. He had been in the compound, I was told, just walking away from feeding the guard dog, Big Boy, when the blasts had started going off. He had been pummeled around by the explosives wrecking his plant and was lucky indeed to be alive; they had given him a checkup at the hospital. He spotted me across the room as he was being led up the stairs. He asked weakly, "You hear about Jimmy?"

The conversations were low and desultory. Occasionally, someone would describe the instant of the explosion. One of the Gruccis said she had been making a tomato sauce for the lunchtime coming up, pouring the thick paste from one pan to another; the shock wave had simply taken it out of the window.

A Grucci cousin named Bill Klein told me he was one of the first on the scene. He had just finished raking leaves at Felix, Jr.'s—Butch's—house and was coming down Beislin Road in his truck, less than a mile from the compound, when the ground began to shake under his tires. Immediately he knew it was the fireworks plant. He saw the cloud rise above the trees. "A lot of stuff was going off in the cloud—titanium salutes. I could recognize them. But it was nothing that made you think of fireworks—just a black, ugly cloud rising quickly."

146

He drove down Maple Avenue. Residents were running out of their front doors.

"Did you see any babies being thrown out of windows?" I asked. "That's what they were saying on the radio."

"I didn't see anything like that," Bill said. "Of course, I had my head down, trying to get to the compound as quickly as I could."

The first thing Bill Klein saw when he got there was Felix, Sr., standing in the center of the compound, stock-still in the debris of the first blasts, and behind him, dwarfing him, a great curtain of fire and black smoke.

"We knew we had to get him out. As you know, the compound is surrounded by a tall chain-link fence. The front gate, where I parked the truck, was fastened shut with a big loop of padlocked chain. Jimmy, Donna, and the old man had driven their cars into the compound from the back gate. So I had to scale the fence with a friend of mine, Kurt DeCarlo. Tore the hell out of my arm getting over the wire. It was a miracle Felix was alive. He was standing there dazed with big eight-inch mortars whizzing around like pieces of scrapnel. Jimmy and Donna had died not more than thirty yards from him."

The two reached him and were hurrying Felix toward the compound fence, the old man crying, "What happened? Ruined! Where's Jimmy?" when the loaded vans, in rows behind them, went up in a final titanic blast, hurling them to the ground. Crawling, feeling the great heat behind them, they supported Felix to the locked front gate, where a fireman, staring wide-eyed over their heads at the flaming compound, was clipping away at the chain with a pair of shears to get them out.

"Could you hear the blasts out where you live?" Bill asked me.

"I'm surprised we didn't," I replied.

I did not see much of Butch, Jimmy's brother, at that first gathering. He was busy on the phone in the kitchen, or coming out to talk to officials and police, who came up the steps and stood awkwardly in the small parlor.

I had a chance to see him a few days after the tragedy. He told me he still couldn't bring himself to believe what had happened. He admitted, about making fireworks, that an accident was always vaguely in the back of the mind. "You live with it every day," he told me, "sort of like knowing that nuclear weapons are pointed at you. Except with fireworks you're literally involved. Because in the sheds you *see* the canisters packed in neat rows on the shelves. You see the stars drying on the table. Then you hear a sharp noise, like a window shade rattling up, or the slam of a door, or a car backfiring, and you think it's starting—it is beginning."

"What is?"

"That the shop is beginning to go up. You even prepare yourself mentally, imagining what it's going to be like. But when it really happens, it's nothing like what you thought. I had an idea the sound would be deep and kind of awesome, like being inside a wave, but it was different. It was a ripping and tearing sound, high and piercing, almost a kind of shriek, and much more frightening than I ever thought it would be."

He told me that on that Saturday he was just about to leave home to pay a short visit to the "shop" to do some paperwork. Then he was going to a jeweler's. His wife had given him an identification bracelet on his birthday, the day before, and he wanted to have it fitted properly. The first detonation went off as he was standing in the kitchen saying good-bye to his wife. The floor began to rumble under his feet; the house shook. Butch knew immediately what had happened; so did his wife, who stared at him wild-eyed and then began to sob. Butch dialed 911 for emergency, and then ran out into the street in time to see the mushroom-like cloud rise above the trees.

One fact Butch seemed sure of—that neither Jimmy nor his cousin was responsible for what had happened. That morning at 9 A.M. Jimmy had gone with Donna to load and finish twenty big eight-inch color shells in the assembly shed. Just before 11 A.M. Donna had called her mother to say that the two were cleaning up what they were doing and that she would soon be on her way home for lunch. Both Jimmy and Donna were outside the assembly shed when the shock wave, followed by the fire ball, destroyed them. They could not have been *in* the assembly shed—which would have been the case if either of them had made a mistake—because nothing was left of the shed except the stone steps leading up to the door. The coroner's observations were that Jimmy had turned, startled, to face the explosion and that Donna was beyond him, running, when the holocaust caught her.

"What have you heard?" Butch asked me. "I mean, about the cause."

"Lots of rumors. Arson. Saturday, when it happened, is an arsonist's day. No one is supposed to be working. Then," I said, "I heard from a friend of mine in the Pyrotechnics Guild who thought it might have been spontaneous combustion from a shell that had got wet, left out in the rain, perhaps in Korea, and then got packed away in a crate and slowly, in there, became volatile."

All week that image had been in my mind—a firework behaving like the antagonistic symbiosis of a cancerous cell. It was awful to consider—a single shell, packed in amid its fellows, slowly, in the darkness of the warehouse, changing its internal composition until now, a deadly instrument, it awaited some delicate shift of atmospheric pressure, or a certain degree of humidity, to be triggered into that first puff of smoke.

"Well, that's the point," Butch said. "A chemist will tell you that it's a million-to-one shot. And the kind of humidity you'd need to cause that type of reaction would happen only on a hot, muggy August day, not a cool November morning."

I then mentioned what a lot of people had talked about—that the tragedy had been the result of friction from some of the neighbors who did not relish the idea of their homes being next to a fireworks factory. Attempts earlier that fall had been made to rezone the area and force the Gruccis to move their operations elsewhere. Could the accident have been caused by someone trying to tip the scales by setting off, oh, just a small explosion, a little symbolic blast to dramatize the issue, not realizing a huge chain reaction was a possibility? I told Butch I could imagine some kid hearing the matter discussed at the breakfast table—"It's just a damn shame that those people are still being allowed to build bombs"—and deciding on his own to nudge things along by rattling a few windows . . .

Butch nodded and said that one of the curious bits of debris discovered in the aftermath was a charred arrow, sticking in a blackened shingle off a shed.

"It's crossed my mind," Butch said. "If that's so, then there must be someone walking around with a terrible conscience. It would be more weight than I could ever carry."

Butch could not get the behavior of the guard dog, Big Boy, out of his mind. A "mutt police dog," as Butch referred to him, he lived in a large fenced-in pen in the center of the compound. On the morning of the twenty-sixth Big Boy had somehow clambered out of the pen, which had happened only once before in the ten years the Gruccis had owned him. Jimmy was scared of the dog, and when he arrived with his cousin at 9 A.M., he telephoned his father, who was the only one in the family able to get close without the dog baring his teeth.

His father arrived and, soothing Big Boy, was able to get him back into the pen. After he had done some work in the office shed and had gone down to check on Big Boy, or perhaps to feed him, abruptly his little empire went up around him.

"What's crazy," Butch said, "is that a lot of dogs along Maple Street, which runs along next door to the shop, were acting erratically that morning. We got a lot of reports. Not only that," Butch went on to say, "but I got a report that last year, just at this time, around Thanksgiving, a small fireworks plant in Ohio, family-run, had a couple of Doberman pinschers who went erratic just like Big Boy and the dogs on Maple, and, just after, the plant blew up. What do you make of that?"

I said I had no idea. It suddenly occurred to me that Bill and Sue Hoyt's home had blown up in the dawn of Thanksgiving Day the year before.

"Could it be ultrasonic sound waves?" Butch was asking. "New weapons in the Army planes that fly off the base? Laser beams? They make dogs nervous."

I said that I had heard of such things. Butch shook his head. "It shows you how crazy this whole business can make you."

I asked how the town was reacting. Butch said that some townspeople, especially those who had lived in Bellport for a generation or so, had said, despite everything, how proud they had always been to have the Gruccis' fireworks factory in their midst. After all, Grucci was such a familiar name in the community—the barbershop was run by a cousin, James Grucci; the radio-and television store by an uncle, Pete; the liquor store had been Grucci-owned. On the Fourth of July all these Gruccis closed up shop to fire displays. No one in the Gruccis, Butch told me, had ever bolted, whatever their actual feelings, from the family responsibility, which was to fireworks. He was sure it would stay that way.

Others in the town, of course, were bitter. They made crude signs and came and picketed the ruined plant. There was one woman—the report was that she lost a glass cabinet full of figurines—who shouted through the fence at Felix Grucci, Sr., looking half-heartedly in the rubble for his dog, who had been missing since the explosion: "Y'bum, how can you go and sleep at night?"

"Frightful."

"It's going to be hard to find a place to start up again," Butch said. "And we're going to miss Jimmy so much. You know, he loved making real big shells, an eighteen-inch shell with ten or fifteen salutes in it, but after it was done he'd become a little afraid. It's odd. He'd break out into little sores around the mouth. Do you remember the Fat Man on the Indian River? Jimmy had some big fever blisters *that* time. It's inherited. Our mother often breaks out before a big show."

"I didn't know that."

Butch thought for a moment. He said, "The thing you love kills you, doesn't it? Isn't that how the saying goes?"

I remembered and said that the famous phrase—it was Oscar Wilde's—was that "each man kills the thing he loves."

"He got it wrong," Butch said.

"It would seem so. It's the other way around, isn't it?"

I had not seen the compound until my wife and I drove to Bellport for the funeral services on November 30. We drove over and stared through the chain-link fence. The landscape had simply been tortured by the blasts into a rubble that appeared to belong to photographs one remembered of the trench warfare of World War I. Indeed, at first I saw nothing in the debris that gave evidence of human involvement. Finally I could make out the chassis of a blackened storage trailer, the steps that led up to a building no longer in existence, the yellowish hulks of the burned-out Grucci family cars in the center of the compound, iron mortars lying askew, and at my feet I could distinguish parts of aerial fireworks—the round disks used to make shell bases, the burned-out husks of paper fuses. There was a brisk wind blowing, so there was just the faintest whiff of burnt powder.

About a third of the town—Bellport's population is just above three thousand—seemed to be at the service. Many fireworks people came from around the country—the Semenzas from Ideal Fireworks in Pennsylvania, Fred Iannini, an old-timer just a year or two junior to Felix, Sr., the Girones from New Jersey, the Rozzi family from Tri-State in Loveland, Ohio, and one remembered that Joe Rozzi, the father, had lost *his* brother in an explosion. They all wore black suits that seemed a bit too snug around the shoulders as they settled themselves heavily into the camp chairs set up in rows.

The casket stood in front of the congregation and had been borne in by seven Grucci employees wearing dark blue T-shirts emblazoned with a spray of fireworks and the legend *Fireworks by Grucci*. It was what they wore when they fired displays. The family sat in the first two rows, swaying toward each other in grief. Butch Grucci had asked me to deliver a tribute to Jimmy. I worked on one for a couple of days. I could not imagine that Jimmy would have wanted its tone to be solemn. Among other things, I said:

"Jimmy Grucci was an honored member of a remarkable profession—craftsmen whose artistic function is momentarily to change the face of the heavens themselves, to make the night sky more beautiful than it is, and in the process give delight and wonder to countless hundreds of thousands. It surely can be said that Jimmy Grucci designed, and prepared, and fired fireworks shows that were witnessed by more people in his lifetime than any contemporary artist I can think of—including the great concert virtuosi, even the most fashionable of the pop stars. Over a million people watch the annual 'Venetian Night' show along the Chicago waterfront; over two million watched the 'Brooklyn Bridge Centennial' this past May; 'Fireworks Night' at Shea Stadium has invariably filled every seat. Countless millions watched this last Inauguration's fireworks on television. And Jimmy Grucci, of course, has been an integral part in making Fireworks by Grucci responsible for these beautiful and mammoth displays. One of them, designed by him, won his family the championship of the world in Monte Carlo.

"But I don't think these honors and renown—the fact that Grucci has become a household word—mattered to him as much as the simple and wonderful art of fireworks themselves. Of his family Jimmy was the one involved to the point truly of passion. He worked in the fireworks assembly area for as many as ten hours a day, six days a week. He loved making shells. He turned and admired a fireworks shell in his hand as a collector might relish a statue of jade. His favorite was the split comet—perhaps the most famous American shell ever made—in the sky, tendrils of gold that split at their ends, and then once again, until the entire night sky seems like latticework. He also liked noise, of course. Big reports. He would be letting the tradition down, certainly the Italian tradition, if there weren't a loud report or two, preferably nine or ten, to accompany things. He understood that curious aesthetic balance that comes with the combination of beauty and harsh concussion.

"In the evening, after work, after all those hours of making fireworks, Jimmy would reach home and immediately telephone his brother just down the street to talk—fireworks. His recreation after dinner was to relax and sit and watch tapes of his favorite Grucci fireworks shows on the great curved extra-sized television screen at the foot of his bed. What woke him in the morning—and I might add everyone else in the Grucci household—was an alarm-clock system rigged to that same TV screen. At the wake-up hour it burst on and showed the climactic moment of the Tchaikovsky 1812 Overture as played outdoors by Arthur Fiedler and the Boston Pops—the fireworks booming and echoing over the Esplanade. There was no yawning and stretching in the Grucci household, his brother, Felix, once told me, no wiping the sleep from one's eyes. At the first sound of that alarm system, everyone was up!

"What joy fireworks gave him, and what joy he gave us with them! Perhaps Jimmy's most remarkable characteristic, I think, was not only his enthusiastic nature but his attitude about fireworks and the public—his abhorrence of even the thought of not giving the public their money's worth. In a profession where it is easy to shortchange the populace, how often I have seen him put an extra four or five shells in a show to give an audience just a bit more than what was necessary. It was as if he were saying, perhaps these extra shells will ignite something in you which will make you understand what the sheer wonder of it is—to take an inanimate object, a canister, a thing of chemicals and minerals, and, like a magician, an alchemist at his astonishing best, illuminate the skies with its performance.

"There is a famous early nineteenth-century essay by William Hazlitt about the death of a great athlete of his time, John Cavanagh, in which Hazlitt says that when a person dies who does any one thing better than anyone else in the world, it leaves a gap in society. But fireworks is an ongoing and perpetuating art that will continue to have its great craftsmen. Jimmy is one of a great tradition. He is one with Claude Ruggieri, Martin Beckman, Peter the Great, Vigarini, Brock—artists all. His family will continue in that tradition. They will not allow a gap to be left in our society.

"Artists are perhaps fortunate in that they leave evidence after they have gone—books, concertos, paintings, ballets—and who here in this church will not remember Jimmy Grucci and what he brought to this art when they see an especially lovely shell blossom in the night sky.

"In the ancient Greek scheme of things, mortals were penalized by the gods when they went beyond the bounds and became god-like themselves. In those times, the people would have said about the terrible tragedy of last week that the gods were taking exception, vengeance, because Jimmy Grucci was doing better with the heavens than they could ever dream of."

GLOSSARY

Battle in the Clouds The name of a shell especially popular at Italian feast-day celebrations. It carries up a number of fused salutes timed to explode in a series of loud reports—giving an effect not unlike a fusillade of musketry. A large eight-inch shell will carry as many as ten salutes.

Black Powder A ground-up mixture of potassium nitrate, sulfur, and charcoal. The proportions of its ingredients have remained very much the same over the centuries: 75 parts by weight potassium nitrate, or saltpeter as it is called in the fireworks industry, 15 parts charcoal, and 10 parts sulfur. It burns briskly when ignited but does not have any properties of thrust, nor does it make a noise, unless confined. It is said to have been discovered by the Chinese, probably around A.D. 1000. When somebody realized a projectile could be thrust out of a barrel by confining the powder at one end and lighting it, the mixture became known as gunpowder. Because of its tendency to corrode gun barrels, and because of its bright flash and clouds of smoke at ignition, a different propellant (smokeless powder) is now used in modern ordnance. But black powder continues as a main ingredient in fireworks, both as a propellant and a bursting charge within the shell.

In the nineteenth century the Chinese used curious ingredients to make the charcoal for their black powder—bamboo knots, coconut shells, eggplant, grasshoppers, and snakeskin. One of the traditional rules in Chinese workshops was that loud talk was forbidden, so that the capricious "soul" of black powder would be "soothed."

Black or **Blind Shells** An apt designation given these shells whose time fuses fail to ignite the bursting charge and fall back to earth without performing. It is a very rare occurrence. Sometimes, though I have never seen it, a shell falling back to earth will be set off by the shock of its landing, especially if the bursting charge has chlorate mixtures in it. It may also be set off from sparks clinging to the inside of a jammed fuse being thrust into the shell by impact.

In a nineteenth-century French fireworks factory, employees fabricate bombes *by hand, wrapping them with Italian twine just as their successors do in many parts of the world today. (Roger-Viollet)*

Break Fireworks people refer to the explosion of an aerial shell as a "break." "It broke low" would be how one would complain about a shell that had exploded before reaching its apogee. Oriental shells are almost all single-break. Multi-break shells, a feature of the United States and European countries, will break four or five times (usually concluding with a sharp report), though some have been made which break as many as ten times. At one of the Pyrotechnic Guild International meetings I heard of a shell built with twenty-two breaks in it.

Burns In the early days of fireworks, when an explosion burned or maimed someone, a curious sixteenth-century euphemism referred to the victim as having been "spoiled."

As in: "My God, what happened to him?"

"He got spoiled."

An early remedy for being "spoiled" was offered by the French *artificier* Amédée François Frezier, the author of *Traité des Feux d'Artifice* (1747). It was to boil fresh pork fat over a moderate flame. "Then remove it," he writes, "and expose it to evening dew for three or four nights, after which place it in an earthen pot and let it melt over a low fire . . . wash it several times with clear, fresh water until it becomes as white as snow. Then place in an earthen vessel until the occasion arises when you may need it."

Bursting Charge The interior charge which when ignited by a flame from a time fuse breaks apart an aerial shell at the top of its climb and ignites the stars (q.v.) contained therein.

Case (often called **Niagara Falls Tube** or **Cascade**) A large tube containing a composition designed to create a long-lasting flow of white aluminum sparks, the effect of a number of them resembling a curtain of fire.

Catherine Wheel The designation given those set pieces (q.v.) which use revolving wheels to achieve their effect. The wheels are outfitted with drivers (q.v.) for propulsion and different color combinations.

The Catherine of the wheel, incidentally, is the beautiful and brilliant proselytizer of Christianity in fourth-century Alexandria who was condemned by the Roman emperor Maxentius to torture on a spiked wheel in an attempt to get her to recant. Many scholars had already tried to dissuade her of her views, and when they failed, Maxentius had *them* burned alive. Rough customer! According to the legend, the spiked wheel of torture flew into splinters at Catherine's touch, after which she was beheaded.

The most extraordinary Catherine wheels I have seen (admittedly on film) are those displayed at festivals on the island of Malta. In their intricacy—wheels within wheels and arranged so that literally the whole edifice appears to pulse and throb as if alive—the color patterns and effects match the best that can be observed through the eyepiece of a fancy kaleidoscope. At the Pyrotechnics Guild International meeting where I saw the films, everyone wondered if manpower was involved in turning the devices (as in the miserable "sunburst" at the Royal Wedding fireworks in London in 1981 which was worked by a man, quite visible through the smoke, turning a crank), or whether the entire effect was achieved by the use of drivers. The consensus was that the Maltese works were entirely pyrotechnically driven.

Chaser A variety of fireworks which, upon lighting, swooshes briefly along the ground with a whistling effect. A prefix is often added to denote an ethnic or racial slur; most recently, during the hostage crisis in Teheran, a U.S. brand of firecrackers was titled "Khomeini-chasers."

Cherry Bomb An illegal firecracker, banned in this country in 1966. The United Fireworks Co. in Dayton, Ohio, is credited with inventing the cherry bomb. When they were legal (the "good ol' days" as fireworks people refer to them) they came in half-gross cartons bearing an airborne eagle with a lightning bolt in its beak. The device inside was (or *is,* since they continue to be manufactured illegally) a small red sphere about an inch in diameter containing about two grams of flash powder. The cherry bomb and the postwar M-80 are largely responsible for giving a bad name to fireworks. They cause the biggest percentage of fireworks-related injuries.

The M-80, the military designation of an item used to simulate the sounds of gunfire (its official name is "military rifle fire simulator"), looks like a tube, its fuse sticking out the middle.

In England firecrackers containing flash powder were called "thunder-flashes." In 1960 their sale was outlawed. The public was limited to buying a black powder firecracker colorfully known as a "banger." In 1963 the explosive content in a banger was reduced from forty milligrams to about twenty-four milligrams—this by voluntary agreement within the fireworks industry itself.

Choke The choke is a variation of the tapered nozzle modified by the great rocket-inventor genius, Robert H. Goddard, in the early part of the century to increase the thrust and efficiency of a rocket motor. Specifically, in rocketry it is the hole in a clay device at the base of a rocket through which the gas formed by the burning of the black powder escapes and thus puts into effect Sir Isaac Newton's Third Law of Motion—which states that for every action there is an equal and opposite reaction. I had always thought that the thrust against the air was what pushed a rocket up into the sky, what Claude-Fortuné Ruggieri, the great fireworks maker (who did not know any better either), referred to when he said that a rocket's gases "lean on the air." Not so, of course. Air *impedes* the motion of a rocket, which would, in fact, much prefer to perform in a vacuum such as space. The "tail" streaming from a rocket in flight has no more to do with its flight (as Alan St. Hill Brock puts it so nicely in his *A History of Fireworks*) than the exhaust has to do with the momentum of an automobile.

Choreography In recent years, fireworks choreography has become an important adjunct to the pyrotechnic science, due largely to electrical firing, which allows preset effects. A throw of a switch can send up a skyful of split comets, say, whereas, previously, a fireworks man would reach in the bomb box, drop a shell into the mortar, light it, and then often would be just as surprised at what blossomed in the sky above him as the spectators. These days, a large show is choreographed beforehand on a tally sheet. The shells are put in the mortars and wired on the afternoon of the display. The entire show sits waiting in its mortars for the evening and the jolt from the electrical impulses from the relay box which ignite the squibs (electrical "match heads") and send the shells up on their way in predetermined patterns.

A magnificent aerial show bursts over a set piece formed by the Jefferson Memorial in Washington, D.C., during the Bicentennial tribute to America's Independence in 1976. The French firm of Ruggieri was responsible for the splendid choreography of this fireworks spectacular. (© Fred Maroon, 1976/Louis Mercier)

These advances have meant that a fireworks choreographer can arrange a show to fit a particular theme—a patriotic display, say—or a show to a particular piece of music. The increasing interest in "theme" shows was one of the reasons that the French firm Ruggieri was picked to provide the main fireworks displays in Washington, D.C., for the U.S. Bicentennial in 1976—a choice which at once outraged American pyrotechnical firms but also made them realize that a skyful of fireworks was not enough to impress their customers. American firms in the bidding for the $200,000 Washington contract had offered a prospectus with the usual "Red-white-and-blue Salute to the Nation," a "Liberty Bell," "American Flag" set pieces, and a "rousing" finale, along with an opaque reference to "special deluxe bombshells" made especially for the occasion. The French, on the other hand, put together a most ambitious proposal, whose theme was "The Triumph of Reason and Order over Chaos and War." These trumpeting words introduced an extraordinary script for the selection committee to mull over. It was full of symbolic references: ". . . fireworks representing riot and revolt leading to the calamities of war and the resulting chaos. Next, the wrath of God [will be] symbolized and then, after a calculated silence, the return to calm and reason . . . Last of all, an enormous, radiant sun [will] burst . . . the final apotheosis, the grand gironde . . . symbolizing in a last burst of light the triumph of culture over violence!"

It was no wonder that the selection committee, a group with the innocent name *Happy Birthday, U.S.A.*, fell for this sort of thing, and opted for the French.

Not only is the science of choreography advancing, but increased attention is being given to the aesthetics of individual shells. Perhaps the most remarkable treatise in these matters is by the Japanese fireworks specialist Dr. Takeo Shimizu—a book entitled *Fireworks: The Art, Science, and Technique*. Here one reads about the "feelings" that are evinced by different shells and color combinations. Shimizu writes that the perfect chrysanthemums, especially those with flashes at the end of the petals, provoke *tension,* whereas flower shells with "rounded shoulders," like the willows, or with dusty, ill-defined tendrils, promote *relaxation.* A variety of willows called the *yugen-biki* (it means "mystery of willow") are made of stars which fall in thin, weak tendrils of amber and these produce, according to Shimizu, *a deep, still feeling.* The reaction one gets seeing a shell called the *akisakura* (or autumn cherry blossom) is that of *elegance.*

Shimizu is very sensitive about color combinations—stating, for instance, that red and yellow "sometimes succeeds," but that red and green "looks dirty."

A great deal of attention is given the circle made by the burst of the shell, what the Japanese refer to as the *bon,* which means "round tray." Their shell designers go to considerable pains to make sure that the *bon* is not only perfectly formed, but that it is sufficiently filled with stars to be pleasing aesthetically. As Dr. Shimizu writes, "the diameter of a round flower must be correct. If it is too large, the density of the stars is low and the flower feels lonely." Often, in this case, presumably to give the viewer the sense that company is on the way, the designer will add a burst to fill the interior of the *bon,* what in flower shells is referred to as "the pistil."

Any number of principles are offered by the good doctor, who likes to refer to fireworks choreographers as "drama directors." A flower must increase from small to large, the stars increase their brightness from a weak to a strong level, color changes must go from cold (blue, green) to a warm chroma (red and yellow), and there must be a decrease in speed from quick movement to stillness. If any of these progressions are reversed, Dr. Shimizu warns that the display is "unstable and can give unpleasant feelings." He gives an example: a pistil in a chrysanthemum must be of a cold color; the momentum must be from small to large. It must vanish before the petals ignite. Otherwise: *unpleasant feelings.*

Ogatsu in his volume on fireworks is no less demanding. He writes of a choreographer: "If a thudding sound comes from his fire-flowers when thundering roar was expected, he would lose his face." As for a star not performing in the proper circular configuration of a chrysanthemum or peony, Mr. Ogatsu describes the situation as being "as if one petal of a flower is missing or has been eaten by a caterpillar."

The Japanese have a number of choreographic effects derived from *how* they put their shells in the air. Among these are *kasane-dame,* which is the somewhat perilous practice of putting two shells in the mortar at the same time. If all goes well, the two shells perform aloft instantaneously. A much safer variation of this is called *tsuiuchi,* or "paired shootings," in which a pair of similar shells are sent up from different sites. *Oiuchi,* or "chasing shooting," is the practice of putting shells in the air so they explode immediately after the other—a choreographic one-two. The practice requires fine timing and very accurate time fuses, because the effect is obviously dissipated if the shells perform at intervals either too short or too long.

Danuchi is what is called the firing of the same shells but of different sizes—extraordinarily effective when the shells, especially the willows, appear to bloom in tiers. The most dramatic firing practice is what is called *kayauchi,* which is the rapid firing of shells one after the other until the sky above is filled with their bursts.

Classification The system employed by the U.S. Department of Transportation to rank different types of fireworks, using the amount and type of pyrotechnic composition as the criteria.

Class A explosives: Bombs, etc., or, technically, solid explosives that can be made to detonate by a blasting cap, such as dynamite, TNT, tetryl, amatol; also types of high-explosive liquid that detonates on impact; also detonators such as blasting caps, and almost all ammunition with the exception, interestingly enough, of that for pistols, rifles, and shotguns, which are in the Class C category along with toy-pistol caps. Thus, ironically, the Class C category in peacetime, because of handguns, is responsible for many hundreds more fatalities than Class A deaths.

Class B: These are explosives which function by rapid combustion rather than detonation. Components, such as black powder, are used from the Class A category but in very restricted quantities. This category includes all the aerial fireworks one sees in a licensed public display.

Class C: This category includes what is left—devices manufactured from Class A and B components but in very limited amounts. Class C products are intended for general public and backyard displays.

As of this writing, all Class C fireworks are allowed in eight states, but there are restricting clauses. While these devices are limited to fifty milligrams of black powder, propellants are allowed, so that Class C includes shells and rockets—items that go up into the air. Nineteen states restrict fireworks to a category referred to as Safe and Sane—namely, devices which do not leave the ground or move. These are fountains and cones, and various types of novelty fireworks. Tanks, motorcycles, the Ground-blooming Flower, the Egg-laying Hen are all Safe and Sane; some of these devices may move, but they do so laterally. The extraordinary Chinese-made aircraft carrier, bobbing on a pond, would be a Safe and Sane item if it were not for its two little paper helicopters which, by lifting off and humming up into the sky, reclassify the aircraft carrier as Class C. Sixteen states allow neither Class C nor Safe and Sane. No Chinese aircraft carriers in Putnam Valley, New York! No Egg-laying Hens, either!

The "Safe and Sane" July 4 is better than no fireworks at all, but it has proved to be a difficult concept for many fireworks enthusiasts, especially the older generation remembering the pleasures of the Fourth as if a whiff of the punk sticks they lit early in the morning of that day of their youth was still caught in their nostrils. One of the more poignant descriptions of the Fourth of July fidgets was described by Max P. Vander Horck, a San Diego resident in his sixty-third year who is the founder of the Pyrotechnics Guild International. In his magazine, *American Pyrotechnist,* he wrote of a Fourth in San Diego where even sparklers were banned: "As the day wore on, punctuated by only an occasional blast from the vicinity of an apartment house on the street below us where a young boy or girl could be seen scurrying in and out to replenish their supply of what must have been 1½-inchers from across the border less than 20 miles south of here, not to mention the even louder racket from a house on our street where someone was playing rock-type soul music at about a 95-decibel level all morning, I became more and more frustrated with this 'Safe and Sane' Fourth of July. At one point, in fact, I seriously considered wiring our stereo speakers out in the yard and playing our ear-chattering record of the Tchaikovsky 1812 Overture conducted by Zubin Mehta, complete with Charlie Marsh's Civil War cannon blasts, at the full 50-watt output!"

Fireworks in Moscow in 1962 to honor the Russian cosmonauts. (Time-Life Picture Collection. Photograph by Stan Wayman © Time, Inc.)

OVERLEAF *Fireworks for the American Bicentennial, 1976. (Contact Press Images. Photograph © 1976 Bill Pierce/Contact)*

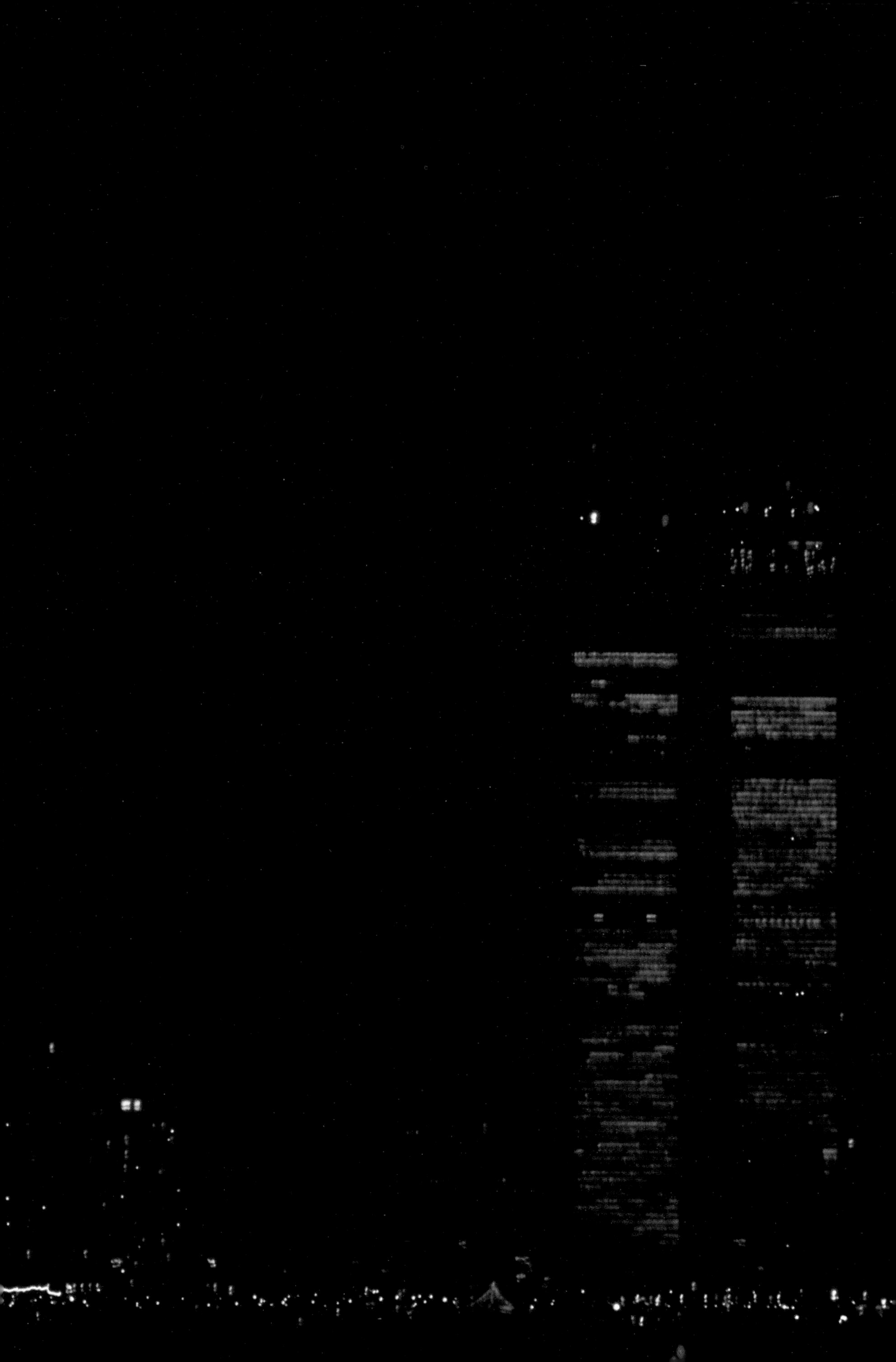

Early in the afternoon Mr. Vander Horck blew up a paper bag and popped it; he also shot off a roll of Mattel caps in his old Hubley cap pistol. That evening he invited the neighborhood over to watch a Glittering Snake perform on a brick, an illegal "sparkler display," and two Happy Lanterns spinning, one of which fell off its string and which Mr. Vander Horck held aloft until the illuminating device inside went out, as his friends commented on how much he looked like Diogenes.

Even this somewhat anemic display made Mr. Vander Horck wake up the next morning "feeling that our Fourth wasn't so 'dumb' after all and that the latest of the 'good old days' had in fact been yesterday."

Colors Six different basic colors can be used in fireworks. These are white, produced by magnesium or aluminum; yellow, by sodium salts; red, by strontium nitrate or carbonate; green, by barium nitrate or chlorate; blue, by copper salts in the presence of a volatile chlorine donor; and orange or amber, by charcoal and other forms of carbon, or iron, and which was, along with an off-white, for a long time the only fireworks colors seen by audiences. The white of those long-ago times was produced by varying the properties of the basic gunpowder ingredients and adding an excess of sulfur.

In the 1630s a French chemist named Jean Appier suggested adding verdigris—copper sulfate—to produce a green texture. By the middle of the eighteenth century a greenish blue was produced by the use of powdered zinc metal. Lavoisier, the great French chemist who first prepared oxygen—and who was guillotined by angry citizens during the Revolution for having been a tax collector—identified zinc as being used by pyrotechnists *"pour leurs feux bleus"* as late as 1792. More color effects were developed in the early nineteenth century. F.-M. Chertier first described a systematic approach to pyrotechnic color in 1836. Claude-Fortuné Ruggieri published a pamphlet of color formulas in 1845. He described salts still in use today—barium for green, calcium for orange, copper for blue, sodium for yellow, and strontium for red. Magnesium appeared in 1865 and aluminum in 1894.

Blue shells were once the most difficult shells to make. They required a mixture that is not only comparatively volatile during the manufacturing process but used a copper-based chemical that irritates the skin and leaves an odd and displeasing taste in the mouths of those who handle it. While new blue formulas are much safer, John Conkling of Washington College in Chestertown, Maryland, who works full-time in fireworks technology, has said, "The creation of a deep-blue flame that is, at the same time, bright is one of the great unsolved problems of pyrotechnics."

Fireworks in Paris on the anniversary of VE Day, 1965. (Time-Life Picture Collection. Photograph by Dominique Berretty)

Fireworks rise off the breakwaters of the harbor at Monte Carlo, Monaco, in 1979, the year the Grucci family of Bellport, Long Island, won the annual fireworks competition. (London Daily Telegraph Colour Library. Photo by Anthony Howarth)

Benny Bello of Elkton Fireworks was famous for his blues. Mysteriously, in his broken English, he used to say that if you felt it in the belly it was a good mixture. When asked where he had come by his formulas for blue, he would reply, "Out of my grandfather's trunk."

Cost Spectators often wonder what it costs to put on a fireworks show. Usually the estimates are much too high. I have heard people propose figures for a relatively small country club display that would rank with bringing in the Kirov ballet from the U.S.S.R., all expenses paid. In fact, a twenty-minute show, featuring aerial shells, a few set pieces, including a sign that spells Good Night in red fire, and a healthy barrage finale at the end costs in the neighborhood of four thousand dollars. That, of course, includes operators, insurance, and so forth. Mammoth shows, such as Chicago's Venetian Night or the Brooklyn Bridge Centennial celebration, can cost well over $100,000. The PL show near Osaka, Japan, involves the most spectacular expenditure—in the neighborhood of a million dollars (see Chapter Six).

The cost of individual aerial shells varies according to size and the complexity of what the shell has been programmed to do. To make an eight-inch shell, which is a very large shell indeed, weighing about ten pounds, and which would be used as a finale effect to extract a large last yell from the crowds, the cost would break down approximately as follows:

1. 38 oz. of lifting and bursting charge of black powder at $1.80/lb.	$ 4.28
2. Various paper components, including paper for casing and paper cover cap for the fuse	3.00
3. Fuse or match six feet at $3.00/60 feet	.30
4. 7 lbs. stars composition at $1.25/lb.	8.75
5. Paste and glue	.50
6. Fiber disks	.25
TOTAL	$17.08

A shell of this size would be retailed for about eighty dollars—to return a profit after payment for labor (the biggest cost), insurance, and other ancillary expenses involved in shooting a show.

Crackle An aerial shell whose noise effect has been likened to the ripping of a giant shroud in the sky. The sound is produced by including magnalium in the composition of the star formulas. Ladyfingers set among the stars will produce somewhat the same effect. The Japanese produce the crackle by putting a tiny explosive core in the center of their round stars. Each star on its ignition produces a sharp crack, and hundreds of these exploding within a second produce the characteristic crackling sound.

Cross-match A method of ensuring that the main time fuse or leader of a shell ignites and that it will, at the apogee of the shell's flight, ignite its contents.

This is done by punching small holes through the time fuse and inserting two short pieces of quick-burning fuse—one outside and one inside the shell.

Dark Fire (also called **Relays**) A composition that gives off hardly any light when it burns. It is set between the coatings of color on a color-changing star (q.v.) so that the effect in the night sky is of one color, say red, winking out, and then, after a second or so, after the dark fire burns, another color appears—a lovely effect, giving the stars of a bouquet a sudden afterlife one had not expected.

Daylight Shells A shell (q.v.) designed to perform in daytime light. The Japanese, who are especially noted for their daytime fireworks, identify three types. The first is the Report Shell, which simply goes up and gives a bang, and is useful (as one Japanese catalogue describes it) for "invigorating people."

The second designation is referred to as Flag and Figure Shells. These are shells which discharge parachute-like balloons, made of a thin, light tissue paper known as Gampi, open at the bottom and weighted, some in the shape of flags, others as animal-like configurations, which slowly float down over the spectators and end up usually as nice souvenirs. The Marutamaya Ogatsu Fireworks Co. of Japan has a category of daylight shells entitled "Comic Shells" which open with parachutes from which dangle any number of representational figures, often oddly spelled, which one can order from the catalogue. Among the animals are: The Rabit, The Tigar, The Ziraffe, The Tartois. Under the category "The Mankinds" are a Buglar, a Man in Tuxedi, a Pitcher of Base-ball, along with a Cather, as well as Mikky Mouse.

The third category is the Smoke Shell. There are two kinds. One is a parachute shell that supports a smoke pot, which tends, as it comes down, to draw haphazard smoke designs in the sky. A father can point them out to a skeptical child as resembling a dragon ("You see, there's the *tail*"). Indeed, the shell itself is called "Smoke Dragon Shell." The most common variety of Smoke Shells are the Smoke Willow and the Smoke Chrysanthemum Shells. At the burst, the shell appears to spew out ribbons of color (white, red, yellow, blue, purple, or black). The lines of smoke, if not dissipated by a strong wind, hang in the sky, if somewhat messily, for many minutes at a time. The largest and fanciest is the "Drifting Flower Shell: Smoke Chrysanthemum with a Stem and Leaves" in which a green color is introduced to suggest the stems and leaves. In truth, a daytime display begins to pall, since there is neither the variety nor the beauty of a nighttime show. After a while, in the daytime, the sky resembles an artist's palette rather than a painting—a messy hodgepodge of ribbons and whorls.

Drivers (or **Turnings**; also **Pushers**) These are the tube-like devices, cigar-sized, that emit a jet-like stream of sparks and provide enough power to turn the set-piece wheel on which they are attached. The composition inside a driver is very much like that which drives a rocket—charcoal, iron and steel filings, titanium and other granulated substances incorporated to give different color effects as the wheel turns.

163

Explosion An explosion is a very fast chemical reaction, but not as fast as a detonation. Explosive force is expressed in terms of *brisance,* or velocity of detonation. Nitroglycerin explodes so rapidly that, if it were in a container a foot across, the explosion would be over in 1/25,000 of a second. Such a force is, of course, shattering. If a stick of dynamite—which is composed of nitroglycerin and sawdust—were placed on the top of a boulder, it would shatter the boulder even if the explosive were not confined. As the book I read on the subject of explosives expressed it nicely: "The boulder simply cannot get out of the way in time." Nitroglycerin—along with TNT, dynamite, and compounds used in military ordnance, such as a bomb—is called "high explosive" as opposed to the less *brisant* of explosives, which are referred to as "low explosives." The latter *push at* rather than shatter the immediate surroundings. Gunpowder, the most familiar of the low explosives, goes off at a speed of only 1/10 of a second per foot. That same boulder would show no effect from a charge of gunpowder set off on its surface. The "low explosives" are, naturally, those employed in fireworks.

Firecracker A small noisemaking cylinder, usually up to an inch and a half in length, often strung together with others of its kind and fused consecutively. It is the well-known staple of Chinese New Year's street celebrations—the firecrackers spitting on the pavement as the serpentine parade figures move by. Incidentally, Gum Lung is the name of the firecracker dragon which is used in San Francisco. He's 120 feet long, with the head of a camel, the horns of a deer, the eyes of a rabbit, ears of a cow, neck of a serpent, belly of a frog, the scales of a carp, and the talons of a hawk, with twenty-two men inside making him work. While the number of firecrackers fired at Chinese New Year's celebrations is huge, the largest known string of firecrackers is undoubtedly that fired at the Pyrotechnics Guild International conventions—numbering over three hundred thousand firecrackers in a single gigantic roll. (See Chapter Five.)

Actually, the first firecrackers *(p'ao chu)* did not have black powder in them. They were simply joints of bamboo thrown on a fire. The noise of their exploding is graphically described by Marco Polo, who reports that if the young green canes are put on a campfire "they burn with such a dreadful noise that it can be heard for ten miles at night, and anyone who was not used to it could easily go into a swoon and even die. Hence the ears are stopped with cotton wool and the clothes drawn over the head, and horses are fettered on all four feet and their feet padded and the ears and eyes covered, for it is the most terrible thing in the world to hear for the first time."

I wondered upon reading this (it is recounted in J. R. Partington's *A History of Greek Fire and Gunpowder*) if perhaps what Marco Polo heard was a very large bamboo joint filled with black powder. Bob Cardwell, a fireworks scholar, has in the interests of research burned joints of green bamboo; he tells me that they tend to emit steam and then burst with quite a respectable bang. But he agrees that the report is hardly anything that would require the tethering and blindfolding of a horse, much less the swooning and demise of a human being. He agrees that Marco Polo can be suspected of hyperbole.

Fire Marshal An authority on fires, who thinks of fireworks as anathema, a tinderbox, a prime cause of what he has been trained to fight, namely fires, but, in truth, an official who often knows very little about fireworks. A case in point: a fire marshal in Washington, D.C., authorized to grant permits for the fireworks to celebrate Ronald Reagan's Inauguration in 1981, asked Dave Opperman, the executive secretary of the American Pyrotechnics Association and who had helped plan the festivities, "Mr. Opperman, what is the weight of what goes up?" "It depends," Opperman answered him. "Some shells, the big eight-inch, or ten-inch ones, might weigh ten, fifteen pounds." The marshal lifted a finger to indicate the portentousness of the next question. "And what is the weight of what comes down?" "Well," Opperman said, after a few seconds of reflection. "Do you mean if the shell doesn't go off? Well, in that rare case—I mean it almost never happens—if thirty pounds went up, thirty pounds would come down."

"No, I mean after it explodes."

"Well, then," Opperman said, "nothing would come down."

"Nothing?"

"A bit of ash. Flecks of paper. Maybe a patch of cardboard."

"And how much would all this weigh?" the marshal asked. He had the stump of a pencil poised above a notepad.

"Perhaps a tenth of an ounce . . . give or take a bit."

The marshal dutifully wrote this down; Opperman wondered if that minuscule amount would turn up somewhere on a government form.

Such authorities from anti-fireworks agencies and associations are formidable foes. One death in a National Fire Protection Association report was attributed to fireworks because the victim, an employee of the California Department of Forestry, had died of apparent heatstroke suffered while fighting a fire "caused" by fireworks. There are those who wish to rid the country entirely of even professional shows. The fire marshal in Detroit, Bernard F. de Coster, spent years trying to do away with the Hudson Department Store show on the Detroit River. He would announce that sixteen people had been killed on the Hudson River in 1953, blithely adding fourteen to the true total. A typical statement—this also from the National Fire Protection Association—ordains: "We believe that fireworks, not some fireworks, but all fireworks, should be taken out of the hands of the public . . ."

In response, in the pro-fireworks journals such as the *American Pyrotechnists News,* the mail is just as vehement: "They strain at gnats and swallow elephants. They should ban pork. They should ban whole milk. Cholesterol! They let any sixteen-year-old kid who can come up with $5,000 buy a car that will go 150 mph and go out and run over people. But an inch-long firecracker? I have never heard of a kid getting hurt with one yet."

Spinoza is quoted: "All laws which can be violated without doing anyone any injury are laughed at."

Thus the fireworks industry seizes upon anyone of official stature who promotes the idea of fireworks, especially Class C, which would allow the public to buy them. In a 1966 industry newsletter published in Saginaw, Michigan, an article from *Medicine at Work* was reprinted which suggested that fireworks had a therapeutic value. "The Fourth of July," the article ran, "used to be a lot of fun, a day when we could celebrate not only our nation's independence, but also our personal independence. Fireworks are a wonderful way of getting rid of tensions. People ought to have a chance to blow off steam once in a while. Watching professional displays just is not personal enough."

The article was by Dr. William E. Schumacher, the director of mental health for the state of Maine, a gentleman who not only endorsed but spent a considerable time promoting a bill to legalize the sale of Chinese firecrackers, Roman candles, and sparklers in his home state. It went nowhere.

Fireworks Any of a number of devices designed to produce visual or audible effects through combustion or explosion. The generic term "fireworks" should not be confused with "firecrackers," which are a specific kind of firework.

Fireworks Artists Fireworks in recent years have been used—often in a somewhat rambunctious manner—by any number of serious artists, mostly of the conceptual school: Jean Tinguely, Dennis Oppenheim, Pierre-Alain Hubert, among others. Perhaps the most famous is the Viennese "self-impersonator" Franz André Heller, who embraces fireworks as an art form very much as the artist Christo has monopolized the practice of wrapping large objects such as bank buildings, bridges, even coastlines. In 1983, Heller put on a huge theme show—it was rumored to have cost in the neighborhood of $800,000—in Lisbon, Portugal, on the Tagus River. It was divided into thematic acts with such titles as "The Creation of the World," "The Invention of War"—symbolized by two Portuguese deep-sea fishing boats got up as *Violence* and *Hate* firing Roman candles at each other—and "Phantasie," which was the concluding section. "Phantasie" involved a parade of ten barges, on each a large set piece depicting a Heller artist-hero—including a lance-work facsimile of the obscure French novelist Raymond Roussel—the whole to end with an epilogue in which the word PAX would burn for a full minute. The spectacle was supposed to last for forty-five minutes. Instead, before seven hundred thousand spectators, largely because of misfires and electrical disconnects, the display sputtered on and off for about five minutes. *Hate* and *Violence* were swept apart by the tides and never got off a shot at each other. The "Phantasie" section blew up out of sequence. Of the barges carrying the artist-heroes, only two illuminated, one of them the mysterious Raymond Roussel; the word PAX never ignited at all. Nonetheless, Franz André Heller's reputation as a fireworks artist has not diminished. He is of that avant-garde school where catastrophe only seems to embellish an artist's stature. Fireworks professionals tend to look upon such artists with bemusement (actually, Ruggieri's specialists were on hand to help Heller with his Tagus River show), but it is quite likely that fireworks choreography will increasingly be directed by fireworks technicians working with artists.

Fireworks Industry An estimated one hundred and fifty firms are engaged in various aspects of the fireworks business in the United States, with retail sales estimated by the American Pyrotechnics Association to reach well over $100,000,000—the large percentage of this in Class C or Safe and Sane items, known in the industry as "Toy" fireworks. Seventy-five percent of this material is imported—from Japan, China, Taiwan, Hong Kong, Macao, France, Brazil, Korea, England, and Germany. The four-to-one ratio is approximately what a spectator can expect from an aerial fireworks display in this country—three quarters of it foreign-made. Some American firms, notably Illinois Fireworks, try to redress the balance with a much larger percentage of American products—a somewhat self-sacrificing gesture since the imports, both in terms of cost and quality, are useful to the variety (a typical Japanese catalogue lists over five hundred different items) and splendor of an evening's show.

Flare (or ***Fusée***) The baton-like implement—which retails as a highway flare or a railroad flare—most commonly used to light professional fireworks. It is exactly the same device with its bright red flame that one sees set out on the road to warn motorists to slow down. There are various sizes. The one that burns for about twenty-five minutes is the type usually used by fireworks people.

The flare has a scratcher-matched ignition. The scratcher fits over the head end of the flare. The pyrotechnician pulls it off with a slight pop of suction, turns it over, and strikes the exposed top end of the flare with its surface, which is composed of various proportions of lacquer, pumice, red phosphorus, and butyl acetate.

What it strikes against is called the match head, which consists mostly of chlorates, shellac, and a pinch of quartz, wood flour, marble dust, and charcoal. The friction created by the two surfaces being rubbed together ignites the match head with a sharp crack; the flare burns with a bright red flame, intensely luminous, and perfect for touching to the fuses of Class B fireworks.

In other parts of the world there are different methods of ignition. The Japanese light their shells by dropping them into the pipe, where the shell fetches up against a red-hot coil at the bottom of the mortar, which sets off the lifting charge. The shell spends very little time in the pipe.

The Japanese also employ a very different kind of manual lighting. A cut star (about 3mm by 3mm by 30mm in size) called a Sindoro (very likely from the English word "cinder") is used. It is ignited with a joss stick and thrown into the mortar, where it ignites "powder spray" dusted over the shell, which in turn lights the lifting charge under the shell, igniting it, and thrusting the shell out of the mortar. With very large *tama* shells, the Sindoro is hung inside the mortar and is attached to a fuse. After lighting it, the operator can remove himself to safer areas. The fuse ignites the Sindoro, which then falls down the length of the mortar and begins its business.

I am told it is an infallible method. A flare is supposed to be a surefire device too. It is not. I recall a misty New Year's Eve in Long Island setting out a small (illegal) fireworks show on the beach with a big eight-inch Chinese shell to climax things at the stroke of midnight. A crowd of friends waited out on the lawn in front of the house, expecting to see the shells rise at midnight from beyond the dunes. With a few minutes to go, I lit a twenty-five-minute railroad flare; its bright red glow lit the sand and the line of mortars. I handed the flare to a friend, a literary agent named Tim Seldes—out there to assist—while I did a last check of the shells.

Timothy asked, "How long do these things last?"

"Twenty minutes," I said. "Plenty of time."

"I don't know about this one," Tim said. As I turned, I saw the arrow point of the flame splutter and expire. We stood gazing dumbly at the dead flare, its length dim in the darkness.

"What did you do to it?" I asked frantically.

"Nothing," Tim said. "I was just holding it."

"Jesus," I said. "We have no way of lighting the show."

A wind was blowing down the beach. The only hope was to shield a cigarette-lighter flame and try to ignite the fuses with it. The stroke of midnight came and went. I could hear the derisive hoots of the crowd, and the thin blasts of paper horns as the crowd waited in a driving mist. I sent for a cigarette lighter. A near-extinct Bic arrived. I crouched in the sand next to a six-inch mortar and tried to push the lighter's wan-like flame at the fuse of the shell. It was not a pleasant sensation—to be with one's face to the sand that close to the mortar, knowing that it would belch forth a shell before I could get to my feet and scramble away. Sometimes it took a minute of spinning the tiny flywheel to get enough flame to light a fuse. The show, which was supposed to last a minute, with the shells going up in quick succession, lasted for ten minutes or so, sporadically, as if each shell were being *made* on the premises and then loaded up. I vowed, sprawled on the sand, always to have a reserve flare on hand. Perhaps a couple. Perhaps even a Sindoro *and* a joss stick!

Flash Powder A mixture of potassium chlorate or potassium perchlorate, sulfur, and aluminum powder developed early in the twentieth century. It is unsuitable as a propellant; nonetheless, it explodes with a large flash and bang and is thus just the thing for reports and salutes. In Class C fireworks, which are limited by law to fifty milligrams, flash powder is invariably used since it is more virulent for its weight than black powder. The flash is especially satisfactory. Indeed, a payload of flash powder was suggested by Robert H. Goddard in a paper published in 1919 as the means by which astronomers could tell that a rocket had reached the moon.

Flights (or *Volleys*) The pyrotechnical term for sending up a number of shells at the same time, usually of the same variety. The beauty of a single shell, say a split comet, is considerably enhanced by filling the sky with them. Electrical firing has increased the use of flights, since the click of a switch on the firing board can send up a dozen or more shells simultaneously. Shells that are especially effective in flights are palm trees, serpents, hummingbirds, parachute shells, whistles, twinkling leaves and strobe shells, meteors, circle shells and the lovely *kamuro* shells from Japan. Ideally, the mortars should be fanned slightly in their troughs so that the width of the display is increased; equivalently the mortar-size diameters should range from four to eight inches so that an increased vertical size of the shell bursts is achieved.

Flowerpot The name given by pyrotechnicians to a shell that malfunctions and explodes inside the mortar. Almost invariably, unless there is a large salute in the shell, the mortar withstands the shock and the ignited stars erupt from its mouth in a colorful "flowerpot" effect. Indeed, very often crowds do not appreciate that something untoward has happened. Heavy salutes, on the other hand, are capable of shattering the mortar, sending it in shards across the landscape; it is the one kind of accident during a public display that a pyrotechnist would fear most. It would be referred to as a "detonation," not a "flowerpot."

Fountain A device—for both commercial and professional use—shaped like a cone or a cylinder (usually with a base for stability) out of which erupts a tall shower of sparks.

Fuse The fireworks' "wick." The older type, still used in some Oriental fireworks, consists of tissue paper rolled around black powder. A more advanced type employs a string of woven threads which contains a train of gunpowder grains. The word "fuse" is derived from the Latin *fusus*, "spindle."

Gerb A variety of fountain (q.v.). From the French word *"gerbe"* which means spray or a sheaf of wheat, which is what its effusion of sparks resembles. Gerbs are usually used by fixing them into a set piece (q.v.) at various angles.

Girandole The "flying saucer" of fireworks. Its history goes back to the fifteenth century. "The revolving one" it was called. Originally, it spun on a pole like a horizontal Catherine wheel, but then rockets and lifting planes were added so that it would spin off a center pole into the air like a whirligig top. Michelangelo was supposed to have designed a girandole display at Rome's Castel Sant' Angelo.

Girandoles come in different sizes. Felix Grucci, Sr., remembers one so large that it was carried by four men who heaved it up one-two-three-*ho!* on its center pole, and then backed off hurriedly when the fuse was lit. The contraption began to revolve slowly, then faster, dropping a circular curtain of fire around it like a skirt as the lifting rockets ("they had four hundred of them under it, I swear") began to turn the huge disk and move it up the pole, then off, free in the air, spinning it like an eerie flying disk as it rose high into the air, changing hues on the way.

The airborne girandoles are no longer as popular. The smaller models have a tendency to tip and scale off in odd, unpredictable directions and even the big ones, however stable, can be blown off course by a wind, or the rockets fizzle on one side, so that it tilts alarmingly, and then starts to come down slowly, still functioning busily, the spectators looking up and yelling and abandoning their picnic baskets and fine quilted comforters with the wine bottles propped up on them as the immense fiery disk settles comfortably down in their vicinity like a starfish descending on an oyster bed.

Greek Fire A mysterious artificial fire for military use, supposedly introduced by Greek soldiers during the Arab siege of Constantinople at the end of the seventh century. It was very likely a jelly-like material—an ancient precursor of napalm—containing distilled petroleum along with sulfur, resin, and pitch. Early military people spoke of it as being ejectable from "siphons" and "ballistas"—devices very much like primitive flame-throwers. Anna Comnena, the daughter of the Emperor Alexius I Comnenus, describes Greek soldiers in Rhodes in the early twelfth century blowing Greek fire out of blowpipes with "violent and continuous breath" so that it "falls like a fiery whirlwind on the faces of the enemy." Greek fire, of course, had none of the properties of an explosive.

Green Man The symbolic figure adopted by fireworks people, more specifically by the amateurs who tend to be more concerned with the history and traditions of fireworks than the professionals. The "green" or "wild" man was a figure in seventeenth-century England appointed to lead processions to clear the way and advertise the presence of a parade by shooting off ceremonial fireworks. The "green" was very likely derived from the leaves on his hat and clothing to protect him from sparks. The Pyrotechnics Guild International uses a woodcut of a Green Man as its logo; its members usually sign their letters to each other with the phrase "Stay green." The husbands refer to their wives occasionally as "green ladies"—a sobriquet which is not especially appreciated.

Hangfire A fuse that starts to burn slowly instead of at its usual speed. Such a fuse may resume burning at its usual rate.

This woodcut served to illustrate the title page of one of the earliest English treatises on fireworks, John Bate's The Composing of All Manner of Fireworks for Triumph and Recreation. *Dated 1654, it shows the medieval Green Man who, dressed in green with a headpiece of leaves, carried a club of fire, leading the parade for May Day festivals. The first recorded reference to this famous character is from a report of Anne Boleyn's coronation in 1533. At the head of her procession was an enormous fire-breathing dragon heralded by "terrible monstrous Wild Men casting fire and making a hideous noise." (Courtesy, Hagley Museum and Library, Wilmington, Delaware)*

The composing of all manner of

Fier-Works

For Triumph and Recreacion,

Plainly and Exactly taught

By JOHN BATE.

LONDON
Printed by *R: Bishop* for *Andrew Crook*, at the Green
Dragon in Pauls Churchyard. 1654

Green Men came in various guises. These examples are from recipe books used by sixteenth-century fireworks masters. (All courtesy Hagley Museum and Library, Wilmington, Delaware)

Happy Lantern A remarkable Class C firework from China. In appearance it looks something like a flattened opera hat. Hung from its string, ignited drivers (q.v.) begin to spin the firework, spraying a curtain of sparks that change color three times; then suddenly the disk-like object drops open and a Japanese lantern magically appears, red rice-paper walls, and silk tassels hanging from its base. Incredibly, inside the lantern a little fireworks display takes place—a pair of magnalium-bright lights dancing briefly. When it is finally extinguished, this wonderfully ingenious firework is attractive enough to keep around the house as a decoration. It costs five cents in China. Exported to the United States, it costs a dollar or so, depending on the size.

The Happy Lantern's ancestor in the Orient was a device known as the Drum. According to accounts of the early 1800s, it looked more like a squarish sea chest. It was hauled by pulleys up to fifty feet or so, at which point

its base dropped open, letting loose a string of lanterns, from which in turn other lanterns would spill, until ultimately five hundred or so hung in a triangle pattern from the chest, each with a flame, just as with today's Happy Lanterns, burning inside. This was not all. The traveler who described the chest wrote that it also let loose "a correspondence of boxes containing squibs and firecrackers of various sorts which concluded the overall effect with a volcano-like eruption." The traveler also wrote that "it involved the gardens for an hour in a cloud of intolerable smoke."

Hummers A small tube carried aloft in numbers by a shell. When expelled by the bursting charge, the device works by spinning under its own power so fast that it makes a screaming or humming sound. English displays are often dominated by the hummerstars, often called hummingbirds, or bees.

Insurance The insurance is a substantial part of the cost of a fireworks show—usually the premium for coverage is in the neighborhood of 8 to 14 percent of the cost of the show. The range is from fifty dollars a day for the Cleveland Indians fireworks, which celebrate a hometown homerun, to twenty thousand dollars the Gruccis paid for a six-million-dollar policy to cover their mammoth Brooklyn Bridge extravaganza. Claims against insurance companies are referred to as "occurrences." A big bother in claims are people who say their cars need a two-thousand-dollar paint job because of a flaky dusting of fireworks fallout after a show. Almost invariably the aggrieved is offered two dollars and fifty cents for a car wash and there the matter ends.

Ladyfinger A small (¾-inch) firecracker. An interesting use of this device is to involve it in the manufacture of stars, so that the shell's burst is accompanied by a great crackling roar.

Lance A small tube (about ⅜ inch in diameter and up to 4 inches long) filled with color-producing chemicals which on ignition produce a steady flame. Connected with quick match so that the lances ignite at the same time, these are the staples of set pieces (q.v.), their flames outlining portraits, flags, or such sentiments as "Good Night" at the conclusion of a display.

Lasers The laser beam, often used in fireworks shows, is an extension of the kind of spectacle provided by searchlight beams. During Ronald Reagan's Inauguration there was an interesting display when all the national monuments in Washington were linked with a bright spiderweb of lasers. Lasers can also be used to project designs—most satisfactorily against a low, dense cloud cover acting as a kind of large-scale projection screen. On July 4, 1980, at the Macy's show on the Hudson River, a laser company named Science Faction Corporation used an instrument called a Laseriter to project the name of the sponsoring company—Macy's—against the cloud cover. To me, lasers do not come close to having the display qualities of fireworks. After all, to see the name "Macy's" written against a cloud is a phenomenon that tends to fade in interest after the novelty has worn off.

Leader The length of quick match attached to a shell or other device. It is the fuse one touches off with a flare.

Living Fireworks A *divertissement* at the turn of the century in which men dressed in asbestos suits and rigged up with fireworks performed various dramatic roles and capered about while rockets, gerbes, fountains, pinwheels, and other devices worked busily on their persons. At one sorry period in fireworks history (during the eighteenth century), animals (bulls, dogs, donkeys) were similarly outfitted and ignited. They ran through the crowds pell-mell until the last device on their backs had burned out—this in the name of commercial entertainment.

Machine (or **Temple**) A large, often very ornate temporary structure especially constructed to backdrop, even contain a fireworks display. The history of the machine lasted for about two hundred years (into the mid nineteenth century). It was phased out in part because the fireworks got better, and the *artificiers* began to use permanent backdrops such as the Palais de Chaillot, or perhaps, most famous, the Crystal Palace at Sydenham for their displays.

A blazing set piece spells out a familiar motto below the American eagle. This marked the finale of a fireworks spectacular to usher in the NRA enrollment drive held at the foot of Washington Monument in 1933. (The Bettmann Archive, Inc.)

On Bastille Day, 1950, the Eiffel Tower was used as a "machine." Maître Ruggieri (he had by then—in deference to his considerable prestige and that of his company—dropped his first name) did the show personally. He stood on the second level in front of a twelve-button electrical panel to set off almost two thousand pyrotechnical devices. "From all three of its balconies," wrote Janet Flanner of *The New Yorker* who stood with a few people at the base, "burst an apotheosis of fireworks in showers, balls, streamers, rockets, and what looked like silver and gold clouds of burning snowflakes . . . the finale was a magical, thunderous bombardment of explosives, going off in artfully patterned flames, and above them the Tour seemed to rock peacefully in the night sky."

Master Blaster Pastor This is the descriptive name given the Reverend Ronald Lancaster, a fireworks authority and manufacturer, and a teacher at the Kimbolton School in England. He was once known more simply as the Blaster Pastor, but after putting on a considerable display for British Royalty at Buckingham Palace to mark the twenty-fifth anniversary of the Queen's Coronation he became known as the *Master* Blaster Pastor. He continues to teach at the Kimbolton School. After the 4 P.M. bell he heads down to work in the converted sheds at the edge of the school grounds. His specialties are giant Roman candles and spider bombs.

M-80 See *Cherry Bomb.*

Mine A tubular Class C device, balanced by a wooden or plastic base, which is designed to propel any number of items aloft—stars, whistles, or even a parachute.

Mini-bag An aerial shell without a lift charge, so that the shell explodes in the mortar, intentionally, and produces a geyser-like effect. It feels soft to the touch, since it needs no integrity.

Misfire A shell in which the quick match burns away after being lighted but nothing happens; a live shell is left in the mortar. Not to be confused with a black shell (q.v.) or dud that leaves the mortar but fails to perform.

Mistakes I have rarely seen a fireworks show in which everything worked exactly as it should have. Often the choreographic effects are not what one expected—jarring colors, the bursts too closely lumped, or shredded by the wind; sometimes the timing is off, usually because a shell does not emerge from its mortar; a shell will "flowerpot" (q.v.), or it may burst too low; a pinwheel on a set piece will refuse to turn; the finale will stop in midpace and have to be relit; an O in GOOD NIGHT will not burn.

The reason for this is that despite the material's being largely hand-crafted, there are any number of circumstances and variables—from the quality of the shells to the inconsistencies of weather—which keep the displays from being paragons of perfection. A number of odd examples come to mind. I am not thinking of the accidents, of course, which are discussed elsewhere in this volume.

Perhaps the most infamous mishap was during a fireworks celebration of Queen Victoria's Silver Jubilee. A huge portrait (it was 200 feet long and 180 feet high) of the Queen and the Royal Family had a small but devastating technical problem: the right eye of the Queen began to blink uncontrollably, as if she were winking at the enormous throng.

Sometimes nature takes a hand. Part of a Rozzi show, preset in its mortars, and protected by plywood covers from an approaching storm, went up when a lightning bolt hit nearby. The shells burst in one frightful instant through the wood covers, harming no one, but offering a magnificent show to the few hurrying by who cared to look up from under their umbrellas.

Reverend Brian Bergin, the American equivalent of the Master Blaster Pastor (see page 106). (Photo by Buz Swerkstrom)

More often, human error is involved. In Philadelphia's baseball park, with a huge crowd on hand in anticipation of Pete Rose's surpassing Stan Musial's total of 3,630 lifetime hits, the Phillies' executive vice president, Bill Giles, who was to give the signal for a considerable fireworks celebration when it happened, shouted, "No! No! No!" as a roar went up in the first inning when Rose's ground ball was bobbled by the Cardinal shortstop. The fireworks people out beyond the ballpark's walls heard the roar and thought Giles had said, "Go! Go! Go!" They sent up the display—without doubt, the largest response ever produced by a shortstop's miscue.

A most curious example of the best-laid plans going awry occurred at the preparation of the extraordinary 1983 Brooklyn Bridge display. While the great Niagara was being prepared underneath the roadway of the bridge, a fireboat came by and shot up a powerful, exuberant, celebratory plume in the air, dousing Phil Butler, of the Grucci clan, who was working on the line of Niagara cases. Indeed, he was nearly picked up by the water's force and poised on its plume, not unlike a Ping-Pong ball on a hotel fountain spray. The cases were thoroughly soaked, so that part of what was to be among the most dramatic effects of the night could not ignite.

Mixing The first process in the making of pyrotechnic composition used in such ingredients as stars (q.v.). Originally, hand-sieving was the common practice, the composition dropping through various-sized meshes adjusted to the size of the particles. Now, two types of mechanical mixes are in general use. One is a drum with internal baffles which is turned, the powders inside being tumbled and thus mixed. The other is a stationary, closed container which has paddles within that blend the contents. Enormous care has to be exercised in the design, construction, and operation of these mixers. No heat must ever be generated by friction, or flakes of powder trapped between the moving parts—since an explosive reaction is a constant possibility.

Mortar (also ***Gun*** or ***Pipe*** or ***Tube***) The tube-like device out of which aerial shells seen at public displays are launched. Made of iron, aluminum, heavy cardboard, or plastic, the tube functions very much like a military mortar. The shell, launched by its propellant charge, emerges like a projectile fired from a gun. The shell must be the right size for the mortar. It should slide easily down to the bottom of the mortar and yet it should be what Canadian fireworks people refer to as a "sliding fit"—that is to say, snug enough so that it will be propelled smartly out of the pipe when the lifting charge goes off. A six-inch shell (six inches in diameter) can be set into an eight-inch mortar with great ease, of course, but the gas from the exploding lifting-charge will escape around its edges and thus enfeeble the thrust necessary to throw the shell far up into the air. In such a case, the six-inch shell will probably come out of the mortar, but not go very far up, and will then fall back to the ground and create its chrysanthemum burst, or whatever, among the mortar tubes and the people working them. I have done this by error once. It is not a pleasant experience.

The size of a mortar will range from two inches in diameter (the usual size of shells sent up in a final barrage is three inches) to forty inches across the muzzle, which was the size of the mortar into which the Fat Man series was settled. Mortars, of course, can be used many times; along with shells, they are the largest inventory item in a pyrotechnic outfit.

The mortar is either embedded in a sand-filled trough, or put in a barrel, or buried in the ground—which protects the firing crews in the rare instance of a shell exploding "in the pipe" (as the expression goes), which could shred the mortar into dangerous flying shards. In the Orient, fireworks people do not seem to worry about this possibility: the mortar is set on top of the ground attached to a supporting stake.

Actually, the mortars in Japan were originally made of wood—not all that surprising when one remembers that early cannons were similarly made. The method was to hollow out a pair of tree trunks like twin troughs and then join the two halves together and bind them with hoops of bamboo. The result stood up against the concussion of sending a shell aloft. The black gunpowder used then as a propellant had less explosive power than today's, which allowed these wooden barrels to survive the emergence of a shell.

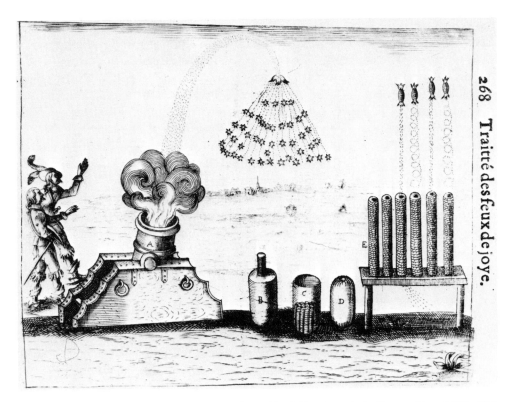

A variety of mortars as illustrated in François de Malthus's Pratique de la Guerre *(circa 1630). This is a page from a section entitled* feux de joie—*fires of joy—as the French once termed fireworks. (Jean-Loup Charmet)*

Mortar Cleaner A stick with a nail in the bottom which is used to spear pieces of paper, some of which might still be smoldering, from the bottom of a just-used mortar to clear it for the next shell.

Music Recently, the art of matching fireworks and music has monopolized the attention of fireworks choreographers—too much so, it seems to me. At meetings of the Pyrotechnics Guild International, seminars are given in which the claim is made that a shell burst can be timed to coincide within a hundredth of a second of a musical beat. I have argued that even if this were so, the sound of the explosion would reach spectators spread over, say, a half mile, at a variance (considering the speed of sound) of almost two seconds (unless they were all listening to transistors), a discrepancy enough to drive any orchestra conductor batty and which surely emphasizes that the melding of fireworks and music is hardly an exact science. Even the visual effects (the burst of a chrysanthemum on the final chord of a symphonic piece) cannot be precise because of the slight difference in fuse lengths. About the most music can do for fireworks, or vice versa, is to reflect moods or pacing, or to illustrate what the music score calls for—as in the cannonading in Tchaikovsky's *1812 Overture*. The background of Japanese music—lute sounds and pipes—to the bursts of chrysanthemums, especially those that rise on tails to the enormous heights Oriental shells achieve, is a breathtaking combination. But, pyrotechnically, not much more can be asked of music.

Naval Battles These were very much a fad in the early days of both English and French fireworks displays—in a sense, a dramatic use of waterborne "machines." Dummy ships were usually used, but on occasion real vessels were manned by firemasters. One wonders how many firemasters took to the water in the conflagrations! In 1610, at the investiture of Henry, Prince of Wales, there was a "sea battle" on the Thames, and three years later another such spectacle celebrated the wedding of James I's daughter, Elizabeth. Accounts of the time described the sea fight as so realistic that the God of Battle might have "been there present." In 1814, to celebrate the sixteenth anniversary of the battle of the Nile (the entrepreneurs must really have been stretching to find a reason for fireworks!), there was a three-hour naval "engagement" on the Serpentine in London's Hyde Park.

Actually, the lovely combination of fireworks over water makes such scenarios a sight to relish. I can recall with great vividness a "sea battle" arranged a few years ago in Newport, Rhode Island, an arching exchange of fireworks between a group on a small island named Gooseberry, whose owner, Beverly Bogart, had allowed us to set some fireworks mortars in the bluffs, and an old-time brigantine, *The Black Pearl*. Her owner, a gentleman named "Buzzy" Warburton, occasionally charters *The Black Pearl* to film companies making pirate epics. As the sun went down, she sailed in to "attack" us—her square sail set and a dull orange in the sunset. She tacked slowly back and forth in front of Gooseberry until the darkness came; an aerial shell arched up from her decks and burst above us. Warburton has a very loud and English voice, even when he is talking across a small table, and at sea it is truly stentorian, embellished by a large vocabulary of ancient sailing terms. His cries rose above the tumult: "Back down the top-mizzen and wear 'round, ye scurvies, and, by your leave, Mister Cushing, sir, will you run out your guns and give them a whiff of the grape!"

He had a small brass cannon on board *The Black Pearl* and a row of three- and four-inch mortars set in barrels on deck. I had given him a rather extensive lesson in how to use them and a small amount of aerial fireworks shells.

"More, more," he had said at the time. "You can't expect me to do much with this measly allotment of shells! And bigger! How am I to run under the range of the Gooseberry long toms with these little things? Give me an eight-pounder, sir, and we'll singe the blackguard's whiskers," etc., etc.

This scene of a mock naval battle, a common attraction in seventeenth-century fireworks shows, strongly recommends the safety of shore as a vantage point. The actors in the drama can be seen on board, running through the fireworks, waving flaming swords. The experience must have been particularly frightening, being long before the invention of fireproof clothing. (Edimages)

page 68 and 69

This machine for a mock land-sea battle was designed by master pyrotechnist John Babington to celebrate a naval victory of Charles II. Babington wrote in his 1635 instructional treatise Pyrotechnica: "Having a space appointed for your worke, (which must be in some spacious River), you shall seek the most convenient place on shore for placing a Castle, which shall be furnished with all manner of works, as well as fire bals, as rockets, with divers small Ordnance to give a more grace for the worke; . . . you shall also make another Castle on the water, on certain boats chained and lying at anchor and you shall provide ships which shall be ready to make a sea fight." (Courtesy, Hagley Museum and Library, Wilmington, Delaware)

A detail from Babington's Pyrotechnica, *1635. (Courtesy, Hagley Museum and Library, Wilmington, Delaware)*

Detail showing the inner workings of one of Babington's ferocious dragons. (Courtesy, Hagley Museum and Library, Wilmington, Delaware)

On Gooseberry, the mortars were angled so that the shells burst above *The Black Pearl,* far above, and perfectly safe, the bright magnesium star clusters illuminating the ship's spars and rigging, and those in red making her glow as if afire.

The people who had brought their picnics down on the rocks on the shore drew in their breaths collectively—we were told later—when the ancient lines of *The Black Pearl* would suddenly emerge in the light, floating on the quiet bay, as if in the glare of a sudden moon.

When the "battle" was over, Warburton anchored *The Black Pearl* just off the rocks. Laughter drifted from her decks. He held a mock trial and, to impress the children seated in rows on the rocks ashore, he had Howard Cushing, a large cousin of mine, walk the plank for "treason." He made a considerable splash when he hit the flat, dark water. He has five daughters, and the youngest of them, sitting on a beach blanket, began to cry until she heard her father call out, "Christ, Buzzy, it's cold. Get me up!" and we saw his shape, luminous in the half light, being hauled up the dark sides of *The Black Pearl.*

Warburton "hanged" a seaman, too, that night for "moral turpitude" in the face of the enemy cannon. Those on the picnic blankets could hear the indictment across the water—that the poor wretch was guilty of "flinching" and "hiding his head" during the engagement against the "blackguards of Gooseberry." Presently, we heard Warburton call out, "May the good Lord have mercy on your miserable soul," and, sure enough, close on the bang of the brass cannon, which made us all jump, a rather dumpy figure like an overstuffed Halloween scarecrow rose jerkily at the end of a line to the yard-arm. Warburton had made his effigy belowdecks—some pillows, a coat, trousers, and apparently a pair of his own shoes. One of the shoes dropped off as the dummy was being hoisted aloft. We heard it land with a sharp slap on the surface of the water, and then Warburton's voice calling out, "Sweet God, that's my *shoe!*"

At the end of the evening, one of the Cushing daughters poised on the rocky shore with the last sparkler, its fitful light illuminating her face until she threw it out in the darkness in the general direction of *The Black Pearl,* the hiss of its expiring lost in the soft sift of the sea against the rocks.

Warburton's voice drifted in from the dark mass of his ship. "All right! All right!" he cried in mock despair. "We'll strike our colors . . . but not until I've finished this martini . . ."

Pa-Boom A single-color shell (a potato, q.v.) with a salute added, more properly a "one break and report"—so-named for the sound effect it creates in the sky.

Photography Being unknowledgeable about cameras and their use, I am grateful to Ben Harriman, from whose article in the *American Fireworks News* (issue #76) I have gleaned the following for the relative layman:

In this engraving from an Italian pyrotechnical manual of 1819, a tree has been turned into a "living" set piece with barrels filled with slow-burning oil, a curious "added attraction" to a nineteenth-century fireworks display. (Courtesy, Hagley Museum and Library, Wilmington, Delaware)

1. *Selection of camera* Any camera whose shutter can be held open will do. This feature is usually indicated on the shutter by the marking "B" (for "bulb," where the shutter stays open as long as the release is pressed) and "T" (for "Time," where the shutter opens on the first pressure and closes on the second). A cable release is essential, and so is a sturdy tripod on which to set the camera.

2. *Film* For still photographs, the following films are recommended:
For slides—Kodachrome II, Type A, used without filter.
For prints—Ektacolor, Type S, used with 80B filter.

3. *Aiming the camera* Most shells—at least those fired in a community fireworks display—tend to burst in the same general area in the sky. The first burst of a display will define the target area. The bursts will vary in altitude, so a camera of rectangular picture format should be mounted on its side on the tripod to give it more vertical range. The magnitude of the display and the size of its shells will determine the distance the camera should be placed from the firing line. For a show limited to shells under six inches in diameter (which would tend to be quite a small display) the camera tripod should be placed about five hundred feet from the mortars, with the camera angle about thirty degrees above the horizontal. For larger displays and shells, the camera will have to be moved back as many as fifteen hundred feet from the mortars.

4. *Firing* Set the lens opening at f/5.6. For aerial shells set the focus at "infinity" (usually marked by the symbol for infinity). Open the shutter as soon as the shell leaves the mortar—that hard, audible *thump*—and close it when the last stars of the shell's burst have died away. Simple as that!

It is possible to record more than one burst on a frame to fashion a composite of aerial bursts. It is essential, of course, that the camera is motionless *during* a burst, or the print will end up with wiggly-looking star trails.

For ground pieces, use the same lens aperture (f/5.6) and ¼ to ½ second exposures. Roman candle barrages and nonstationary effects require several seconds or more.

5. *Movie cameras* For movies, Kodachrome Type-A film exposed at sixteen frames per second with an f/2.0 aperture works practically without fail. Aluminum effects (like a Niagara Falls) require an aperture of f/2.8 to prevent overexposure. The newest camera models with through-the-lens viewfinders (which tend to "sop up" light) require opening the aperture to f/1.8, generally the widest stop on the lens.

6. *Processing* Rarely are slides and transparencies affected by the photofinisher. But often when prints are ordered from color negatives, a slight wash or pinkish cast is deliberately added to make the flesh tones more pleasing— the less expensive labs being notorious for sprucing up the color tones of one's loved ones. Harriman recommends sending one's most promising work to Eastman Kodak, which is more expensive but tampers less with color balance. For the enlargement of a particularly good print, it should be sent to Kodak with the transparency as a color guide, which will mean a reproduction of absolute fidelity. Glossy print surfaces, rather than the "silk" finishes, should be specified, since the delicate details of an aerial burst will be more faithfully preserved.

This fire-belching lion is from a French design for an aquatic fireworks display in 1650. (The Bettmann Archive, Inc.)

Pillbox A type of star carefully hand-set into a shell so that the effect in the sky is that of a large burst of long-burning, extra-large balls of color, often magnesium.

Portfire The designation in the foreign countries of the British Empire for the flares used in the United States to light professional fireworks. In those countries, a "flare" is a thin paper tube into which colored fire compositions have been lightly taped. Groupings of them are often used to show off buildings or groves—an effect called "Illuminations." Small versions were used at one time to light cigars.

Potato The industry name for an aerial shell that goes up and simply breaks in a spray of color. It is the most humble of shells.

Punk Pressed wood, molded into a thin, pliable rod like an incense stick, which, when ignited, burns slowly and just intensely enough to be a perfect instrument for lighting commercial or "toy" fireworks. Usually a packet of punk arrived with the Fourth of July assortment, much as books of matches are tossed into an order of cigarette packs.

Quick Match A special kind of very quick burning fuse used to light set pieces (q.v.) and other kinds of fireworks that require near-simultaneous ignition. The fast rate of burning is achieved by enclosing a regular fuse in a straw or paper tube which keeps the temperature inside so high that the fuse burns along its length extremely rapidly.

Recipes What fireworks people call the formulas involving the display properties of their craft. The recipes are zealously guarded; often committed to memory, they are passed down from one generation to another via oral communication. The earliest recipe book known in which the formulas were written down is an ancient manuscript entitled *Liber Ignium ad Comburendos Hostes,* or the *Book of Fire.* It contains thirty-five pyrotechnic recipes collected from the mid-eighth (preceding the discovery of gunpowder, of course) to the end of the thirteenth centuries. One of the recipes (one part resin to six parts of saltpeter) is recommended to be put "into a reed or hollow wood" and lit. "It flies away suddenly to whatever place you wish and burns up everything." Odd ingredients turn up in recipe books—including brandy, wine, ink, onion juice, and dung.

Recipe books are not that common. More typical is the kind of secrecy described in an account by Emanuel Farrugia of Malta writing recently in *Pyrotechnica* of a fabled Maltese fireworks man in Mqabba he remembered from his youth. Known as Qonsru, this artist specialized in very large set-piece wheels, ten feet or more in diameter, which he would place one behind the other to revolve in opposite directions, which gave the illusion of an eight-pointed flower, "the beauty of which I haven't seen since."

"One morning in 1936," wrote Mr. Farrugia, who is himself a member of a Maltese fireworks dynasty, "we were in school and heard a terrific explosion. Instinctively, we all knew what had happened. Qonsru's factory blew up and three people died. Apparently, he had been charging the red-fire drivers to be used in the wheels. I have often heard it said that his color formulae were so sensitive that after he charged them into the casings, they would go off within forty-eight hours *whether he fired them or not.* Qonsru had never taught anyone his technique . . ."

I can see why. I must say if Qonsru had a recipe book I am not sure I would rush to snap it up. Imagine making a firework with the built-in properties of a ticking time bomb!

Rocket A cylinder, with a cone-shaped head, referred to as the cap or head, filled with pyrotechnic materials, attached to a long stabilizing stick. Upon ignition, the gases from the propellant erupt out of the choke (q.v.) at the bottom of the cylinder, and the rocket rises with a familiar *whooooosh* high into the air. A time fuse reaches the bursting charge and pops the cap apart at the apogee of the rocket's climb. Since much of the pyrotechnical material in a rocket is used in getting it up there, not much can be carried aloft, not more than a few stars. The size of rockets varies—from the Class C bottle rockets (so-called because they can be launched from a bottle set on the ground) to

Although F. de Malthus's famous Pratique de la Guerre, *published in France during the seventeenth century, was primarily a manual for pyrotechnical warfare, he included a section entitled "Traitté des feux de joye," with descriptions for making fireworks for festive occasions. One of the illustrations shows a pyrotechnist preparing to fire a rocket. (Jean-Loup Charmet)*

TROMBES, FIRE-POTS AND BOMB.
(*VALLO*, 1529.)

The crossed rockets, firepots, and bomb in this print decorated a sixteenth-century fireworks treatise. (The Mansell Collection)

the "six-pounders," which is the weight of the rocket usually fired in professional shows. There are larger ones in the history of fireworks. The Siamese developed immense rockets—the canisters as long as ten feet, mounted on bamboo stabilizing sticks over forty feet in length.

The pyrotechnical material within the pot is known as the "garniture," and also (in an apparent bastardization of the word) the "furniture." Thomas Kentish in his *The Complete Art of Fireworks* (1905) describes a "furniture" of three parachutes ejected along with suspended flares.

Rockets were traditionally used much more than they are today. In the last century the "bouquet of rockets"—in extreme cases of showmanship, especially on the Continent—numbered as many as ten thousand, and were considered the most important feature of a display. Bernie Wells of Pyro-Spectaculars in California recalls prewar displays in England in which rockets were sent up in flights of a hundred—one-pound rockets rising twelve hundred feet in a curtain of gold before puffing open in an individual triad or so of stars. The reason for the decline of rockets is, of course, that the payload is minuscule, compared to that capable of being carried by a shell sent up from a mortar. There is also the hazard of falling sticks and cases.

Roman Candle A cardboard tube, usually brightly packaged for consumers, measuring from six to twelve inches in length, which contains alternating layers of compacted black powder and single stars. The user is warned in the directions not to hold the candle but to stick it in the ground. When lighted, the stars pop out one at a time and rise like colored balls to a height of fifteen to fifty feet. The largest Roman candles, made for commercial use, measure two inches in diameter and send up a star two hundred feet.

The most interesting theory on the derivation of "Roman candle" is in a Ruggieri treatise published in 1801—that carnival throngs in Rome would light and relight their *chandelle romaine* from another, thus giving the torch the additional life that is suggested by a continuing series of stars, rising one after the other.

Safety I do not ever remember Felix Grucci, Sr., seeing his sons off to shoot a show—men who had spent their lives in the business—without his calling after them, "Be careful! Be careful!" Thus, the awful irony of the twenty-sixth of November, 1983. One of the terrifying adages in the fireworks industry about a bad accident—namely an accidental explosion—is not *if* there will be one, but *when.*

What Felix Grucci called after his sons is an echo of what has been stated for centuries. Casimir Simienowicz in *The Great Art of Artillery* advises anyone handling gunpowder to do so with a "continual Eye upon Heaven . . . For the accidental Shock of two Stones, the hasty Attrition of two Strings, nay the very impetuous Rubbing together of two Straws, may be the Death of you . . .''

The work in a Japanese or Chinese fireworks factory is usually done with the employee sitting on the floor with the components and tools spread out

around. It is considered the safest position since tools cannot drop off a table surface and strike a spark.

The effect of fireworks going off uncontrolled can be devastating. In 1930, a fireworks factory exploded in Devon, Pennsylvania, with a force reported to have derailed and partly wrecked a passing train. In 1953, a fireworks company in Fort Worth, Texas, went up in a frightful flash, injuring seventeen people, destroying a number of motel cabins, and igniting a wayward rocket, which landed in a distant field and started a prairie fire that burned down an airport hangar.

Powder mills "had explosions" with startling regularity. The Whipple Mill of Lowell, Massachusetts, blew up in 1820, killing four men, with a report that was heard for thirty miles. The following year, in June, it blew up again, killing three men, and then in August, up it went once more, though this time there were no fatalities. Not surprisingly, the mill owner, considering the trouble at that site, built another plant on the Concord River, a short distance from the first, and immediately the facility suffered a whole series of explosions, the worst in 1826 and 1830. The product being milled, known as Boston gunpowder, was considered of the highest quality—that is, once they were able to get it into the guns.

One reads literally scores of accounts of such powder-mill accidents, very often ending with such a sentence: "the factory was demolished with the exception of one chimney."

To take an accident at random from the volume *A History of the Explosive Industry in America,* in 1886 a man named Wilson P. Foss, the manager (at 125 dollars a month) at the Plattsburgh, New York, plant of the Clinton Dynamite Company was standing twelve feet from nine hundred pounds of nitroglycerin sitting in a wash tank when it exploded, set off by an accidental gush of live steam from a faucet. The building in which Foss was standing completely disappeared, leaving behind a crater thirty feet deep. Mr. Foss himself ended up around the bend of the Saranac River on the ice. When the plant employees hurried to the site of the detonation they assumed they were not likely to find more of Mr. Foss than perhaps a bit of shoelace. To their astonishment Foss appeared, striding around the river bend. All his clothes below the waistline had disappeared. He had approximately two hundred spruce splinters in him. According to witnesses his first remark was, "What's the matter?"

His experience did not deter Foss in the least. He went on to build a number of dynamite factories and was a considerable figure in the industry—looked upon with some awe, I would have thought, considering what had happened to him.

Usually, such incidents occur in the mixing rooms—the result of a spark, or friction, or the volatility of the chemicals. There have been some odd exceptions. On July 4, 1854—could the date have had something to do with his act?—William Bixby, a worker in the Spencer Mill near Worcester, Massachusetts, decided to do away with himself. After one last drink, he walked into the mixing room puffing away on a lighted pipe, and succeeded.

In this photograph, taken in 1906, an employee in a French fireworks factory is filling Roman candles. (Roger-Viollet)

The cause of such accidents is not usually as easy to discern. Inevitably, there is very little evidence left for investigators to comb through. I have read a report (written in 1931 by a fireworks importer and manufacturer named W. E. Priestley, who started a number of factories in the Orient) that inevitably the *devil* was thought to be responsible for accidents; after an explosion it was very important to exorcise him. When one of Priestley's factories blew up in Hong Kong, killing thirty girls, he was told that the devil had been seen entering the building just before the explosion and was still in there looking for victims. Mr. Priestley describes the rite he was very firmly asked to initiate:

"I found myself at the damaged factory in the company of two Taoist priests, who were to perform the ceremony while I served as acolyte. Two priests, dirty and unkempt, spoke no English and looked at me with a malevolent expression.

"The first thing was to heap up thirty small piles of stones, each containing a few sticks of joss. Then the priests cut the throat of a black dog and caught the blood in a dish. Acting under their instructions I took this blood and, with a small brush, painted some Chinese characters on the door of the factory. I did not know what the characters meant, because I copied them from a piece of paper supplied to me by the priests . . . but as nearly as I could tell from my associate Ah Duck's explanation, the writing was to protect the local village people from the devil.

"The next thing was the most important. I had to go to the door of the room where the devil was confined and open it. For a reason that I did not discover until later, no one would accompany me on this mission. I found the door [in the ruins of the factory] but could not open it, so I had to smash in some of the panels. The devil was supposed to come out of this hole. When I returned and reported what I had done, the priests appeared satisfied and packed off with their goods and chattels, but Ah Duck was melancholy. He explained that when the devil came out of the room, he took the first man he met and that I was sure to be dead in a week.

"While Ah Duck watched me anxiously from day to day, I was busy with the practical aspects of the affair. I had to pay thirty dollars for each girl who was killed, a sum I considered quite reasonable. The British officials were very courteous, but suggested that our operation should be removed from the Crown Colony of Hong Kong."

Of far more interest to the general public, of course, are accidents related to the setting *off* of fireworks rather than their manufacture. The statistics out of the past are almost unbelievable. On July 4, 1903, when the population of the United States was well less than half what it is now, fireworks accidents killed 466 and injured almost four thousand people. One of the particularly lethal firecrackers of the time was a foot-and-a-half-long cardboard casing filled with saltpeter, carbon, and sulfur that went off with a blast that shivered the leaves on the trees for an acre around. Because of such devices, nearly as many people died celebrating independence—around four thousand over the years— as actually died fighting in the War of Independence itself. The glorious Fourth

This cartoon appeared in London's Punch *on November 6, 1912, the day after Guy Fawkes Night. (Mary Evans Picture Library)*

became known as the "Bloody Fourth" and, because of the large number of severe infections from burns, the "Carnival of Lockjaw."

Reactions to such statistics were inevitable. In the 1930s a number of anti-fireworks campaigns were launched, an especially effective one by Edward W. Bok's *Ladies' Home Journal,* which printed scores of pictures of maimed children. Individual states began to pass laws. Federal regulations started to ban the descendants of the huge firecrackers of the early 1900s—the cherry bomb of the '40s, and then the postwar M-80, with its stiff fuse sticking out of the center of its silver-colored cylinder.

So effective and far-reaching were the laws in some states, notably in the Northeast, that sparklers, Roman candles, and even the party snappers in the colorful cylinders with the paper hats inside, which children had enjoyed at birthday celebrations, were outlawed. One Connecticut legislator, arguing unsuccessfully against such stiff laws, mourned that the Fourth of July had "become a day of red, white, and blue lollipops."

Substitutes for fireworks were tried. By Congressional resolution in 1963, bells were to be rung throughout the United States (a project entitled "Let Freedom Ring"), but the idea never caught on.

At present, household fireworks come under the jurisdiction of the Federal Hazardous Substances Act, which is now administered by an independent regulatory agency known as the Consumer Product Safety Commission. Its five commissioners listen to petitions and testimony from groups such as the National Society for the Prevention of Blindness and the National Fire Marshal Association, typical of organizations that wish to bar all types of fireworks. To date, the agency, after reviewing considerable data, has refused to do this. Instead, it has concentrated on setting safety standards for all household fireworks, and especially for the firecrackers (still the primary cause of accidents), limiting the latter to only two grains of powder, which is approximately the amount that goes into the kind of Chinese ladyfinger firecracker that seems to split itself into little shreds of red paper on the pavement rather than explode.

The big bang down the street that startles the neighborhood on the Fourth and sends the family dog whining under the porch is invariably an illegal firework sold out of the back of a station wagon by a bootlegger. He is a retailer for a nationwide clandestine operation devoted almost entirely to turning out silver salutes and M-80s which use as much as forty to fifty grains of flash powder per firecracker. Nowhere in the United States are these devices legal.

The responsibility for ferreting out the manufacturers of these firecrackers falls chiefly on the Bureau of Alcohol, Tobacco and Firearms, whose operatives are the famous T-Men (who bemusedly refer to their wives as T-Bags). The T-Men arrest a dozen or so bootleggers a year, a typical haul totaling perhaps fifty thousand M-80s and silver salutes from an operation set up in a barn, usually, or a farmhouse, though in one instance in an apartment complex in Baltimore.

Injuries due to fireworks have dropped drastically in recent years. Indeed, the Consumer Product Safety Commission now ranks 131 consumer products more dangerous than fireworks—including grocery carts, beds (which rank *eighth* on the list—do that many people fall out of them?), key rings, high chairs, golf equipment, tricycles, and plumbing fixtures. Fireworks would rank even lower if it were not for the illegal cherry bombs and M-80s.

Safety Rules The list is long, but these are the major points to keep in mind:

1. *Buy reliable fireworks.* Look for a manufacturer's label. If there is none, the firework has probably been made illegally.
2. *Always read directions.* The most common cause of injury is misuse.
3. *Have an adult present.*
4. *Never experiment.* Do not take fireworks apart or mix anything with the contents.
5. *Ignite outdoors.*
6. *Have water handy.* Keep a bucket of water at hand for dousing misfires.
7. *Light one firework at a time.*
8. *Keep a safe distance.* Be sure others are out of range before lighting.
9. *Never give fireworks to small children.*

10. *Dispose of properly*. Do not try to relight or handle a firework that malfunctions. Soak with water and then bury.

In Canada, according to the official manual there, the preferred manner is to burn the duds individually in a bonfire! The text does remind the reader that the firework will behave as it is supposed to in the heavens, and that thus it is important that the bonfire should be located in a "sandpit or like depression." *I'll* say.

Safety Cap A tube of heavy paper that fits over the bared quick match at the end of the leader and is removed just before ignition by the operator.

Salute (or **Maroon** or **Aerial Flash Bomb** or **Amusement Bomb**) A cylinder filled with flash powder or a titanium mixture and added to the components of a display shell to provide noise—usually a single loud report and flash to punctuate the shell's performance. Some shells, often those used to complete a show, carry only a salute. Usually the salutes in the barrage of a finale are three-inch shells. A single salute filling an eight-inch shell is the largest I have heard of and makes truly a massive concussion. The use of such noisemakers is peculiar to Occidental rather than Oriental displays.

English pyrotechnicians are more prone to use the term "maroon" than salute, or report. The word is pronounced like the color; in fact, it derives from the French for chestnut—*marron*—a charming descriptive, from the loud pop that chestnuts make burning in a fire. In Japan, the salute is referred to as a "thunder" and a number of them as the "ten thousand thunders."

The Japanese speak of "invigorating" a crowd with this device. In 1902, while running for Congress, William Randolph Hearst used fireworks to gather and invigorate *his* audiences, but he made the mistake of passing out generous quantities to the people who came to listen. Halfway through his speeches, his audiences could not resist setting off what they had at hand, which meant that, until he stopped his largesse, the ends of his speeches were lost to pyrotechnical thunder.

Hearst never seemed to have much luck with fireworks, though he loved them. On November 4, 1902, ten thousand spectators gathered in Madison Square to watch aerial fireworks in celebration of his election to Congress. Somewhere in the line of unburied mortars—three to nine inches in diameter—a shell started a series of sympathetic explosions. Mortars toppled every which way, turning into field guns, and sent a barrage of shells into the crowd pressed close around. Fifteen people were killed and eighty seriously injured.

Serpents Small tubes carried aloft in a shell and which, charged with a fiercely burning composition, shoot in erratic streaks across the sky. In England they are called "whizz-gigs."

FOLLOWING PAGES *This scene, from the* Illustrated London News *of 1874, of a celebration in the harbor at Reykjavík, Iceland, handsomely depicts a rocket being fired, but also the breaking of just about every safety rule. (Mary Evans Picture Library)*

Set Piece A wooden framework set on the ground studded with lances that, when ignited, will outline a portrait or a picture in colored fire. Set pieces range from small sizes ("Good Night") to large edifices, replete with moving parts that can show in outline quite complex configurations, such as a Mississippi riverboat or a horse drawing a carriage. Set pieces may never again reach the enormous size and popularity enjoyed in London's Crystal Palace at the turn of the century, but displayers continue to employ them, especially in stadiums and enclosed areas where the public can be charged admission. A set piece can be shown exclusively, which is hardly so with an aerial shell that goes far up, is visible for miles around, and thus can be enjoyed by a nonpaying crowd outside the stadium.

Historically, the largest set piece ever built was the *pièce de résistance* at the Crystal Palace in 1898. Built by Messrs. Brock and Co., it represented the destruction of the Spanish fleet in Manila Bay on May 1, that same year. The scene covered sixty thousand square feet of a structure seven hundred feet long made of cane and wood and bristling with nails on which the lances were secured. Accounts of the day suggest the great care for similitude. The foun-

The famous pyrotechnical firm of Brock's pioneered a tradition of set pieces which became the distinguishing trademark of English fireworks of the nineteenth century. Set pieces evolved from faces of royalty, similar to this one of King George VI and Queen Elizabeth, opposite top, to the elaborate display designed to commemorate Queen Victoria's eightieth birthday, opposite bottom. Below, the Brock team is seen at Lübeck on the Baltic in 1890 as they take time out from their work of constructing an elaborate set piece. (Top: The Mansell Collection. Bottom and Below: The Brock Collection)

dering of the battleship *Antonio del Uliva,* her colors nailed to the mast, was portrayed with startling vividness. The outlines of the battleships were obtained from photographs and sketches; as a Brock official said at the time, "the artist is *not* permitted to rely upon his imaginative faculty for his effect." Indeed, a set piece representing the Taj Mahal and fired in India by Brock's on one of its tours was so realistic that the Hindus, when it went off, prostrated themselves before it.

Some of the Crystal Palace devices were supposed to provide mirth, and apparently did. One of the most popular was a donkey that reared back and kicked the cart it was hauling, knocking out its contents, including the driver. Another was a huge representation of the British lion which winked and lashed its tail, which was enough, apparently, to get an audience, according to the *Windsor Magazine,* "roaring most enthusiastically."

One of the most picturesque and famous tableaus produced at the Crystal Palace was one called "The Avalanche." The scene was of the Alps, their peaks outlined in fire, with a railroad train moving along at the base, disappearing in and out of tunnels for almost a minute until suddenly a huge mass of fiery snow (the white smoke must have given it an extraordinary life-like appearance) thundered down the side of the tallest mountain and swept away a little chalet at the base, just missing the train skedaddling into a last tunnel.

What is truly amazing about the great Crystal Palace set pieces is that on some occasions they were actually used to illustrate contemporary events. When the Sino-Japanese War broke out in 1894, C. T. Brock knew that a decisive battle would surely take place, very likely at Port Arthur, the Chinese naval base. Accordingly, Brock assembled every photograph he could find of the place and began work on what would be the backdrop for the battle. Then the word came in that the battle had indeed taken place, but not at Port Arthur. Hasty alterations were made. Only ten days after the event, "The Battle of the Yalu River" was reproduced at the Crystal Palace in a tableau about six hundred feet long.

Portraiture was also a staple of Brock's set-piece fireworks—huge structures of lancework to outline a recognizable celebrity of the day, very often visiting royal personages who would have the honor of igniting their own visages with an electrical switch in the royal box.

Portraiture was once a considerable part of American public fireworks too, one of the traditions of a turn-of-the-century Fourth of July being the fiery visage, moustache and all, of "Theodore Roosevelt, Our President" burning above the infield grass in baseball parks. Some of the set pieces of those times worked like moving cartoons: a donkey kicking a horse whose head would fly off and explode with a *pop;* an elephant dipping his trunk into a pail, rising up, and spraying a fountain of fire into the air.

Today's set pieces often combine to have projectiles which move along a wire—a baseball, for example, whacked off the bat of a baseball player who is outlined in lances. In Canada, one of the favorites of this kind of firework is a race along a wire between an "elephant and a pig." Fireworks of this sort have an ancient history. In Queen Elizabeth I's time, one of the favorite devices—she was a great fancier of displays—was a fiery dragon propelled by rockets that traveled the length of a rope spewing out different fireworks. Such movable fireworks were known as "pigeons," or "line rockets."

Shell (Old-timers refer to it as a ***Bomb***) The canister fired out of a mortar into the sky and which contains the various pyrotechnic compositions referred to as stars (q.v.) used in aerial displays. It came into common use at the end of the eighteenth century, beginning to supplant the rocket. Claude-Fortuné Ruggieri writes of a shell with a lifting charge and the stars all in one container, just as today's, back in 1812.

These days the size of shells ranges in diameter from two inches to the forty inches of the Fat Man; in weight, from a few ounces to Fat Man's seven-hundred-odd pounds. In most displays, the shells range from three to eight inches in diameter, the weight from one to fifteen pounds. The casings are made of thick Kraft paper or plastic materials which disintegrate at the shell's burst. In the sky, American shells, which are cylinder-shaped, tend to burst in a more random pattern with lingering color effects and often with a series of "breaks" built into their performance, often with a report at the end. Oriental shells are ball-shaped and burst in a single thistle-like pattern familiar to anyone who has seen a large fireworks show.

There is a great variety in the kinds of shells. For example, the Japanese divide their night display shells into three categories—parachute shells, diadem shells, and star shells. The parachutes suspend various effects, including flares, colored chains, or illuminated flags; the diadem shells break in the air and eject cardboard-like strips or disks which flicker brightly as they fall in a cluster—the effect like the silvery flickering of a tiara's jewels caught in a beam of light. The star shells, of which there are many varieties, rely on the performance of the stars ignited at the shell burst. Willow shells have stars which burn long enough to trail long branch-like tendrils as they fall. The loveliest of the willow shells is the *kamuro* (it means "boy's haircut" in Japanese), usually fired over water, since its tendrils reach almost down to the ground before winking off. Pattern shells, by the exact placing of stars within the globe of the shell itself, make recognizable designs in the night sky when the shell is detonated. The stars are thrown out into the shapes of crosses, circles, cherry blossoms, butterflies, bouquets, even letters.

The most familiar of the star-burst shells to U.S. audiences are the floral shells, particularly the peonies and the chrysanthemums. If the stars do not have trails as they burst out from the central core, the shell is a peony. Those with trails—a fuller, more thistle-like configuration in the sky—are called chrysanthemums.

Some Oriental shells are fitted with powder bags at the neck of the shell which, as the shell flies up, ignite and puff open into various effects—pine leaves, small bouquets, small flowers, a branching of comets, even whistles. The Japanese refer to the practice as *kyoku-do*. Another effect to enhance a shell's ascent is to give it a tail. This is done by pasting a comet or pellet of powder firmly to the shell; it ignites as the shell comes out of the mortar. The Italians and Spaniards are also masters of making a shell perform while ascending.

Usually the blossoming of an Oriental shell in the sky is comparatively

A crowd gathers to watch a fireworks display as painted in watercolors by the English artist James Wilson Carmichael, during the mid nineteenth century. (The Yale Center for British Art, Paul Mellon Collection)

quiet compared to Western shells. In the West, designers feel they must punctuate their artistry with a large exclamatory boom. I can remember trying to persuade Gordon J. Davis, then the Commissioner of Parks in New York City, to allow a large display of Chinese shells in Central Park to commemorate the opening of a large exhibition of Chinese art at the Metropolitan Museum of Art. He had been very skeptical. We had shot an international show from Central Park a year or so before whose Italian segment, with all its concussion, had provoked telephone calls from as far away as the borough of Queens asking what had happened to Manhattan.

"I don't think I'm going to allow you to do this," Davis had told me.

I said, "Well, the interesting thing about the Oriental shells is that many are almost silent."

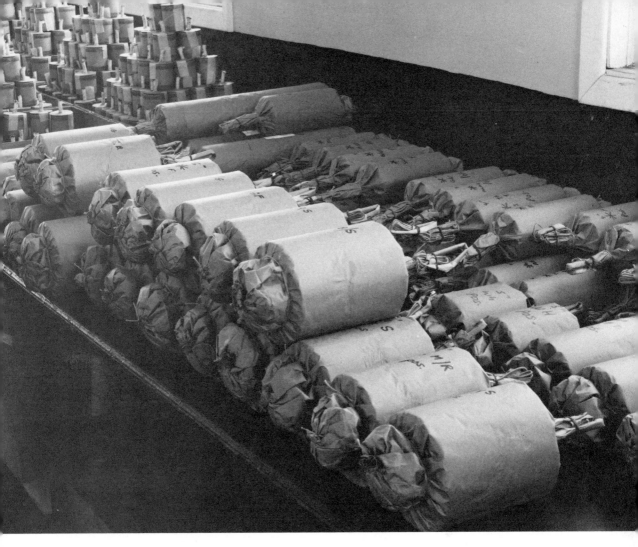

Shelves at the Grucci compound are stacked with aerial shells in various stages of construction. Those in the foreground have been completed, their long fuses folded back and secured with elastic bands. Note the bulbous lifting charges at the base of each shell. (Photo © Ken Clark, 1980)

"You're not going to tell me that they are inscrutable," Davis said.

He agreed to an afternoon test. A brisk wind was blowing. I managed to station the Commissioner upwind from the mortar. A six-inch shell thumped up into the afternoon sky. The shards of white smoke that appeared at its burst were swept away almost soundlessly, though downwind from us faces turned abruptly among the trees, and mothers bent to their alarmed infants in their baby carriages.

"Well, well," said Davis. He had not noticed. "My God, they *are* inscrutable." He allowed us to fire the Museum show.

Actually, Oriental shell-makers have a line of *tama,* or big bombs, which *do* make a sharp report when they explode aloft—what the Japanese call *saki-ware.* We heard some of them in Tondabayashi at the PL display. Professor

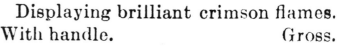

RUBY LIGHTS.

Displaying brilliant crimson flames.
With handle.   Gross.
No. 3. 1 gross in package _ _ _ _ _ _ _ _ _ _ **72**

GRASSHOPPERS.
Gross.
1 gross in package _ _ _ _ _ _ _ _ _ **72**

ASSORTED LIGHTS.

Displaying variegated colored illuminations.   Per box.
3 gross assorted in box _ _ _ _ **72**

Girl holding a sparkler. From a fireworks catalogue of the 1880s. (The Bettmann Archive, Inc.)

Ogatsu says that the process of making these shells is so perilous that only "fire-flower masters" are capable of working on them. I did not mention these to the Commissioner of Parks.

Sparkler A steel wire six to nine inches long, of which the bottom third serves as a handle. The rest of the wire is coated with a pyrotechnic composition which when ignited showers gold sparks—which cool almost instantly and hardly prickle the skin. As every child knows, the way to ignite a sparkler is off the glowing white tip of another.

Spectator Tragedies The most fateful fireworks-related accident occurred on May 16, 1770, when the city of Paris was celebrating the marriage of the future King Louis XVI to Marie Antoinette. The crowds were so thick in the unfinished Place Louis XV (today's Place de la Concorde) that at the end of the display a crush developed as the crowds left, turning into a panic in which approximately eight hundred people were killed. The collapse of a building scaffold was responsible for many deaths. The tragedy is listed in the *Guinness Book of World Records* among the "Worst Accidents and Disasters," under the category "Fireworks." It struck me that a more accurate listing would have been to put the tragedy under the heading "Panic," since it is hard to see how the fireworks were responsible other than to gather the people there in the first place. Those eight hundred deaths would have been small potatoes compared to what *does* win in the "Panic" department in that book of records: *four thousand* people perished in an air-raid shelter in Chungking, China, on June 8, 1941.

Squib A device which, by an electrical impulse, produces a spit of flame and is used to ignite fireworks. Also called an "electric match head."

Star Mines Star mines are similar to shells and are often used in finale racks. The stars ignite immediately. Unlike the consecutive firing of a finale in this country, that is to say, one shell after another in a building crescendo, the star mines, connected with quick match, are set off simultaneously, so that a curtain-like effect is achieved in the night sky. The Japanese tend to utilize the

Sparklers from a fireworks catalogue of the 1880s, advertised as "Brilliant Stars." (The Bettmann Archive, Inc.)

BRILLIANT STARS.
An attractive penny and nicl

star-mine curtain. Its effect is concussive and quick as opposed to the crescendo effect of the Occidental finale.

Stars The pellets—of varying sizes—which are packaged in a shell and ignited by the bursting charge at the height of a shell's climb; the stars provide the patterns and effects of an aerial firework. Hundreds of stars may be employed in a single shell.

Here are some formulas for a star—the first for a silver star, and the second for a red star:

SILVER		RED	
Potassium chlorate	60%	Potassium perchlorate	70%
Aluminum "fine flakes"	20%	Red Gum	9%
Aluminum "very fine dust"	20%	Charcoal 150 mesh	2%
Dextrin, the binder	(6)★	Dextrin, the binder	4%
		Strontium Carbonate	15%

★*Certain silver effects, such as a cascade; do not need the binding agent.*

Potassium chlorate, incidentally, mixed with pipe tobacco apparently produces a hashish substitute. Dr. Herbert Ellern has looked into this ("had occasion to study the original article") in his work *Military-Civilian Pyrotechnics*. He supplies the caveat that the side effects are so unpleasant that the spread of such usage is unlikely.

In a Japanese shell the center of a star is the seed of a green leafy vegetable called *natane* from which the oil has been extracted. This grain is dipped into a thick soupish mixture of chemicals and a coloring agent; the resulting clump is rotated on a "star-shaping machine" until it assumes a perfect spheroid form. After drying, the ball can be put in as many different coloring-agent mixtures as the fireworks master wants his star to show different colors. The larger the ball, the greater number of times—as it burns to the core—the colors will change.

The simplest kind of star is known as *kakeboshi*. It gradually diminishes its brilliance as it burns out. A more refined star is known as *kiriboshi,* which has a cube-like core that allows the star to burn with a consistent brilliance and then wink off abruptly, like a candle flame being blown out. This is considered an important aesthetic attribute—to have the shell's display in all its parts suddenly extinguish against the sky without leaving a trace of a spark.

Stringless Shells In 1954, Felix Grucci, Sr., and his brother, Joe, very likely using stringless Oriental shells as models, perfected a casing that could stand the stress of firing without being held together with bound lengths of string called Italian twine. The problem with string was that it was often ignited by the bursting charge; strands would drift down, afire, and cause damage—especially to automobile surfaces at the drive-in movies and racetracks where the Gruccis often shot displays. After two years of experimenting, canisters were fashioned of varying sizes—depending on the size of the shell—of card-

FIG. 4. A FIXED WHEEL UPON A POST WHICH WILL
CAST FORTH MANY ROCKETS INTO THE AIR.
(*RICH CABINET*, 1677.)

This seventeenth-century woodcut shows a fixed wheel on a post for use as a multi-rocket launcher. (The Mansell Collection)

board liner, heavier Kraft paper, with Elmer's Glue substituting for the Italian twine. Most American companies continue to use either stringed shells or plastic casings for their aerials.

Strobes One of the latest aerial effects—purportedly developed by the Chinese in the 1960s. A shell appears to let loose a cluster of silvery lights which float down . . . slowly enough to make one wonder if they are not suspended from individual parachutes. The effect is done by pasting a magnalium composition on small rectangular pieces of paper. This results in a flashing strobe-like phenomenon as the paper falls slowly through the air. The Japanese have a similar color effect which they refer to as "falling leaves." The Spanish have a lovely rocket which contains a persistently twinkling golden star called *lentejuela magnalium* (magnalium spangles) which is related to the "falling leaves" of the Orient.

Timer The delay fuse that burns within the canister as it lofts upward and which will ignite the bursting charge when the firework reaches the top of its climb. Fireworks people speak of the timer being "top-" or "bottom-fused," that is to say, the timer is either initially ignited at the top of the shell when the quick match is lit, or is ignited by the lifting charge at the base of the shell. A long-standing argument exists as to which is preferable. The Oriental shells are all bottom-fused. The problem is that sometimes the blast of the lifting charge is so violent that the timer never gets a chance to light, so that the shell goes up "dead" and will eventually fall back to earth like a stone—a so-called "black shell." It is also more likely with bottom-fusing that fire can get into the main body of the shell and cause a premature explosion, often just over the mortar mouth, the dreaded "blooming over the gun" that was responsible for the Hudson River accidents in 1953 in which two men were blown off a barge and drowned.

The time fuse in a Japanese shell is called *oyamichi*. It is timed to reach the bursting charge at what the Japanese call the "ball's seated position," which means the shell, high in the air, is going neither up nor down. It is particularly important for a Japanese shell to burst in this poised position—much more important than for the shells of other countries, which do not depend to such a degree on producing a symmetrical floral design. If a Japanese shell bursts on its way up or down, its floral bloom behaves in a kind of conical configuration. The *hanabi* people refer to these instances disparagingly as "fire-flowers of half-closed umbrellas."

On the other hand, proponents of bottom-fusing say that their method is safer because there is no chance of the shell going off *in* the mortar. They would point to the Bellport explosion of Fat Man I as an example of what can happen with top-fusing.

Actually, most fireworks people, if faced with a choice, would rather have the shell go off in the pipe and "flowerpot" rather than have one burst just over the top of the mortar. Fortunately, electrical firing renders the argument moot, since the personnel are far enough away so they are safe no matter what happens on the firing line.

Titanium A metallic element used in salutes (q.v.) which leaves a distinctive silver burst in the sky. It is one of the most recently developed of color effects.

Torpedo A device that consists of a minute quantity of fulminate of mercury mixed with grit and twisted up in a piece of tissue paper. Thrown against a hard surface, it pops satisfactorily. In India the torpedo is especially common, but rather than fulminate of mercury the manufacturers there use potassium chlorate and yellow sulfide of arsenic—a very sensitive mixture indeed which has been responsible, as Brock reports, for an "enormous number of accidents among Indian fireworks makers."

Tourbillon The French word for "whirlwind." It was an early nineteenth-century fireworks piece. It had a revival in the United States in the early 1940s, known then as the "flying saucer" or the "whirlybird." The gas emitted turns a propellor which lifts the tube-like device; jets on either end of the tube cause it to rotate, so that the whole spins high into the air like a flying wheel-top.

Vantage My own preference as a spectator is to get as close as possible to the firing line, at least near enough so that the lowest shells are bursting at a forty-five-degree angle of sight. At this distance, the effects of noise and color seem at their best, and the viewer is close enough to feel the sharpness and concussion of the larger shells. The "prettiness" is tinged with a kind of *frisson*—the realization that the beauty is provided through an explosive property. Spectators who watched the Brooklyn Bridge display from inside office buildings, sealed in by unopenable windows, missed the concussion, though the windows rattled in their supports. One of them told me it was like watching a football game from a weatherproofed press box, where the loudest sound is the clacking of a typewriter.

It is not easy to persuade people that it is better to be close. I remember a Bastille Day demonstration in New Orleans in 1980 for which a large party had taken over a river steamer for the evening. When the fireworks started we were almost a mile away from the barges. We could see the quick burst of light and after a while we could hear the distant thump and crackle of the shells drifting across the water. I ran for the pilothouse and, looking up at the captain through the big window frames, I pleaded with him to move the paddle-wheeler closer. We were so far downstream from the fireworks barges that we weren't going to *see* anything. The captain looked down wordlessly, a slight frown of confusion on his face as he pondered the thought of someone trying to get him, for God's sake, to *park* his steamer amid an upward rush of rocketry.

He raised his eyes and stared stolidly out over the bow at the distant city waterfront. Slowly he continued to back the paddle steamer down. The spectators on the foredeck shifted uneasily, and some of them went below to dance. Those who stayed on deck mentioned how "pretty" the fireworks were at that distance.

Equivalently, the Macy's show in New York on the Fourth of July has been marred by being shot off barges in the vicinity of the Statue of Liberty, which is fine for the people in nearby boats, or photographers on assignment trying to get the statue's uplifted arm against a chrysanthemum of stars, but an inevitable disappointment for spectators standing over a mile away at Battery Park on the tip of Manhattan. A great improvement occurred in 1983 when the display was moved to the East River and shot off barges between Fortieth and Twentieth streets in the midtown area.

Weather Rain is the most dismaying weather, for not only the pyrotechnician, who may lose all his shells because of the damp, but also, obviously, the spectator. Honoré Daumier, the French nineteenth-century illustrator, once drew a cartoon entitled "Evening of a National Celebration," showing a couple trudging along gloomily, the father carrying his child piggyback. The caption reads: "It never fails. You go to see the fireworks, and the only thing that works is the rain."

Some pyrotechnicians, especially the Italians, prefer a high cloud cover. It seems to shield the ground from moonlight, and the distraction of stars, but more particularly it confines the sound, so they say, and thus increases the bombardment's sonority and effectiveness.

But rain, fog, and wind, these are what produce murmurs of impatience and frustration. In 1774, Samuel Johnson, the lexicographer, went to a fireworks performance at the outdoor pavilion at Marylebone Gardens in London. A slight rain was falling. The crowd was small. When the performance was abruptly canceled because the fireworks were said to be damp, Johnson shouted loudly that the postponement was because the crowd was not large enough. "This is a mere excuse," he shouted, "to save their crackers for a more profitable company!" and he urged those around him to threaten to break the colored lamps around the orchestra pavilion unless the show went on as scheduled. Though apparently the fireworks were indeed damp, a group took Johnson at his word and went on a rampage that had to be contained by the police.

Weeping Willow An aerial effect made by adding an excess of charcoal to the composition of a star. Since charcoal has a relatively long burning time, the stars continue to burn an amber hue as they fall—the effect, one of the loveliest in fireworks, being to outline the delicate drooping branches of the willow. The Japanese *kamuro* shell is this type at its most breathtaking.

Wheel A framework turned by a number of cylinders called "drivers" (q.v.) placed strategically and fired simultaneously with quick-match fusing. The combined thrust of the drivers spins the wheel. Sometimes the drivers are placed and ignited so that the wheel changes the direction of its spin during its performance.

Whistle Shells These are noisemaking tubes that give off mild, sad shrieks as they dart across the skies after the shell burst. The Japanese refer to them as "mad lions." They were invented and patented by Ronald G. Hall in 1955, and perfected subsequently by Benjamin Brock. The sound of these fireworks is not produced by the passage of wind over an opening in the casing as it whizzes through the air (which I had always supposed—like the principle of the flute) but by the plastic or paste resins which produce a high keening whistle as they burn. The chemical used in a whistle is sodium salicylate, which is closely related to one of the ingredients in aspirin. When I found this out, I burned a Bayer aspirin on the edge of the bathroom sink in the hope it would produce a whine of sorts. Alas, it burned very slowly and soundlessly.

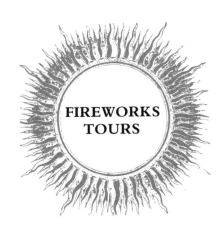

FIREWORKS TOURS

I have never heard of anyone planning an extended trip or vacation based on going to "where the fireworks are" as a coed might head on Easter vacation to "where the boys are." Fireworks tend to be thought of as an extra fillip for the traveler. One is startled by the distant thump of the shells and pulls aside the gauze curtain of the hotel room to step out onto the balcony to discover the fireworks in the evening sky, arching out over the dark waters of the bay.

But why not? If a trip can be planned to take in cathedrals, or antique shops, or famous restaurants, just as lively a reason to hurry on ahead to the next town would be to sit out on the hotel balcony to enjoy a fine display of fireworks. Perhaps night after night of them on an itinerary might be taxing, though I, myself, would doubt it. Certainly in a foreign country one could take in at least *one* fireworks display. Perhaps the tourist could even plan a vacation around the best show that the country offers. It would be absurd to be in Spain in the springtime and not visit the pyrotechnical hullabaloo that is Valencia's during Easter week, or in Italy in the summer and not watch the Feast of the Redentore from a Venetian gondola, or in France on Bastille Day and not see the Paris shows. One can also see the Monte Carlo Tuesday nights in late July and August, and the great rose-red display at Carcassonne. In Japan in August it would be criminal not to pay a pilgrimage to the town of Tondabayashi near Osaka to watch the million-dollar Perfect Liberty show shot off the golf course.

The following pages include a listing of fireworks festivals and displays in various countries which occur on a regular basis. It is by no means a complete list. Fireworks nearly being a universal art, it would require a lifetime of devotion and travel to thoroughly check out fireworks shows worth seeing. Japan itself is worth a year or so of investigation. Also, fireworks people are notoriously protective of their contracts. This is especially so in the United States, where annually there is competitive bidding for most large displays. It

215

is also a practice elsewhere. Kyosuke Ogatsu, the president of one of the major Japanese fireworks firms, was once asked by George Zambelli, Sr., who contracts for more displays than anyone in the United States, how many shows Ogatsu's company fired in a year. Ogatsu conferred with an aide, and then another, and, after considerable verbal palaver, turned to Zambelli, who thought he was about to get a detailed list, and announced, "Lots."

It is a fair bet that many countries not listed in what follows have fireworks traditions, especially as part of their national celebrations. Pains, the English pyrotechnic firm, lists, among others, Zanzibar, the Seychelles, Singapore, Grenada, and the Isle of Man as being among the out-of-the-way places where its operatives have shot off fireworks on national holidays.

In sum, a sensible procedure before going off on vacation and hoping to include some fireworks-viewing would be to contact the particular country's cultural attaché's office. In every instance I have tried, the office has been of considerable assistance. Cultural attachés who know nothing of their country's fireworks are engaged in the wrong line of work.

ALASKA

On the third of July there is a big parade in Juneau, with the fireworks shot off as the strokes of midnight die away—an expeditious time to do it since the midnight sky is about as dark as it gets during the summer of the midnight sun. Not only do Alaskans celebrate the glorious Fourth in its first few seconds, but fireworks are of considerable consequence in Alaska. On occasion, the Grand Marshal of the parade has been a pyrotechnician, Larry Parker, riding in splendor on the lead float, throwing little torpedoes into the street among the crowds.

AUSTRALIA

The subcontinent has a very rich tradition in fireworks. Almost all the festivals, celebrations, and the fairs put on by "agricultural societies"—no matter how small the community—incorporate a fireworks show. The annual festival at Alice Springs, for example, the only community in a remote area of Central Australia, attracts the entire population of not only the town but outlying territories covering twenty thousand square *miles*. The festival—not surprising considering the people trekking in hundreds of miles over the barren flatlands—is called "The Camel Cup."

The size of any fireworks display is, naturally, governed by the sponsoring organization's finances. In Australia there are three exceptionally large shows, all put on by Howard and Sons, one of the most important fireworks concerns in the world. The New Year's Eve fireworks display over Sydney Harbor opens the annual City of Sydney Festival. It starts at the stroke of midnight and features a thousand shells from three to twelve inches in size, as well as a thousand rockets—rockets being a distinctive Australian specialty. The display can be seen from many locations on Sydney Harbor, but the best would be from the Opera House frontage, or, even better, out on the water on one of the hundreds of pleasure craft and ferries that turn up for the occasion.

Every year in March the Mooba Festival takes place in Melbourne—ten days and nights of various cultural entertainments. Fireworks displays both open and close the proceedings. The fireworks are fired from barges under tow along the Yarra River and can be viewed from either bank. The river is not particularly wide—which gives spectators sitting on the banks the advantage of close viewing of the great variety of fireworks effects involved, which include shells, mines, Roman candles, extra-large fountains, huge set pieces, as well as a 250-foot Niagara suspended across the river.

Finally, the Adelaide Festival of Arts, which is held every two years and runs for one month, features a fireworks display—both aerial and ground pieces—in the parklands on the banks of the Torrens River. Commemorating the cultural aspects of the Festival, it features a mammoth set piece of an artistic picture done in lances and sparklers.

This is not to suggest that these three shows are all that there is to see in Australia. The Royal Agricultural Societies have festivals in all the major cities—usually holding them in stadiums, which means that the fireworks choreographers, while limited in the shell sizes, show off a vast number of ground pieces, set pieces, and low-burst shells and effects. The best of these are the Sydney Royal Easter Show (March–April), the Brisbane National Royal Show (August), the Adelaide Royal Show (August–September), and the Melbourne Royal Show (September), as well as the Royal National Show in Canberra (February).

BELGIUM

From Baudelaire on, travelers have complained how boring a country Belgium is; however, it has a fireworks tradition that goes back hundreds of years. When known as Flanders, it was under the control of Spain. Diego Ufano, a Spanish artilleryman who published a book on fireworks in 1612, was of the opinion that Spain was responsible for the high state of the art, "civilizing" the inhabitants of Flanders in matters pyrotechnic. Thus, if there is a day to go to Belgium, it would be on July 21, the anniversary of the arrival of the country's first king, Leopold I, in Brussels. Fireworks displays take place all over the country. One interesting sidelight—I am told by Robert G. Cardwell, the editor of *Pyrotechnica*—is that there is a great rivalry between the Flemish and the French-speaking pyrotechnicians regarding fireworks display techniques. So a traveler can experience two different schools of pyrotechnic thought as well as two languages.

CANADA

The major fireworks shows in Canada take place on Victoria Day, the Monday preceding May 25, throughout the provinces, with the largest at Ontario Place in Toronto, and on June 24, Quebec's *fête nationale,* also known as Saint Jean Baptiste Day, which is celebrated throughout the province in association with major exhibitions in Ottawa, Toronto, Edmonton, Calgary, and Vancouver. Then comes the largest celebration of all—Canada Day, the national birthday, which takes place on July 1. Major displays are scheduled in a number of cities, including Toronto, Montreal, and Ottawa. Responsible for firing these displays is the largest manufacturer of shells in Canada, the Hand Chemical Industries, Ltd., of Mississigud, Ontario, a company that has been in the fireworks business since 1873. Interestingly enough, only Canadian shells are seen on the occasions mentioned above, since the import duty on non-domestic shells is prohibitively high. But no matter. The Canadian shells— Hand makes over two hundred varieties—are very good, especially their willow trees and palms, which incorporate a uniquely bright effect using magnesium powder. Hand makes military flares requiring enormous candle-power, a company skill exquisitely adapted to many of their commercial shells, which are so bright as to seem to light up every blade of grass as they perform high above.

CHINA

At present, due to the austerity programs, there are no longer large fireworks shows in China—an obvious irony since most authorities consider China the birthing ground of fireworks. In modern times, up until the death of Mao Tse-tung, large displays were held on occasion in Tian An Men Square in Peking, now Beijing. These have been halted. All large display fireworks are exported—indeed, Chinese shells often comprise a large portion of a typical large civic display in *this* country.

Still on sale in the government shops throughout China are firecrackers (in plain red wax paper), fountains, and Roman candles. At night, one can see an occasional shower of pyrotechnic sparks across the darkness of a river in celebration of a wedding or a birthday. Surely, one day, the large displays will return, and the Chinese will once again be able to enjoy the artistry of the craft they originated.

Imports from that country started following Richard Nixon's visit in 1972 and the subsequent reestablishment of trade relations. Robert Jani, a fireworks choreographer and importer, was one of the first representatives from Disney to travel to that country. With him he carried the Abrams coffee-table book *The Art of Walt Disney* to help him try to explain who his employers were to the Chinese. In the northern part of the country the Chinese had never heard of Walt Disney. Jani told me: "Even the motion-picture makers had never heard of Mickey Mouse. I showed them the pictures of Mickey from the book. He was really quite hard to explain." "Did you try Goofy on them?" I asked. "I stuck with the mouse," he said.

ENGLAND

The big fireworks day in England is, of course, Guy Fawkes Night—November 5. Ninety percent of the fireworks manufactured in England are expended on that date—the anniversary on which Mr. Fawkes unsuccessfully tried to blow up the House of Commons with thirty-four hundred pounds of explosives smuggled into the cellar through a tunnel. Indeed, the British fireworks concern, Pains, which, with the apparent withdrawal of Brock from pyrotechnic manufacture, is the best-known fireworks company in the country, reflects its Fawkes connection with perhaps the most curious of advertising inducements in its catalogue. "We have plenty of experience," the statement reads, "even Guy Fawkes himself in 1605 actually used gunpowder made by our own Mr. Pain!"

The fourth of June, the birthday of George III, was for years during the eighteenth century and into the nineteenth century an occasion for pyrotechnic rejoicing. The day is still celebrated at Eton, where a fireworks display follows the famous procession of racing shells in which the crews nervously stand up alongside their upright oars in a considerable, and occasionally successful, feat of balance.

Other fireworks events in England take place on special occasions such as royal weddings, or birthdays, or a jubilee. Gone, sadly, are the great regularly scheduled events of the Crystal Palace days, as is the Crystal Palace itself, which burned down.

While November 5 is the date associated with fireworks in England, the tradition goes further back to the pre-Christian era of the Celts and Saxons. November 1, marking the beginning of winter, was noted with lighted bonfires, and parades in which torches and firebrands were carried—a kind of Festival of Light to drive away evil spirits, quite similar to the ceremonies the Hindus hold to this day with their celebration of Divali in October. Sometimes a lighted bale was pushed off the peak of a hill—a tumbling ball of fire bounding down, creating quite an effect, I would have thought. In England, often the tradition was to start a display with the rise of a fire balloon. As it disappeared into the twilight skies, a rocket would go up, as if in search of it, and the fireworks would begin.

England's candidate for the invention of gunpowder is Roger Bacon (1214–1294), a friar also known as *doctor mirabilis*. His qualifications are especially intriguing in that they appear in his defense against an accusation of practicing witchcraft in 1242. But—like the Chinese—he was only aware that the ingredients that make up gunpowder explode. He never imagined using the mixture as a propellant at one end of a barrel.

FOLLOWING FOUR PAGES *The English firm of Brock's Fireworks supplied life-size exploding figures for Guy Fawkes Night celebrations for over a century. (Courtesy of The Bettmann Archive, Inc.) Children and adults paraded through the streets and countryside with these fireworks-scarecrows by day. After sunset the effigies would "come alive" with the crackling sound of firecrackers while bonfires burned throughout the November night. (Mary Evans Picture Library)*

FRANCE

France has always had a great fireworks tradition. True, Madame Pompadour loathed fireworks. On one occasion one of her famous white hats caught fire from a spark and smoldered black during a Ruggieri display. On the other hand, General Charles de Gaulle once stopped a regularly scheduled train en route to the 1968 Olympics near Grenoble so that he could watch a fireworks display against the mountain snow.

Chronologically, the best shows are as follows. In May, there are three large festivals involving liberal use of fireworks. In Rouen, a commemoration of St. Joan of Arc is highlighted by a huge laser-beam portrait of the saint—a centerpiece for an elaborate *pyromélodie* fireworks show. At the picturesque harbor-resort of La Trinité-sur-mer a *festival de la mer* features a harborful of artfully decorated craft, strung fore to aft with lights, and a magnificent fireworks show to cap things off in the evening. And May, of course, is the month of the Cannes Film Festival—traditionally concluded with an elegant gala night featuring a considerable fireworks show shot up from barges in the sea off the Carlton Hotel.

In June, perhaps the loveliest display is the feast day celebration of St. John the Baptist on June 23–24 in Perpignan near the Spanish border. I have not seen it myself, but I have been told admiringly of the illumination of the *castille* of that medieval town under the soft glare of fireworks.

There are two June displays in the suburbs of Paris—one in Viry-Chatillon, the other in Massy-Paliseau, which are distinguished by laser beams and synchronized music along with the fireworks. At Montpélier at the end of June there is a two-hour show referred to as a *"pyromélodie gala"*—the music being of particular importance and to which young composers are invited to contribute choreographic effects. I would like to see that one.

July is, of course, the month of Bastille Day, the fourteenth. Paris is traditionally the place to celebrate. For years, Bastille Day fireworks were fired from the Pont Neuf and its proximities. Now, displays have been decentralized to cut down on traffic and pedestrian congestion; they are fired throughout the entire city. The many locations include:

Sacre Coeur de Montmartre
Parc des Buttes-Chaumont
Parc de Montsouris (near the Cité Universitaire)
Jardins de Chaillot

In the center of Paris, the Dome des Invalides and the Place de la Concorde were once firing sites, but traffic problems became insurmountable and fireworks are no longer shot from those locations.

The best place to view the Paris Bastille Day show would be from a rooftop overlooking the city, perhaps a private roof garden with Japanese lanterns strung from the potted orange trees, a table set out with wine, and a balustrade to lean against to watch the evening darkness envelop the city. Of the public facilities, the first level of the Eiffel Tower is a splendid viewing spot, but too many people know about it. Up above the station in Montpar-

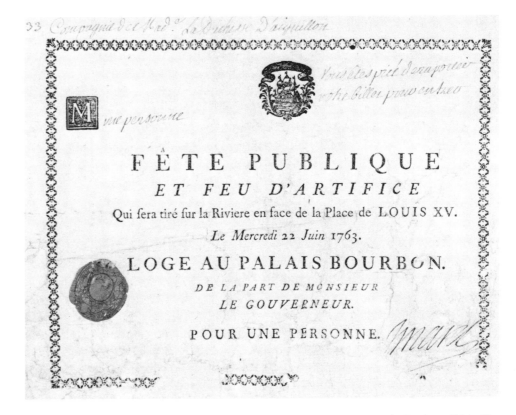

This invitation to attend a Fête Publique, *complete with fireworks, was sent to the Duchesse d'Aiguillon by Marie Antoinette in 1763. The queen's guests were requested to show this ticket in order to gain entrance to the palace where the royal company assembled to watch the extravaganza. Her signature is visible at lower right. (The British Architectural Library/RIBA, London)*

nasse or from the Tour de Montparnasse is the best place to see the fireworks coming up from the Jardins de Chaillot. The *bateaux mouches* on the Seine, despite the pleasure of an evening's boat trip, are not good for fireworks-viewing since the narrowness of the river precludes setting off fireworks from barges; the quais would block the sighting of all but the highest shells shot up from elsewhere in the city.

The other great Bastille Day show is the fireworks extravaganza at Carcassonne, the vast walled medieval hilltop city restored by Viollet le Duc in the nineteenth century. It is one of the few fireworks shows that are best viewed from a considerable distance. Most of the 150,000 to 200,000 spectators station themselves as far away as two kilometers in order to get a panoramic view of the fortress-city. The show lasts for about half an hour, all of it choreographed with the fortress very much in mind. First, the walls are illuminated by hundreds of fountains while aerial shells illuminate the parapets and towers from above in an increasing profusion. About twenty minutes into the show comes what everyone is there to see—an *embrasement* of the entire fortress, in which the structure is bathed in a strange red glow. This phenomenon is effected by the lighting of literally thousands of red flares, what the French call *flammes de Bengale*. This extraordinary spectacle is complemented at the last with a huge *couronne* of aerial shells over the city.

The fireworks concern responsible over the past years has been La Maison Lacroix, which is considered on a par with Ruggieri, the other great pyrotechnic company in France. La Maison Lacroix has spent years refining its Carcassonne show, priding itself on the "visual" rather than the sound effects. Indeed, the whole Carcassonne show is carried on in such muted fashion that from two kilometers away one can hear the stir and fidget of crickets above the distant mutter of the shells.

The Carcassonne show may now be the one to watch on Bastille Day because, over the years, the Paris displays have become smaller. The Minister of Culture and the restaurant trade have been especially inhibiting factors in Paris—the minister because of worry that loud reverberations in the narrow streets will damage historical buildings and monuments, and the restaurant people because *(à la français)* they think that their clients should be able to eat without their wineglasses trembling. Thus, the size of the aerial shells is restricted to three hundred millimeters; rockets are not allowed, nor are such novelty shells as parachute flares. Monsieur Tournais, who is the chief technical expert at Ruggieri, believes that far better shows are to be seen in the smaller cities, especially Ancis and Avignon, as well as Carcassonne. His particular favorite is Ancis's "Fête du Lac."

Certainly near Paris the best fireworks shows to watch are those put on every summer at Versailles. The approximate dates are the fourth of July, the fifth of September (Grande Fête de Nuit de Versailles) and the eighteenth of September (Fête de Grand Canal). The tickets, which must be reserved at least a month in advance through the Bureau de Tourisme, are expensive, but the displays are spectacular. They include music, often ballet, and historical reenactments of the galas of Louis XIV's times. The fireworks, many of which have "ascending tails," are reflected in the pools and fountains of the gardens, creating the *mariage idéal* of fire and water which is considered the ultimate way to present fireworks and is typical of the eighteenth-century traditions for which French pyrotechnicians, especially Ruggieri, have been so noted.

An August fireworks show with a considerable reputation among aficionados is the one that takes place in Annecy. The shells rise above the lake with the Alps in the background, a spectacle that attracts thousands from Germany and Switzerland. Another similarly praised show which combines fireworks and an impressive vista takes place in mid-August in a quaint seaside resort near Perpignan called Collioure. The fireworks rise from an old castle which dominates the little town, and the star clusters are reflected in the sea.

Throughout the month of August, Monte Carlo holds its traditional festival of international competition (described in Chapter Three). Five companies representing their countries compete on a succession of Tuesday nights. Every Friday night, starting in June, there is a fireworks display in front of the Sporting Club which starts at nine-thirty.

Another "World Championship" takes place in August, just down the coast from Monte Carlo in Cannes. It goes on over a two-week period—the spectaculars shot from offshore barges. The Gruccis went to an event one evening during their Monte Carlo stay in 1979. They arrived in time to see a shell dart off horizontally from the barge—a mortar must have fallen over in its trough—and come skipping toward the shore like a cannonball bouncing in from a ship-of-the-line. It came up onto the beach into the crowd and injured a few people. Until that happened, the Gruccis had been very impressed by what they saw. The Cannes entries—unlike the Monte Carlo requirements—were synchronized to music. I could not help wondering what the music accompaniment had been for the shell that had skipped inland. The Gruccis couldn't remember, but they remembered the shell. "Two break and report," said Felix Grucci.

Fireworks regulations for public consumption are very relaxed in France. Large shows for state occasions are fired by experts, but smaller shows for a town or a fair are arranged and packaged (along with instructions) so that a mayor or an appointed official can fire them. Citizens can buy prepared boxes for private uses. They are called "Fêtes du jardin." The French sell their equivalents to Class C fireworks usually in their novelty or *farce et attrape* shops. Ruggieri manufactures a "Weekend" package for garden parties. At Christmas time there is a heavy run on sparklers, which the French often display prettily by hanging from trees.

GERMANY

The great annual pyrotechnical event in Germany is known as the "Rhine in Flames." It is made up of a string of fireworks events and effects along a stretch of the Rhine from Braubach to Koblenz, a distance of about seventeen kilometers. The display, which was inaugurated in 1955, takes place in the first week in August and is invariably put on by the Moog concern, Germany's premier fireworks manufacturer. A half million people turn up to watch the proceedings, many of them waterborne on everything from river steamers to small dinghies. The main body of spectators waits in Koblenz for the largest display, which is a huge show over the Festung Ehrenbreitstein, a fortress built in 1815 by the Prussians as a bulwark against the French and which is considered one of the Rhineland's great citadels.

Every firework shot up along the length of the Rhine is purportedly German-made. The reason for this is that Herr Moog, the official pyrotechnician to the Nazi regime, once ordered a whole shipment of shells from Japan which were supposed to contain swastika flags suspended from parachutes. Instead, with Adolf Hitler on hand at some vast ceremonial occasion, the shells popping open high above the stadium displayed hundreds of Japanese Rising Suns. Hitler was apparently furious as the parachutes drifted down. Ever since, so it is said, no fireworks have been imported into Germany. However, I have friends who have seen what they are sure are Oriental shells bursting above the Festung Ehrenbreitstein, so perhaps the ban has been lifted, or foreign shells are being smuggled in.

HONG KONG

Hong Kong's harbor, with its surrounding cone-like hills with the high-rise apartments on their slopes like clustered chimneys on a steep roof, is perhaps the most perfect amphitheater for fireworks in the world. It had not had a show since Queen Elizabeth II's visit in 1974. The Pains company of England was called in to do that one, though the majority of fireworks were from China. The reason for the discontinuation was the emergence at that time of the "Red Guard" movement in China, which unnerved the British authorities to such a degree that explosives of all sorts were banned in Hong Kong.

In 1982 Hong Kong finally did have a fireworks show. It was put on by Pyro-Spectaculars, a company from California. The show was shot from four barges in the channel between Hong Kong and Kowloon. The cost, one million Hong Kong dollars—about $177,000, was covered by the Jardine Matheson shipping company, which decided that fireworks would be a fine method of celebrating the concern's founding one hundred and fifty years before. The long-standing regulations were lifted for the occasion. Just as in the case of the Pains show eight years before, ninety-five percent of the fireworks—the rest were Australian rockets—were shipped from Pyro-Spectaculars's warehouses in Rialto, California, to Hong Kong . . . a classic case of carrying coals to Newcastle, since a major portion of the show was composed of Chinese and Japanese aerial shells manufactured on the Hong Kong side of the Pacific.

The date for the show was the night of the Chinese New Year, January 25, the first day of the Year of the Dog. I went over to see it. It lived up to every expectation. Since the city surrounds the harbor on three sides, perched on steep hills, I doubt that a fireworks show has ever been seen by as many people. Estimates were that there were over five million viewers.

The display has become an annual event. The one drawback to being in Hong Kong at the time of the New Year is that the shops are closed. Businesses mark their doors with red-paper greetings and start holidays that last from three days to nearly two weeks. One would be advised to arrive before New Year's Day and leave immediately afterward. The fireworks are the only reason to be in town. When I was there, authorities were wondering if perhaps the annual Day of the Dragon Festival, which takes place in the spring,

Along the Rhine from Braubach to Koblenz, German castles are illuminated and fireworks rise from their ramparts during the annual festival known as the "Rhine in Flames." The largest of these displays takes place in Koblenz at the Festung Ehrenbreitstein seen in the photograph above. (Courtesy of German National Tourist Office)

in which wonderfully decorated craft throng the waterways, might not be a better date. Good weather is more predictable. The shops—which are a prime reason for being in Hong Kong—are open. My own suggestion to the few civic officials I met was that *both* dates should be utilized.

INDIA

The earliest records in India of the use of fireworks go back to 1443 to the reign of Devaraya II, when fireworks were mentioned as being used in the Mahanavami Festival. References in the literature of the times describe their use at weddings, festive occasions, and the dedications of temples. Fireworks also had a curious practical use in India's history. They were used to stem what must have been an awesome sight: an *elephant* charge. The device utilized was known as a *cherky*—one imagines it as a kind of cherry bomb—and it was tossed by people who undoubtedly took to their heels rather than stand around to see if it had worked. Cherkys were also used when elephants got to fighting among themselves at festivals or weddings. When the cherkys were tossed among them, the elephants, ears flattened in alarm, would back off from each other.

Also important in Indian culture was an indispensable article in various ceremonials called the *dipas,* or lamps, which were arranged in predetermined designs, light being a symbol of any number of values, in particular Knowledge and Purification. Obviously, the use of light evolved into fireworks of various kinds.

The great Hindu fireworks festival—indeed, known as "The Festival of Lights"—takes place during the celebration of Divali on October 27 and features huge effigies of the three devils of the Ramayana epic, Ravana and his two brothers, which blaze up merrily when shot by the heroic Rama with the fiery arrow. The effigies are filled with fireworks—waterfall showers, pinwheels, fountains, and so forth—so that when ignited they perform in a most effective pyrotechnic manner. Some of the effigies built in the larger communities are huge—in the more prosperous areas of New Delhi, the figures of Ravana and his brothers tower over a hundred feet. The effigies are everywhere on that day (one is reminded, of course, of the fallas of Valencia and the castillos of Mexico). A smaller neighborhood's thirty-foot Ravana provides just as much pleasure, perhaps more, since the preparation and ceremony involve everyone in the area.

The great effigies are common elements in Indian celebrations. All sorts of things are done to them, but sometimes fireworks are not involved. In the August/September festival of Ganesha, a Hindu deity with an elephant's head, often a huge replica thirty feet high is taken out to the waters of a lake or the ocean and sunk! So, for fireworks aficionados there are places to avoid. For example, in Bengal, in northeast India, during the Divali festival in October (although the tourist guide speaks of it as "the gayest of the festivals") the great effigies, in this case representations of the Hindu goddess Kali, are also taken out and submerged in the lake rather than fired. Nothing in that!

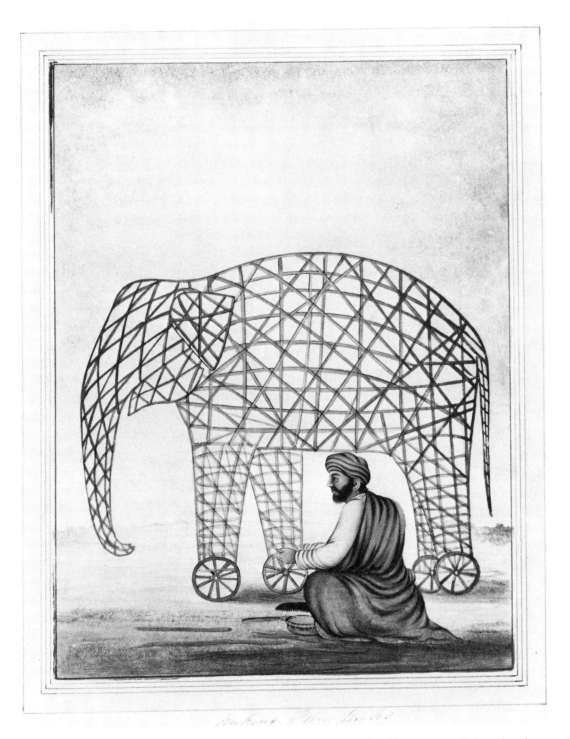

The Mogul craftsman in this small painting (ca. 1815) applies a combustible paste to an elephant-shaped armature soon to be wheeled to festivities in the capital city of Lucknow in Upper India. During the late eighteenth and early nineteenth centuries, Lucknow attracted a wealthy international set. Fireworks provided a popular diversion on every major holiday and for private parties as well. (Private Collection)

Sparks fly from spinning wheels of fireworks attached to these folk figures during an Indian holiday in February. (United Nations Photograph)

During the Festival of Lights, almost every Hindu hangs a ceremonial lantern in his home. Also, for his children he buys what is called an *anar,* a small baseball-sized round earthen pot filled with a composition very similar to what is in the fountains and cones of the Western world, and these when ignited expel a tree-like column of silver and gold sparks. Originally, as in the evolution of fireworks themselves, the *anar* was thought efficacious in driving off evil spirits, just as throughout the centuries in India a peach branch over the door was thought to keep ghosts out of the house.

Another ritual, typical in Bengal, is the "burning down of the old woman's hut," in which miniature huts made of dried leaves are set on fire by the children, at which point, according to my authority—Hovidas Mitra's *Fireworks and Fire Festivals*—"the mosquitoes are asked to go away downstream."

Fireworks are often a feature of Hindu weddings—especially evident in January, which in India is the most auspicious month in which to get married. Also, at the ceremony of "beating retreat," which is held on India's Republic Day, the government sets off barrages of huge Roman candles in the national colors—saffron, white, and green—but it is a fairly restrained display. No, the time to watch fireworks in India is at the celebration of Divali on October 27.

One additional fireworks display should be mentioned. During the festival of Pooram in the spring, a temple celebration takes place at Vadakkunathan (Shiva) on top of a hill near Trichur. The festivities are introduced by thirty elephants carrying tall parasol-like ceremonial umbrellas while being fanned by people walking alongside with huge whisks. The elephants come out through the temple gates and parade around the temple. After midnight, a gigantic fireworks display continues until the break of dawn. The Government of India Tourist Office recommends this display as "the grandest in terms of variety and magnitude."

ITALY

Venice, of course, is famous for its festivals. The one which incorporates fireworks, and to a spectacular degree, is the Feast of the Redentore—the Redeemer—which is celebrated on the third Sunday of July. Part of the celebration centers around the Church of the Redentore, designed by Palladio in the late Renaissance and built in recognition of the populace's deliverance from the plague in 1576. What is world-known is the extraordinary procession of boats of every size and shape, decorated with strings of lanterns and lights. Many will cross the Laguna Venezio to be on hand at the Lido for the sunrise the next day. In the main, the fireworks, a truly magnificent display, appear over the St. Mark's basin. Those who have seen it, either lounging on their backs in a gondola, or standing in the crowds in St. Mark's Square, the great pigeon flocks wheeling above in alarm at the concussions from the lagoon, speak of the fireworks show as being among the most dramatic sights of their experience.

In Rome, the great fireworks display is on the evening of the last day of the Festa de Noanti in mid July in the Trastevere, the neighborhood where the "true Romans" live—or so the Trasteverini themselves claim. The festa offers many features of a carnival—flea-market booths by the hundreds, strolling musicians, boxing matches, street vendors selling roast suckling pig *(porchetta)* and snails—all of this capped by a monumental fireworks show reflected in the flow of the Tiber.

Practically every village in Italy has a festival for its patron saint which features fireworks. The farther south one goes, the more colorful and noisy the display. Almost all such shows are put on by local artisans, often keeping alive a family tradition of fireworks manufacture that goes back centuries. The workshop of the Pinto family in Pianura, outside Naples, was established in 1750. Indeed, in the vicinity of Naples, the unofficial fireworks capital of Italy, there are an estimated seven hundred *fuochisti.* Despite increasingly strict official regulations to protect the public, Naples is notorious for clandestine operations. Apartment workshops have been discovered with enough pyrotechnical material stashed under the beds to blow up the entire building. On occasion this happens—frequently enough so that EXPLOSION ROCKS NAPLES is almost as common a disaster headline for filler stories tucked away in the New York metropolitan dailies as its South American counterpart, BUS PLUNGES INTO GORGE.

The closer to the New Year, the more likely one is to hear a distant detonation. In Naples, New Year's is celebrated largely with noise-making firecrackers and cherry bombs—or "bangers," as the English would say—with considerable effect. In 1978, just to pick a year, ninety-seven people ended up in hospitals.

A more formal and safer time in Naples, though no less tumultuous, is the picturesque Festa di Piedigrotta. Centered around the church erected in her honor in the thirteenth century, the festival starts on the vigil of the Madonna's birthday, which is September 8, and goes on for a week. The event has been celebrated in some fashion since Roman times and now involves various processions, parades of allegorical floats, song fests, and, of course, fireworks—*alla napoletana,* which means, naturally, that a considerable amount of noise will be involved.

Another famous *fuochisti* family near Naples is the Maffettone. They are responsible for the annual Festa dei Gigli in Nola. The patriarch of the family often gets requests to put on shows in foreign countries, but he is always on hand for the feria in his home village, which takes place on the Sunday following June 22. It commemorates St. Paolini, a bishop of Nola who in the fifth century went to Africa to ransom some of his fellow citizens being kept as slaves. The processions in the streets of Nola celebrate his success. Tall, carved obelisks are carried aloft with young musicians precariously perched on them who play rather wobbly music.

Almost all the major cities have traditional displays. One of the most time-honored is in Milan. The ceremony, which is called the Scappio del Carro, occurs on the day before Easter and has been a fixture for many centuries.

The ritual has evolved slowly into its present form. A wire runs from the high altar of the cathedral out through a window to a *carro,* or cart, standing some distance away in a square. On the cart rests a pagoda-like structure composed of various fireworks—pinwheels and such. At the noon mass, at the beginning of the *Gloria,* the archbishop lights a fuse in a rocket concealed in the body of an artificial bird—a symbolic dove—which is attached to the wire. Ignited, the rocket drives the bird along the wire, out the window, down to the cart, where it sets off the display *there.* No sooner does this happen than a second rocket sends the bird back along the wire, through the cathedral window to its starting point and the anxiously waiting archbishop. Great stock has traditionally been taken in the successful completion of the bird's trip, both down and back, and especially in the proper lighting of the *carro.* If successful, it indicated good harvests; if there was any kind of failure, or hitch, a bad year was forecast. Some authorities say that in harsher times—as in the case of the execution of the messenger who brings the bad news—the pyrotechnist whose bird would break down, or whose *carro* would not ignite, would be lynched by a mob. In less severe times, the pyrotechnist's fee was withheld if things did not go off as planned. Brock describes a traveler, one H. Preston-Thomas, who in 1910 saw the bird rocket burst prematurely on the wire, upon which the desperate pyrotechnist rushed forward and ignited the *carro* on his own. The bird never returned to the archbishop, but at least the main display went off in the town square.

The tradition goes back to the first Crusade in 1096 when Pazzino de Pazzi brought back stone chippings purportedly from the Holy Sepulchre. The holy fire of Easter Saturday was started by striking sparks off the relics. It is from this flame that the archbishop lights the dove at the moment of the *Gloria* in the noon mass.

Florence has a more traditional fireworks display on June 24 to mark the end of the feast of San Giovanni Battista (John the Baptist), who is the patron of the city. One of the other highlights of the week-long festivities is the *gioco del calcio*—a curious football match played in Renaissance costumes which originated back in 1530. The fireworks display, which is shot from the piazzale Michelangelo, is of special beauty, since the architectural wonders of the city are illuminated in the fireworks' glow.

Other celebrations of note in Italy occur at Amalfi, the lovely white-walled village that clings to the terraces above the seaport. On June 21 the Amalfitani celebrate with a historical regatta in the port—Amalfi rivaled Pisa and Genoa as a tenth-century maritime republic—and a huge fireworks display is put on to end things. Fireworks are also utilized in a major way in the celebration of the feast of St. Andrew, the patron saint of Amalfi—a double celebration since the Amalfitani are *festa*-conscious enough to have *two festas* in honor of the saint—on June 27 and November 30.

Another fireworks show on the Amalfi coast which attracts considerable tourist attention is the Festa della Madonna delle Grazie which takes place on July 2 in the hills behind Positano at Monte Peruso, a locale known for an enormous natural tunnel in the mountains. Indeed, *peruso* means "hole" in

Neapolitan dialect. The local legend is that the hole was made by the devil in a desperate attempt to flee the Madonna. The story of their confrontation is represented with fireworks—the lighter colors—white, gold, and silver—representing the Madonna, and the darker hues of blue and red supposedly suggesting the devil.

The Festival of Two Worlds—a potpourri of music, dance, drama, and art held in the last two weeks of June in Spoleto, Italy, the old Roman town in the Umbrian hills—concludes with an open-air concert in the central piazza which in turn is followed by a towering show of fireworks over the church of San Pietro.

Other annual feasts in Italy and Sicily which feature fireworks are: St. Agatha in Catania, February 5; the carnival in Viareggio, which takes place in the last week in February; St. Joseph in Rome, March 19; in May, St. Alfio, celebrated near Taormina; St. Christopher in Milan, June 19; St. Anne on Ischia, July 26, which is of particular note because of a parade of boats, bonfires, and the locale of the fireworks show itself, which goes up between Ischia *ponte* and the Aragon castle on its island. Also on Ischia, on August 29, the feast of St. John Joseph of the Cross, is a display which is usually a *competition* between the two best pyrotechnicians in the Neapolitan area. Ferryboat-loads of huge shells (starting with six- and eight-inchers!) are utilized, leading up to truly massive finales in this extraordinary pyrotechnic duel. And, finally, the large fireworks shows should be mentioned that accompany the Festa della Vara, which occurs in August in Messina. It is wise, as has been mentioned before, to check the festival dates, and while it would be unlikely that any tourist—save a member of the PGI—would go to these events solely for the fireworks, it would be possible with checking to ascertain the quality and size of the pyrotechnic displays.

JAPAN

Japan is by far the most enlightened and enterprising nation when it comes to fireworks. The country not only manufactures fireworks of exceptional distinction, quality, and beauty, but also puts on displays as a punctuation to just about every festive and ritual occasion. In Japan, fireworks are set off much as, in other countries, flags are carried in a parade, or a band plays at a political rally, or cheerleaders turn up at a ribbon-cutting ceremony. For example, the grass-burning ritual on Wakakusa Hill in Nara, which takes place in the chill of January and is supposed to rid the area of insects for the next spring's planting, is supplemented by great bursts of chrysanthemums above the burning fields.

The Japanese word for fireworks is *hanabi*. It means "fire-flower." The first time it turns up in Japanese literature is in reference to a display given on August 6, 1613, for Tokugawa Iyeyasu at Sumpu—now Shizuoka—by an emissary from King James I of England. There are records about the same time of Chinese fireworks technicians being employed to display *hanabi*. Fireworks seem to have been entrusted only to foreigners.

But in the eighteenth century the Japanese began to make and display their own fireworks, especially for children's use—*senko-hanabi,* which were miniature fireworks on sticks, and *nezumi-hanabi* or "mouse" fireworks, which scuttled and crackled on the ground.

The center for the earliest manufacture of these items was the city of Edo (now Tokyo), with a population of over a million. The houses of Edo were built of paper and wood, with roofs of highly flammable thatch, except for the homes of the samurai who could afford terra-cotta tiles. The houses were packed in among each other and fires were a terrible hazard. Whole neighborhoods were snuffed out by an errant "mouse" firework. Naturally, just as today, a conflict arose between civic authorities and the fireworks people. Stiff legislative acts were introduced in 1648, 1652, 1655, 1670, and 1680. Common to all of them was the stipulation that anyone found guilty of burning down part of Edo would be expelled from the city!

The city authorities finally restricted the use of fireworks to the banks of the Sumida River. It was here in the mid-seventeenth century that an itinerant farmer named Yaheh from what is now the Nara prefecture set up a shop in Yokoyama-cho Street and founded a dynasty of "fire-flower artists" that lasted for thirteen generations. Yaheh—stuffing pieces of cane and reeds with gunpowder mixtures—started by making the little "mouse" fireworks. His shop was called Kagiya. He was an experimenter in his adopted craft, and apparently a very careful and slow-moving one. Fifty-eight years after his arrival in Edo he shot up his first *hanabi*—this an offering to the water god of the Sumida River. The first of these "fire-flowers" were known as "tiger tails," because of the thick trail of sparks left behind as the firework rose into the air.

Eventually, *hanabi* became a ritual on the river. On May 28, 1733, fireworks were fired to celebrate the first day of the summer river season. The teahouses and the restaurants along the river helped defray the costs. Often, the viewers along the banks or out on the river in boats would call out the name of their favorite "fire-flower artist" in appreciation—such as, "Tamaya!" or "Kagiya!"

The occasional fires continued. In 1843 one of the most famous of the fireworks makers, Tamaya Ichibeh, a disciple in the Kagiya fireworks dynasty, had a fire in his shop near the Ryogoku bridge which burned down the entire neighborhood. It happened at an extremely awkward moment—on the evening of a considerable ceremonial occurrence: the departure of the Shogun to Nikko to pay homage to the occupants of the ancestral mausoleum there. Tamaya was expelled from Edo. He was subsequently allowed back, but his career as a "fireworks master" was never the same.

But the tradition set by Tamaya continues. These days the major fireworks displays take place in the summer months, particularly in August. Indeed, it is difficult to imagine how the pyrotechnicians manage it. It is as if

237

In this magnificent triptych by Japanese printmaker Yeizan Kikugawa, a boating party settles in to watch the fireworks at Ryogoku on the night of the Kawabiraki or River Festival in 1807. (Print Collection. The New York Public Library. Astor, Lenox and Tilden Foundation)

239

in the United States the demands of July 4 were repeated night after night. Of the many shows, one of the most noteworthy is the Sumida River fireworks, which is held in Tokyo on July 26. The river is only fifteen miles long, lined with factories, warehouses, cranes, and yet it is a landmark of Japanese culture, featured in Hiroshige and Hokusai *ukiyo-e* woodcuts, and no less known for its lovely summer fireworks.

The Sumida River display actually has two sites—between the Komagata and the Umayabashi bridges and between the Shirahige and the Kototoi bridges. Both sites are readily accessible—from the Asakusa station on the Ginza line subway or the Toei Asakusa subway line. The shows are done by two different companies. Both are superb displays. The shells, because of the restricted area, are limited to three and four inches in diameter, but they are fired from the barges with great rapidity. An estimated seventeen thousand shells are fired altogether.

About the same time as the Sumida River fireworks is the great Perfect Liberty show at Tondabayashi, described in Chapter Six. Tondabayashi is near Osaka and its show is considered a climactic part of the larger city's summer festivities. The various stages of the rites take up almost the entire month of July, many being purification and washing ceremonies to symbolize the ridding of the plague in the ninth century. It is highlighted by a midmonth procession of huge floats called *hoko*. They are pagoda-like houses, some of them eight stories in height, which are hauled through the streets. In them, small percussion bands play a refrain endemic to the festival and which my authorities tell me sounds as follows: *"ching ching kon kon ching kon kong,"* repeated endlessly. The *hoko* are accompanied by palanquin floats decorated with life-sized scenes from Japanese mythology and history. On the twenty-fourth and twenty-fifth of July, the palanquins are loaded onto barges, one to each. Accompanied by a huge procession of decorated and lanterned craft, the fleet proceeds up the Dojima and the Yodo rivers—the "Shrine fleet," it is called—to a position over which, when it gets dark, a considerable fireworks show takes place. My authorities tell me that the best way to enjoy this spectacle is to go to Nakanoshima at Tenjim-bashi and rent a small rowboat. If you row toward Osaka Castle and around the bend, you'll be right in the middle of things, and directly under the fireworks. A lot goes on out on the river—theatrical performances, various dance troupes, all performed on flat barges, and during the interludes small galleys and motorboats carrying traditional Japanese musical ensembles, and, incongruously, German beer-hall brass bands, career about serenading the spectators in what was described to me as a "wonderful aquatic frathouse frolic, Oriental style."

All of this can be considered a splendid prelude to the pilgrimage to Tondabayashi and the Perfect Liberty event.

The second largest fireworks show in Japan takes place at Gifu, over the Nagara River, on August 2. The number of shells sent aloft is only second to the Perfect Liberty display and it draws a huge number of spectators, nearly a million.

Other large conventional shows worth mentioning occur at Tochigi on August 2 (featuring a Niagara two kilometers long), at Miyazaki (in the Kyushu Province), also on August 2, where the shells are shot up across the width of the Oyodo River (one hundred thousand people come to see this annually); then at Ibaraki on the Tone River, a twenty-thousand-shell display; finally, at Iwate, the Ofunato City fireworks display draws fifty thousand spectators annually—this show on August 5.

There are three great annual festivals famous not only for their fireworks but also especially for launching large fleets of lighted lanterns on the water. The first of these "Big Three" festivals is the annual Nebuta Matsuri which takes place in Aomori in the northern prefecture on August 3–7. The celebration originates from the legend of Sakanoue no Tamuramaro's subjugation of rebels at the turn of the ninth century by the use of *nebuta*—monstrous representations of giants, animals, and winged creatures that apparently struck terror into his enemies. Facsimiles of the *nebuta* are hauled through the streets on carriages. The fireworks display is held on the last day of the festivities. Among the distinctive characteristics of the *nebuta* display is the elaborate use of star mines as well as set pieces.

A second famous lantern festival takes place on August 15 and 16 at Matsushima in conjunction with the Buddhist festivities held at the Zuiganji Temple. Three thousand lanterns are set afloat.

The Miyazu lantern festival, the third, and certainly the largest of the three events, takes place in Kyoto, the ancient capital of Japan, on August 16. Twenty thousand lanterns are set afloat on Miyazu Bay, a ritual that has been going on annually for three centuries, and which provides an extraordinary setting for a large fireworks display.

In Japan, a number of festivals feature the burning of great bonfires. Almost invariably these are accompanied by fireworks shows. Perhaps the most spectacular is the annual Daimonji Okuribi Bonfire Festival which takes place on the five mountains surrounding Kyoto. The date is August 16. The largest bonfire is lit on the slopes of Mount Nyoigadake in the form of the Chinese calligraphic character *dai,* meaning "great." The fires are lit by a group of eighty people who have undergone a week of purification procedures. The event, a very sacred one, is held for the purpose of sending off the souls of Kyoto's dead to Heaven. At eight in the evening all the lights of Kyoto are turned out so the people can see the burning on the mountains.

There is another bonfire and fireworks festival, very much like the one in Kyoto, which takes place on Mount Myojogadake across the valley from Gora, Hakone-machi, which is in Kanagawa prefecture. The Gora summer festival lasts from August 14–16, and the fireworks are on the last day.

Two seaside shows are worth mentioning—a display that is shot on August 1 from Yugawara Beach, which is slightly more than an hour from Tokyo by train, and a show set off from the shores of Zaimokuza Beach on the same day.

Of special interest to aficionados would be a number of ancient, relatively unknown religious ceremonies involving fireworks and the worship of fire. Some of them involve initiation rites for young pyrotechnicians—literally a kind of test by fire in which the participant is often singed. I asked Toshio Ogatsu if he had ever been involved in such a ceremonial, and he replied, "Oh no, no. Very old-fashioned."

One of these takes place in April during the Wind Festival at the Uturu Shrine in Toyohashi City in the Aichi prefecture. The apprentices give ritualistic cries and gestures before lighting cascade flares, which they point toward the Uturu Shrine in an offering to the gods in thanks for the safe use of fire for the year. The evening fireworks show is distinguished by a series of set pieces—not as common a staple in Japan as they are in the United States and Britain—which include such traditional themes as the Buddhist parable of a monkey rushing out to grasp at a reflection of the moon in the water, and a representation of Hokusai's famous wave rising in front of Mount Fuji.

A more frenetic initiation event takes place in October during the Tominaga Shrine festival at Shinshiro City, also in the Aichi prefecture—a two-hundred-year-old ceremony in which the apprentices are required to perform in a series of rites to testify to their manhood and courage. The height of the occasion is when the young men—as many as thirty or forty—dance around in a park near the shrine and spray each other with sparks from their fountain flares. Apparently, burns and injuries are taken for granted. Considering the fallout of sparks and burning paper in a huge show of the type the Japanese often fire, perhaps there is a practical side to the ceremonial: these people become accustomed to being burned.

The Japanese have a tradition of competing in firework contests—which, of course, for the involved spectator provides a fine opportunity to see shell-making at its best. One of the major annual meets is on the shores of the Omonogawa at Omagari in the Akita prefecture. An average of ten companies compete, and they are graded on single shells—very large shells indeed: six to twelve inches in diameter—five judges assessing them on color, burst, originality, quality of sound, etc. The winning company gets a silver trophy that Toshio Ogatsu described to me, considering the expense and effort of competing, as "not so good."

Another major contest takes place in October at Tsuchiura City to which a quarter of a million spectators come to watch. Companies compete for the Ministry of Industry Award and the President's Award from the Japan Pyrotechnic Society.

The annual All-Japan championship takes place at Aichi, often on August 2, the so-called Nagoya meet. In 1980, six pyrotechnic companies competed. A total of twenty thousand shells, two Niagaras, and thirty-five set pieces were ignited, and what was done was watched by a million people.

Another similar meet takes place at Okazaki City at the Okazaki Tourism Festival—also scheduled for August 2. It should be restated that many of these dates conflict with the great goings-on at the Perfect Liberty show in Tondabayashi. There is simply nothing else to be compared with that monstrous show, so all else for the tourist on his first visit to Japan should be dropped in its favor.

MALTA

If there is one country which rivals Japan in pyrotechnic activity, it would be the tiny island nation of Malta in the Mediterranean. The place is in a continuous uproar, a condition which must remind the older generation of Maltese of the wartime years when the Germans tried to bomb the island flat. It is said that every scrap of paper on the island eventually ends up in aerial bomb casings, and even that a man who successfully completes a morning shave without a cut is quite likely to celebrate the feat by shooting a rocket out a window. I cannot attest to this, not having been there personally, but there is no doubt that the fireworks tradition on Malta is a lively one. On August 12, 1980, the year following the Grucci family's triumph in Monte Carlo, the Maltese won the International Fireworks competition there. The company which triumphed was the St. Michael's Fireworks Co. from Hal Lija, Malta, led by the veteran fireworks maker, Carmel Farrugia, better known as "Habugia," and his sons. When they landed back in Malta they were met at the Luqa airport by a large crowd carrying placards ("An honor to Lija and for Malta!" etc.), and the winning pyrotechnicians were carried out of the arrivals lounge on the shoulders of the crowd—something more than can be said for the arrival of the Grucci clan back in Bellport after *their* victory in Monte Carlo.

Malta is a heavily Catholic country. Each community has its patron saint (the village of Zebbug celebrates the feast of St. Philip, Qormi the feast of St. George, Luqa that of St. Andrew, Kirkop that of St. Leonard, and so forth), but almost invariably there is a *second* saint, very often considered by some factions in town to be more important than the first. Thus each village has *two* feast days to prepare for annually—which develops a considerable rivalry between not only various villages, as one might expect, but also the partisans of the two saints *within* a village. Rival clubs represent each saint. Each has its own committee which draws up plans for street parades, the brass bands, the icons and banners that will be carried, and which, most importantly, prepares the fireworks. The two clubs of a Maltese village will usually each have its "factory" where the fireworks are made, but in the larger cities, such as Valletta, where the congestion of houses is such that firework workshops are discouraged, the clubs must buy their fireworks from elsewhere on the island. There is no skimping. One authority on Malta, Jeremy Boissevain, reports that a village of five thousand with a pair of workshops spent thirty-four hundred dollars just for its raw pyrotechnical materials. Imagine what a fireworks show could be put on if a *per capita* expenditure of this kind was the tradition of, let's say, New York or Chicago!

The magazine *Pyrotechnica* has published a number of candid photographs of Maltese fireworks and their artisans. One of them shows the St. Leonard's

Band Club of the village of Hal Kirkop standing in front of a considerable pile of "some" of the fireworks made for St. Leonard's feast, usually September 16—such an abundance of them that I was reminded of those discomfiting portraits of elegant country game-shoots where what has been gunned down is laid out in rows before the gentry standing in baggy plus fours, their shotguns cradled easily in the crooks of their arms. The Maltese bore that smug sense of nonchalant pride—hardly belied by the baseball caps that a number wore or the considerable youth of some of them. One picture, showing four stick-thin boys crouched behind a line of enormous multiple-break eight-inch shells, was captioned: "Their shells performed so excellently that they all got drunk afterwards in celebration!"

The Maltese government has an ambivalent feeling about fireworks. In 1980, two people were killed working with fireworks, one of them a fourteen-year-old boy who was an "expert" at the making of multi-break shells. The police commissioner took an extremely strong stand: he not only banned the manufacture of all fireworks on this island but also refused to let any of the existing stocks be fired until a "study" could be made to determine what had happened and how the industry could be made safer.

The Maltese fireworks people were stunned. It was not long before the great displays of August and September. They held a meeting, and afterward went to the government and pointed out that large quantities of fireworks prepared for the fiestas were still lying around the island—a dangerous state of affairs that would be alleviated if the stocks were shot off. And wouldn't it be prudent, they went on, if the shells were shot off at the fiestas so the tourist trade wouldn't be affected. The government, after consideration, thought this was a reasonable solution—as long as *all* existing stocks were used (they were very firm and admonitory about it), which means that the 1980 fireworks displays were perhaps the most spectacular in the history of Maltese pyrotechnics, so successful and admired that the police commissioner threw up his hands and let the industry alone.

The Maltese, like the Italians from whom their fireworks traditions are derived, are very fond of noise. Almost all their large shells conclude with a loud report. Sometimes their big shells begin with a barrage of salutes from the first break and then a couple of color breaks sandwiched in before the concluding report. Perhaps the most astonishing of their work are the set pieces and Catherine wheels. The intricacy of the effects—the wheels seem literally to throb and pulse with activity—surely have no peer. At a convention of the Pyrotechnics Guild International in Albuquerque in 1982 where I saw a film on Maltese fireworks there were shouts and murmurs of approbation, indeed disbelief, from the members as they watched the wheels revolve and spin on the movie screen.

The best time to go to Malta for the fireworks is in August and September. Originally the fiestas corresponded to the ancient Church calendar and were held throughout the year. Through the instigation of the Maltese government the major fiestas—or *festi* as they are called there—are now celebrated on weekends during the late summer tourist season. The climactic event

A thousand rockets filled the evening skies as the Duke and Duchess of York left the port of Malta in March 1901. The Maltese tradition of fireworks has been long and distinguished. (The Mansell Collection)

of the year is the feast of the Assumption of the Blessed Virgin Mary which on August 15 is celebrated in seven different places on Malta. Tourist buses run from one township to the next, so that it is apparently possible to see a number of these displays. There is almost a universal firing of shows on the celebration of Malta's National Day, which is held on the thirty-first of March. Further information may be obtained by writing the Department of Information, Auberge de Castille, Valletta, Malta. I have no idea what else one does in Malta. I have heard the water-skiing is all right.

MEXICO

Mexico has a strong fireworks tradition. Indeed, it is estimated that more than three thousand festivals a year in that country use fireworks. The familiar centerpiece to any Mexican fireworks show is what is called the *castillo* or castle, very much like the *fallas* of Spain—a kind of minuscule version of the "machine" of fireworks' earlier days. The *castillo* is a derrick-shaped structure from thirty to sixty feet tall, its height and substance depending on the munificence of the community that pays for it. It is ingenuously arranged and festooned with various kinds of multicolored fountains, pinwheels, cascades, and lances. The structure usually takes about twenty days to build. The architects are known as *coheteros*. In the heavily Indian states of Pueblo, Mexico, and Oaxaca there are villages in which dozens of *coheteros* work, but in the less populated areas of the north the *coheteros* are commissioned from afar and turn up on the fiesta days with the ready-made *castillos* in the back of the truck.

In many villages the townspeople carry the statues of saints from the church out to the plaza so the statues can "watch." Late on the night of the fiesta (usually between 10:30 and 11:30 P.M.) the artisans who built the *castillo* light the fuse. The fireworks attached to the edifice start to go off in stages, moving up from the base until finally reaching the top of the structure where the *corona* or crown burns a miniature finale. The process can last for over half an hour.

The *castillo* can perform a number of artistic functions. It can outline *leyendas,* which are slogans appropriate to the occasion, or it can support lance-work effigies featuring the faces of national heroes or saints depending on whether the festival is religious or civic. Sometimes the structure is built in the shape of a devil tied to a wheel. When ignited, the devil spins in a circle and then eventually pops open, showering candy onto the cobblestones of the square—a great favorite, obviously, with village children, who scamper among the spark showers waiting for him to explode.

After the *castillo* has burnt itself out, the youngsters rush around with multisided halberd-like creations called *toritos,* or bulls, which are studded with pinwheels and crackers. They are dashed playfully at the spectators as if to envelop them with noise and sparks. There is quite a lot of frightened crying by young children in their mothers' arms at this stage, along with angry shouts from onlookers calling for less helter-skelter behavior.

What does tend to restore order to the square is the lighting of the *cascada* or waterfall—what American pyrotechnicians call a "Niagara." This string of fountains, often of considerable length, is suspended across the façade of the most imposing structure on the square, usually the church, casting it in the warm glow of golden rain as the *cascada* performs. As the last sparks drift away, the crowd in the square will crane their heads for the aerial shells that will conclude the night's celebration.

While all village fiestas feature the *castillo,* and at least three *toritos* to be carried headlong through the crowd, the *cascada* is a feature of the more affluent communities. Obviously the larger the town, the more elaborate the display.

The great range and complexity of Mexican fireworks is especially evident on the country's two national festivals—the eve of September 15, National Independence Day, and on December 18, the day of the Virgin of Guadalupe. On these days the greatest displays are in Mexico City. A quarter of a million spectators gather in the huge central square, the Zocalo, to watch an hour-long display of various fireworks. At 10 P.M. a government dignitary, usually the President, waves a flag from his balcony to signify that a veritable derrick field of *castillos* in the southwest corner of the square is to be touched off. The *cascada* is stretched along the two-hundred-yard-long Renaissance-style façade of the City Hall. Aerial fireworks conclude things.

On December 18 a number of *castillos* are built within yards of the spot where the Virgin of Guadalupe appeared in an apparition to the Indian, Juan Diego, in 1531. Many of the set pieces ignited on that day in Mexico will depict that apparition scene.

Other fireworks fiestas across Mexico during the year that are worthy of note would include the celebration in the village of San Felipe de Progreso, near Mexico City. On the third Wednesday of every January more *castillos*—as many as thirty—are burned there than any other community in the country. The display lasts for almost four hours.

Almost every Mexican fiesta seems to have its distinguishing features. On May 3 in Tepotz there is a festival at San Miguel de Allende, an attractive colonial town three hours north of Mexico City, which features ten exceptionally large *castillos,* supposedly the largest built in the country. Even more unique is the festival at Chiapa de Corzo, which is a village on the Sumidero River in Mexico's southernmost province of Chiapas. A fireworks sea battle is staged out on the river which is supposed to represent a ship-of-the-line duel off Spain centuries ago. The display lasts for an hour and a half and includes cannon and artillery duels from both boats and the shore. The people watch from grandstands built along the riverbank and from the village rooftops. Chiapa de Corzo is about ten miles from Tuxtla Gutiérrez, which is serviced by a number of daily jet flights from Mexico City.

An additional feature of Mexican fireworks is the Judas wheel—effigies filled with fireworks and suspended from tree branches. They have a long history. Indeed, they were prohibited while Maximilian of Austria was the Emperor of Mexico in the 1860s because his authorities thought the effigies looked too much like the Emperor.

PORTUGAL

Those who enjoy rockets would be advised to attend a *festa* in Portugal where these wonderful devices still predominate in displays. This is partially because of the tradition, but also because of economy—a larger quantity of chemicals being required to make a three- or four-inch shell, whereas the chemicals for the rocket motor—sulfur, saltpeter, and charcoal—are relatively cheap.

One of the principal festivals is the Vespera de São João, on the evening of June 23, the night before the feast of St. John the Baptist, celebrated in both Portugal and Brazil with fireworks. The evening is dedicated to "fire, water, and love."

In the first week in August there is a four-day feast, the feast of St. Walter, at Guimarães, Minho province, which was the first capital of Portugal. Very large "bouquets" of rockets are featured.

One of the most colorful festivals in Portugal, indeed in Europe, takes place at the town of Tomar, Ribatejo province, in the second week of July every odd year; i.e., 1983, 1985, 1987, etc. It is a four-day festival called the Festa dos Tabuleiros, a thanksgiving feast celebrating a successful harvest with the sharing of bread and other food with the poor. Tomar itself is turned into an incandescent wonder for the occasion, its buildings outlined in electric lights, lanterns hung everywhere—and, naturally, there are fireworks. Each night ends with a huge midnight display, featuring rockets, of course, shot from the Templars' castle on the hill.

On the last night of the *festa,* an extraordinary parade takes place. Very much as the Green Men preceded medieval processions, two fireworks *tireurs* move slowly down the street wearing the traditional white shirts and trousers, broad red sashes, and green and red knitted caps. One holds a bundle of rockets, while the other plucks them away one by one, lights them, and then fires them *by hand* toward the Templars' castle. Following these two brave worthies comes a procession of bagpipe players, and then six hundred young women wearing crown-like *tabuleiros* (which literally means "trays") loaded with tall mounds of foodstuffs, loaves of bread and so forth, weighing so much that each has to be steadied by a young man who walks alongside. Quite a show!

On New Year's Eve, the Vespera de Ano Novo, the devout first attend religious services and then let loose at midnight, when in village squares throughout the country there are great outbursts of drums, bells, horns, and especially fireworks.

The greatest of these shows takes place in Funchal, the port-city capital of the island province of Madeira off Africa. There are two reasons for celebration—the year's end coincides with the feast of the city's patron, St. Sylvester I. The display consists of flights of hundreds of rockets at a time. Indeed, many experts rank the Funchal goings-on as one of the major displays of the world.

SOVIET UNION

In the Soviet Union fireworks shows are fired by the fireworks detachment of the Ministry of Internal Affairs. A fireworks spectacular is called a *salyut.* Salyuts light up the Moscow skies at least ten times a year on various national days (these can be checked at a hotel registry). These displays are matched in the other fourteen capitals of the Soviet republics, and in the so-called hero cities of Leningrad, Volgograd, Sevastopol, Odessa, Novosibirsk, Kerch, and Tula. The displays are so common that residents are somewhat blasé about them. When I was there for the 1980 Olympics, one evening fireworks began to go off above the so-called Iron Bridge near the Kremlin, huge blue and orange bursts with very large stars. I began running for them, traveling at quite a clip down the streets, my face upturned, looking for the next burst, and I was conscious of passing people who seemed to be taking no interest at all. It was Navy Day, apparently. The fireworks seemed very impressive to me. The best place to see them would be from the slopes of the Lenin Hills, or from the great parapets in front of the University of Moscow that look down on the city.

There was very little variety in the shell bursts I saw. The colors were red, gold, green, and blue, invariably one color to a shell. A number of the bursts were accompanied by a strange ripping sound, like a piece of silk cloth being torn down the middle. Judging from the size of the star spread in the sky and the thump of the propellant charge, the diameter of the Russian shell was very likely in the large eight-inch class. The colors were brilliant—very likely to compensate for the light evening sky into which, in the summer, in those high latitudes even a late-night show must be shot. Very few pale colors such as silver were used—but mostly deep primary reds, violets, and oranges.

Russia enjoys a lively history of fireworks. The coronation of the Empress Elizabeth Petrovna in 1742 was celebrated by mammoth displays. During his reign Alexander II accompanied his big shows in Moscow and St. Petersburg with choirs and singing. Elsewhere in this book I have described Peter the Great's fascination with matters pyrotechnical.

In his history of fireworks Alan Brock describes an extraordinary episode involving the Russians. In 1881 his grandfather Charles went to Russia on a million-pound contract to prepare fireworks to celebrate the coronation of Tsar Alexander III—surely the largest order in the history of pyrotechnics. The irony that Alexander was being crowned because his father Alexander II had been blown up by a nihilist's bomb earlier that year could not have been lost to Brock, Sr.

While he was in Moscow, arranging for the show, an astonishing plot against the regime was discovered. It was dreamed up by a contractor named Koboseff Bogdanowitsch. He had wangled the job to wire the Kremlin with an electric-light system. What was not known was that Bogdanowitsch was a nihilist whose plan was to install a considerable number of bombs into his electrical circuits. At the ceremonies to initiate the system the Tsar himself would be led to the master switch to turn on the lights. "Here we are, sire," and in the semidarkness, everybody looking forward to the wonder of this new-fangled device, the Tsar, perhaps removing his glove to get a better feel of the switch, would click it forward.

Before this happened—what a scene for a Hollywood thriller!—Bogdanowitsch was arrested and his home searched. Not only were the bombs discovered that he had hoped to set into the sockets of the Kremlin system, but also a number of other explosive devices, purportedly designed to be hidden under peasant capes and thrown from the crowd at the royal carriages if the Kremlin plot failed.

FOLLOWING PAGES *A startled horse disrupts the ceremonies of fireworks to celebrate the coronation of Alexander II in Moscow in September 1856. The display was staged in front of the building of the Corps of Cadets, and featured something quite novel at the time—fireworks to a background of music provided by a band of two thousand instruments and a choir of one thousand singers. (Photo of an anonymous print by Herb Orth/Life Magazine. © 1955, Time Inc.)*

Naturally, all this focus on explosive devices was quite disturbing to the authorities. They explained to Charles Brock that under the circumstances perhaps it was not appropriate that fireworks should be part of the coronation festivities. Brock had to take all his fireworks back.

SPAIN

The great pyrotechnic manifestation in Spain takes place over the feast of St. Joseph in Valencia during the week of the nineteenth of March. The affair lasts for the seven days of that week—with such intensity that I am told getting to sleep in a midtown hotel is almost impossible unless one is equipped with earplugs. Firecrackers, many of an illegally large variety, go off constantly during the daylight hours. In past times one of the traditions was to link great chains of firecrackers together, wiring them along building fronts and streetcar poles so that the city squares were joined by a kind of skein of noise. Ernest Hemingway describes this in *For Whom the Bell Tolls*:

"And what did thee do [in Valencia] when not eating or drinking?"

"We made love in the room with the strip blinds hanging over the balcony . . . and from the streets there was the scent of the flower market and the smell of burned powder from the firecrackers of the *traca* that ran through the streets exploding each noon during the *feria*. It was a line of fireworks that ran through all the city, the firecrackers linked together and the explosions running along on poles and wires of the tramways, exploding with great noise and a jumping from pole to pole with a sharpness and a crackling of explosion you could not believe . . ."

"We have done things together," Pablo said.

"Yes," the woman said. "Why not? . . . But never did we go to Valencia. Never did we lie in bed together and hear a band pass in Valencia."

The firecracker *tracas,* or trains, were largely discontinued a few years ago, because of the considerable damage they did *en route*—especially on restaurant awnings, which had to be doused by waiters with pitchers of water to keep them from being consumed by flames.

At 1:30 P.M. in the main square the official daytime fireworks began—these too with a massive reliance on concussion. As Kenneth Tynan, the dramatic critic, has described the daytime fireworks of Valencia: "If they cannot dazzle you, by God they will deafen you. Puff-flash-boom, multiplied several thousand times, is the outcome: conversation ceases, windows shake, and late-sleeping strangers shoot bolt-upright in their hotel beds, wondering why anyone would choose Valencia for a preemptive strike."

The evening fireworks begin at 1 A.M. During the *feria* they are a nightly event—each carefully choreographed and quite unique, since a number of firework companies, some from other countries, even Japan, compete for a prize of fifty thousand pesetas. Tynan, himself a fireworks aficionado, wrote the following impression:

"Three giant bangs, like the *trois coups* that precede the rise of the curtain in French theaters, announce that the volcano is about to erupt; and the movements are punctuated by single detonations. But these are niceties you do not notice until familiarity sets in, four or five displays later. What you notice the first time is quite simply one of the greatest free entertainments on earth; a prolonged spasm of organized fire animating the night sky in streaks and splashes, so that it looks like an indigo sea reflecting sunlight at noon. There are the solo heavyweight missiles, blown into the air from mortars and descending in quintuple tiers of expanding color, prodigally scattering sapphire chandeliers; the salvos of elemental noise, rising to a percussive crescendo of violence like Philly Jo Jones run amok in your ear; the flaring swarm of marsh lights that whistle, or fizz in circles, or dart laterally like mayflies, or even float down by parachute, illuminating the whole townscape; and always the rockets in their regiments, thrown into battle regardless of casualties, rushing upward to reenact in multiple form the big-bang theory of cosmology—initial flash, bright centrifugal spray, and final decline into darkness. They are images, on the way up, of individual birth, so many spermatozoa squirming for survival; on the way down, of cosmic death, so many cooling stars. You realize that an art superficially childish can be emotionally overwhelming, touching some very resonant chords indeed. Thanksgiving by fire, the element that warms us and cooks our food, must be one of the oldest and most appropriate means of human celebration. Three more explosions signal the end of the show, and the spectators clap their approval (or, more rarely, hiss their disdain) of the pyrotechnics manufacturer who provided it. If it has been a good night, you will observe, as they disperse, that their eyes are shining. So are your own, and strangers look at you in recognition. You have shared with them a glittering, shimmering, shattering, zooming-every-which-way experience; and when the celestial gang bang is over, and you walk home through night air that is dense with cordite, along avenues strewn with the sticks of rockets, it is not uncommon to feel a momentary glow of communal bliss."

Other than the extraordinary fireworks, the feature of the Valencia *feria* is what is called a *falla,* meaning bonfire in Valencia dialect. In fact, the *falla* rather than being the act of burning has come to mean *what* is burned—namely, a wood, wax, and papier-mâché structure ranging from a dozen feet high to a gigantic edifice sometimes topping eighty feet. Each district hires an *artista fallero* who with his assistants in a suburb known as the Falla Artists' City interprets the year's theme with his construction. One year "Sexuality and Politics" was depicted in a variety of wicked caricatures—feminists, hippies, nudism, female football players, Gibraltar (Gibraltar is inevitably involved, whatever the theme), pornographic films, lesbians, Pan-Catalanism, television violence. Thousands of people whose artistic output is limited to a life of three days are employed the year round to produce these huge absurdities. On March 16 the *fallas* are trucked in to the various square and street corners. Prizes of up to four thousand dollars are given for the most original, but only the first-prize *falla* is preserved; the rest, well over two hundred, are burned in the astonishing conclusion to the *feria*.

The burning takes place at midnight on March 19, St. Joseph's Day—what is called the "Nit de Fac," Valencian dialect for Night of Fire—a saddening spectacle to many since such obvious care and artistry has gone into their making. My associate, Margaret Mathews, could barely believe these sparkling papier-mâché figures were destined to be burned. She wrote me: "Watching a *falla* burn is perhaps the most moving part of the festival. It takes only a few touches of the torch to light the base of the *falla*. The papier-mâché figures seem to submit peacefully to their fiery fate. Flames lap around the base and slowly consume the figures. A feeling of sadness descends on the spectators as sparks are carried upward by the winds."

She told me she felt better when she was assured that, though the *fallas* were not directly associated with Lent and Easter, there was a symbolic association with the notion of resurrection and rebirth—that, in a sense, what was being celebrated was the end of winter and the start of spring and the planting of crops.

One of the most interesting of the Spanish fireworks is what is called *una corona de subir y bajar*—a rising and falling crown—which is a spinning girandole device designed to move up and down in the night sky, as if on a rubber band, until finally, with a *whoosh,* it soars up and winks out. It is a specialty of one of the greatest of the Spanish fireworks firms, the Pirotecnica Brunchu, which was founded in 1809. It is one of the three most important Spanish companies, all of which are situated in Valencia, the province which, because of the *feria,* has a particular affinity with the art of fireworks.

Valencia is the major spectacle, but there are other shows in Spain during the course of the year. Almost every festival has its fireworks. Those who follow the bulls will almost invariably find that the soft evening air after the bullfights is graced by fireworks. The San Isidro on May 15 in Madrid features thousands upon thousands of rockets. I can remember walking back to the hotel at night with the roar from above, and hearing around us the soft clatter of spent rocket sticks striking the cobblestones.

The festival of San Firmin in July at Pamplona which Ernest Hemingway made famous in *The Sun Also Rises* is noted, of course, not only for the "running of the bulls" but also for the pyrotechnics, which, like the bulls, must be dodged. Much of the stuff, which is supposed to go up, as in the straight rise of a rocket, tends to move on a horizontal plane, often not more than a dozen or so feet above the cobblestones. One afternoon, I remember, a rocket hissed down a Pamplona street, rose slightly, trailing a thin plume, and suddenly, with unerring accuracy, disappeared through an open window into a darkened third-story apartment—*floop!* We stared at the window in a strain of anticipation, expecting a muffled explosion and a small boil of smoke, but apparently the thing was subdued in there, or had not gone off, because we saw a thin arm materialize and the window come down with a loud angry bang.

Every year, in March, hundreds of fallas like this one light up the streets of Valencia on the final night of the feast of St. Joseph. (Photo © Carl Nagin, 1982)

SWITZERLAND

The Swiss, which one might expect, have a reputation for putting on displays marked by perfect choreographic effects. The best examples are shows during the Fêtes de Genève—festivities which take place usually in the latter part of August on Lake Geneva.

The fireworks season starts on the Monday following the spring equinox (early April) with an interesting two-day celebration in Zürich called the Sechseläuten, whose climactic moment is the "Burning of the Böögy" to symbolize the rising temperatures melting Old Man Winter—the representation of this being a huge snowman made of cotton, saturated with petrol and stuffed with fireworks. The figure is immolated at 6 P.M. on the second day of the festival.

On the first day of summer in June there is a large fireworks display, a Seenachfest (a lake night-festival), in Lucerne.

At Interlaken, all summer long, on Monday and Wednesday nights, there are large fireworks displays on the water, many of them provided and displayed by the Hamberger family, perhaps the best known of the Swiss pyrotechnicians.

The national day in Switzerland is August 1, the day on which, in 1291, the towns of Schwyz, Unterwalden, and Uri formed the Swiss Federation. On that night, bell-ringing, fireworks, and beacon fires on mountaintops occur throughout the country.

TAIWAN

Fireworks displays take place during the Moon Festival, which is in mid August, during the Chinese New Year in February, and in various parts of the country on the birthday of a Buddhist deity named Ma Cha, which falls on May 30.

UNITED STATES

Undoubtedly the first fireworks to be set off in the New World—at least the ones that are chronicled—were by Captain John Smith. He writes in his history of Virginia that on the evening of July 24, 1608, "we fired a few rockets, which flying in the ayre so terrified the poore Savages [the Indians] that they supposed nothing impossible we attempted; and desired to assist us."

More familiar are the words of John Adams about the Fourth of July, written in a letter to his wife, and reprinted in just about every newspaper on the holiday: "The day will be the most memorable in the history of America. I am apt to believe that it will be celebrated by succeeding generations as the great anniversary festival . . . It ought to be solemnized with pomp and parade . . . bonfires and illuminations [by which were meant fireworks] from one end of the continent to the other."

This prophetic statement is in a letter John Adams wrote on July 3, 1776,

A colored woodcut by the American artist B. J. O. Nordfeldt, showing a turn-of-the-century Fourth of July fireworks celebration featuring rockets. (The Metropolitan Museum of Art, Gift of Mrs. B. J. O. Nordfeldt)

just after the Continental Congress proclaimed the American colonies independent of England, and before the final approval of the amended Declaration on the Fourth.

Since the war was still being fought, the first Fourth of July celebrations in this country were constituted more by gunfire than fireworks. In Philadelphia, on July 4, 1776, each warship in the fledgling navy celebrated the day by firing thirteen cannon to honor the new United States. Later that afternoon, according to the Philadelphia *Evening Post,* the local notables of the new republic dined at the City Tavern. A number of toasts were given, "all breathing independence," and at the conclusion of each, outside there was a "discharge of artillery and small arms, and a suitable piece of music," played, it might be added, by a captured Hessian band. Patriots lit their windows with candles. Those of the British Loyalists remained dark. There actually *were* some

257

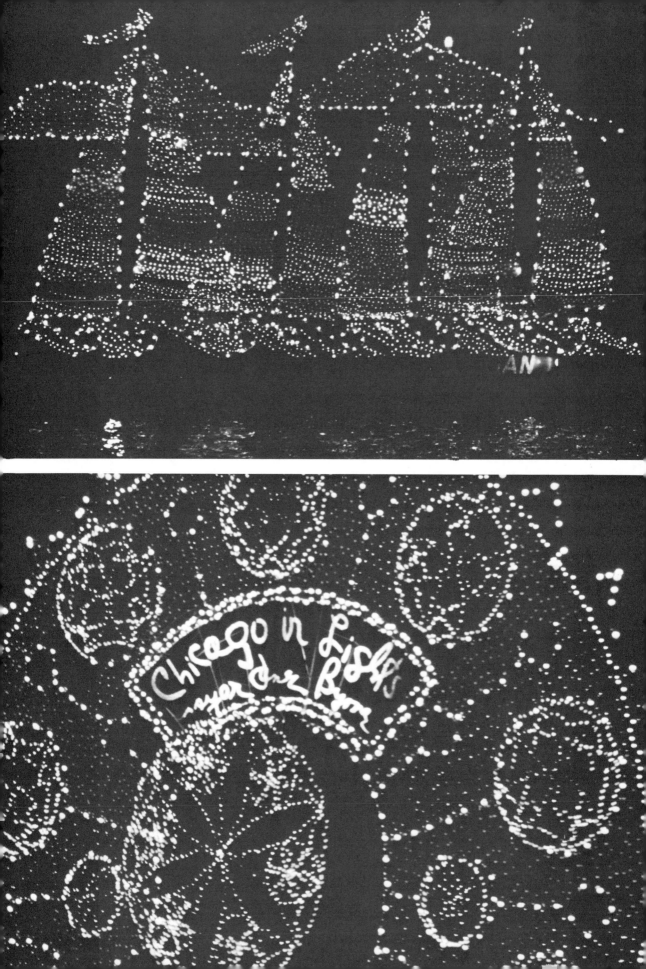

fireworks—an opening and concluding barrage of thirteen rockets shot up from the Commons, a large field west of Sixth Street from Chestnut to Spruce.

The Fourth of July, needless to say, did become the country's fireworks day. Indeed, in Philadelphia, one of its citizens noted in his diary of 1864 that "as a general rule, 30 or 40 houses are set *afire* every 4th of July."

The earliest known manufacturer of fireworks for pleasure in America was the Du Pont family, which had been producing saltpeter and black powder in stone sheds along the Brandywine River near Wilmington, Delaware, since 1802. In 1809 the family started setting off fireworks to celebrate weddings, birthdays, anniversaries, baptisms, and so forth, not only for family members but also for the workers at the Eleutherian Mills. When General Lafayette visited the Du Ponts during his Grand Tour in 1825, a fireworks show was put on in his honor, somewhat marred by an accident during the display. The Du Ponts' manufacture of fireworks continued through the 1940s, and the company supplied the 2F powder that fireworks manufacturers used in their lifting charges until the early 1970s.

Massachusetts was the first state to vote official recognition for the Fourth of July, which it did in 1781. Now, ironically, it is one of the states where it is against the law for citizens to buy or sell fireworks.

Today, on the Fourth of July, just about every geographical location is literally within range of a good fireworks display. George Zambelli, from New Castle, Pennsylvania, has a thousand operatives working for him on the Fourth. Just about every major city puts on an impressive Fourth of July professional show. Perhaps most notable are the displays in Washington, D.C. (with the Washington Monument as the centerpiece), Boston (off the Esplanade), Milwaukee (off the lakefront), and New York City (the Macy's show).

Increasingly, New Year's Eve has come to feature fireworks at the stroke of midnight. That has always been the tradition in the south, but now it has spread northward. In 1983, in Chicago, sixteen locations, including skyscrapers, were used to celebrate the turn of the year with fireworks. Fireworks were fired from three locations in New York's Central Park, and also from Brooklyn's Prospect Park. In New York, the parks are now becoming the place to spend New Year's rather than in the traditional crush of Times Square.

Aside from the Fourth of July and New Year's Eve, fireworks displays, just as they were in the earliest days, are commissioned for any number of occasions for which it is difficult to establish exact dates—state fairs, feast days, municipal dedications of bridges or parks, centennial celebrations such as those held for the Brooklyn Bridge in 1983, or the Statue of Liberty. I once offici-

Chicago's Lake Festival, better known as Venetian Night, has traditionally been the scene of great fireworks displays. The fireworks begin at the conclusion of a parade of colorfully decorated floats and yachts. Over a million people throng the lakeside to catch the proceedings. (Photos © 1982 Diane Graham-Henry, Click/Chicago)

FOLLOWING PAGES *The Centennial celebration of America's Independence was the occasion for these festivities in New York City's Union Square. On July 4, 1876, every building was suddenly illuminated with a dazzling array of lights while rockets were fired from locations around the perimeter of the square. (Collection of Margaret O. Mathews)*

ated—being peppered with snowballs as I did so—at a large show signaling the opening of the World Cup skiing competition in Aspen, Colorado—a lovely show that was shot off the side of the mountain, the violence of the finale making it look as though a volcano had opened a vent halfway down the slope.

There are a few large fireworks shows which are consistent enough on an annual basis to be worth mentioning. The largest of these is Venetian Night in Chicago. It celebrated its twenty-fifth anniversary in 1982, and its date is the last weekend in August. It is enormously and deservedly popular. In 1981, a million spectators gathered on the lakefront, a great half oval of people stretching from the Observatory down the straightaway of Grant Avenue to the Navy Pier. The reviewing stand is directly in front of Buckingham Fountain, just at the water's edge. City ordinances forbid dispensing even beer in the vicinity for fear, presumably, imbibers will topple into Lake Michigan. Those who come with their picnic baskets and hampers bring their wine with them. At 8 P.M. the parade of illuminated floats and yachts begins. Prizes are competed for. The flotilla is got up as dragons, swans, airplanes, peacocks, many of them carrying bands, Playboy bunnies—just about anything to attract the judges' attention. These worthies sit in the reviewing stand. So does the mayor. An astonishing number of contestants feature tributes to the mayor, as if the competition was based on what yacht owner can curry favor most imaginatively. In a city inured by the cult-personality tactics of Mayor Richard Daley, none of this seems to raise an eyebrow. Nor does the fact that the mayor's name is attached to the festival—as in: "Mayor Byrne's Venetian Night." A New Yorker was left to ruminate how long in his city it would take an orange to arch out of the crowd if its mayor—say, Mayor Koch—was ever crazy enough to attach his name to a public event.

The fireworks begin after the yacht parade is finished. It is one of the few fireworks shows in the country in which the budget is over one hundred thousand dollars. In 1981, almost five thousand shells, including twenty twelve-inchers, were fired from four barges moored out by the breakwater of Monroe Harbor. Anyone interested in fireworks in mass employ should make a point of seeing the Chicago show.

Certainly, the annual display on Cincinnati's riverfront is worth mentioning. The so-called "Riverfest" takes place on the Saturday before Labor Day. The occasion was first sponsored by the Cincinnati Symphony Orchestra. Recently, the rock-'n'-roll station WEBN has taken over. Rozzi's Famous Fireworks provides the show. Seventy percent of the shells fired are made in their own compound in Loveland, Ohio, and the rest, as one might expect, are imported from the Orient. In keeping with the pace of rock-'n'-roll, the show is noted for the speed of its deliverance to the sky, ending with a spectacular fifteen-hundred-shell finale. The show is choreographed to rock music (the Who's "Won't Get Fooled Again" started things in 1980), but perhaps in deference to its heritage of classical music the programmers arranged for a part of Haydn's "Surprise" Symphony to put in an appearance that same year. Over 350,000 spectators, most with transistor radios, turned up on the banks of the Ohio between the Beard and Central bridges to watch. The Rozzis being

(Cover drawing by Alajalov; © 1953, 1981. The New Yorker Magazine, Inc.)

one of the premier fireworks manufacturers of the United States, "Riverfest" is one of the great non-July 4 shows.

There are other displays worth noting. Newport, Virginia, has an annual late July "Harborfest"—an afternoon of aquatic events of considerable variety—whaleboat races and so forth—followed by a large fireworks show from barges just off the downtown area.

New London has *its* "Harborfest," also in late July—again off the water. The waterborne fleet is very large; to be in it is the best way to see the show. On the Groton side of the Thames River the crowds are thick on the slope of the hill. Also on the Groton side are the great iron-colored cocoons of the Tridents, the strobe-like flares of the acetylene torches flickering throughout the night as the submarines are worked on in the great hangar-like building sheds. They continue sparking during the fireworks and after—an odd and somewhat sobering counterpoint to the lovely effects out on the water.

The two Disney facilities, Disneyland in Anaheim, California, and Disneyworld in Orlando, Florida, have regularly scheduled small fireworks shows—they last about four minutes—and on special occasions put on more grandiose displays.

Increasingly, baseball clubs across the country have a Fireworks Night to go along with Bat Day, T-Shirt Night, and so forth, and the promotion has been hugely successful, drawing by far the largest crowds of the season. Indeed, my favorite time of the summer as a sports fan is to take my two children to New York's Shea Stadium on Fireworks Night and quite selfishly indulge them in my two favorite pastimes—baseball and pyrotechnics. Afterward, it is a joyous crowd that leaves the stadium, even if—which is usually the case—the Mets have lost. I like the way the ballplayers from both clubs, drawn by the sound of the fireworks, come out in various stages of undress to kneel and watch from the dugout steps. The New York Yankees near the Harlem River cannot put on a fireworks show because a number of municipal buildings are too close to the stadium for regulations to permit it—a supreme irony, since George Steinbrenner, the Yankees' owner, was born on the Fourth of July. For years his management has been trying to bend the rules so that those significant birth dates—the country's and their boss's—can be duly celebrated. New York's fire marshal, perhaps a Red Sox fan, has been unyielding.

As mentioned at the outset, the calendar of pyrotechnic events, with the exception of the Fourth of July, is not reliable on an annual basis. It is best to check—either with local authorities, or, even better, with the major fireworks companies. I have listed twelve of the largest ones below—whose offices would most likely give out the locations of the next scheduled show worth traveling to watch.

American Fireworks Company
P.O. Box 394
Hudson, Ohio 44236
Phone: 216-653-5380

Fireworks by Grucci
Association Road
Bellport, New York 11713
Phone: 516-286-0088

Garden State Fireworks
Carlton Road
Millington, New Jersey 07946
Phone: 201-647-1086

Illinois Fireworks Company
P.O. Box 792
Danville, Illinois 61832
Phone: 217-442-1716

International Fireworks Company
P.O. Box 209
Millington, New Jersey 07946
Phone: 201-647-6522

Keystone Fireworks Manufacturing
  Company
P.O. Box 338
Dunbar, Pennsylvania 15431
Phone: 412-277-4294

Pyro-Spectaculars
P.O. Box 910
Rialto, California 92376
Phone: 714-874-1644

Rich Brothers Company
Box 514
Sioux Falls, South Dakota 57101
Phone: 605-336-3344

Ruggieri U.S.A. Inc.
P.O. Box Q
New York, New York 10028
Phone: 212-772-3003

Star Fireworks Manufacturing Company, Inc.
403 East 14 Street
Danville, Illinois 61832
Phone: 217-442-7665

Tri-State Manufacturing Company
  (Rozzi Family)
P.O. Box 5
Loveland, Ohio 45140
Phone: 513-683-0620

Trojan Fireworks Company
P.O. Box 1170
Norwalk, California 90650
Phone: 213-921-1466

Wald & Company, Inc.
208 Broadway
Kansas City, Missouri 64105
Phone: 816-842-9299

Zambelli Fireworks Manufacturing
  Company, Inc.
P.O. Box 1463
New Castle, Pennsylvania 16103
Phone: 412-658-6611

If this does not work—as mentioned, fireworks people sometimes tend to be cagey about their schedules—you can always call me. I am in the Manhattan telephone directory. I would always direct someone to a good fireworks show. It would make me feel as if I had accomplished a good deed for the day.

FURTHER READING ABOUT FIREWORKS

The literature of fireworks is surprisingly varied and large, considering the extremely specialized nature of the subject. It spans five hundred years and virtually every European language, as well as some Oriental tongues.

The present brief list is confined to works in English either currently in print, or likely to be found in the collection of a typical large city or university library.

BOOKS

Pyrotechnics by George W. Weingart. Brooklyn, N.Y.: Chemical Publishing Co., second edition, 1947

Fireworks: Principles and Practice by the Reverend Ronald Lancaster, M.A., et al. New York: Chemical Publishing Co., 1972

The above two books are concise technical manuals primarily devoted to techniques and formulae for manufacturing fireworks. Weingart's book is the final edition in a series of manuals by that author, the first of which was published in 1930. Though a classic in some respects, it is outdated in others. Its descriptions of "shop goods" fireworks, as sold to the general public prior to World War II, are detailed and interesting. It presents a less accurate picture of the public-display branch of the industry. Lancaster's book, published in 1972, remedies these defects and includes better formulae, although it is less detailed in discussion of technique. A reading of both books together is a good introduction to the technical side of pyrotechny. Currently in print. Order from Chemical Publishing Co., 80 Eighth Avenue, New York, N.Y. 10011.

The Chemistry of Powder and Explosives by Tenney L. Davis, Ph.D. New York: John Wiley & Sons, two volumes, 1941, 1943. Reprinted ca. 1978 by Angriff Press

Dr. Davis was a professor at Massachusetts Institute of Technology and this book was a textbook for his course on the subject. As Dr. Davis was also technical director of the old National Fireworks Co. headquartered near Boston, his book includes a long and interesting chapter on fireworks that reflects his interest and expertise. Much of it is duplicative of Weingart but some information is still to be found only in Davis. This book has been reprinted by Angriff Press and is currently in print.

Pyrotechnics from the Viewpoint of Solid State Chemistry by Joseph McLain, Ph.D., et al. Philadelphia: Franklin Institute Press, 1981

This work is a highly technical study of pyrotechnic chemistry. It includes a chapter on fireworks but does not treat them as its primary subject. It is currently in print.

Fireworks: The Art, Science, and Technique by Takeo Shimizu. Tokyo: Maruzen Co., 1982

This expensive, limited-edition work is perhaps the most exhaustive treatment of *fireworks* (as opposed to the broader subject of pyrotechnics, which includes military and industrial applications) recently available. It is completely up-to-date and discusses both pyrotechnic chemistry and the craft of fireworks-making with special emphasis on the techniques in use among the Japanese. It will benefit most those readers who have absorbed the works of Weingart, Lancaster, and Davis, and who have some practical acquaintance with fireworks manufacturing. Its chapters on the aesthetics of fireworks are, however, illuminating to any person who wants to watch fireworks with a critical eye. Currently in print, but may not be for long!

Although out-of-print, the following books are usually available in libraries:

A History of Fireworks by Alan St. Hill Brock. London: George C. Harrap & Co., 1949

An interesting history of pyrotechny from its origins in the early middle ages through World War II, this book covers social, aesthetic, and technical aspects of fireworks. As a scion of the prominent British fireworks-making family the author is perhaps inclined to overemphasize the role of Brock's Fireworks and of English pyrotechny in general, but on the whole the work is accurate and detailed.

Modern Pyrotechnics by Herbert Ellern, Ph.D. New York: Chemical Publishing Co., 1961

Military and Civilian Pyrotechnics by Herbert Ellern, Ph.D. New York: Chemical Publishing Co., 1967

These are broad surveys of pyrotechnic chemistry with discussions of application primarily in the military and utilitarian civilian fields (e.g., matches). Although storehouses of valuable technical knowledge for the manufacturer of fireworks, they are rather remote for the general reader. The 1967 work contains a brief chapter on fireworks by the Reverend Ronald Lancaster, who later wrote *Fireworks: Principles and Practice*.

JOURNALS

Pyrotechnica, published by Robert G. Cardwell, Pyrotechnica Publications, 2302 Tower Drive, Austin, Texas 78703

Pyrotechnica is an irregularly appearing journal primarily devoted to technical and draft-oriented articles covering subjects in detail and at length. It also carries articles on historical and economic aspects of fireworks and reviews of books and literature about pyrotechnics. As it is irregular in appearing, being published only as suitable articles are submitted, there are no subscriptions. Those who inquire are placed on a mailing list and notified as new issues become available.

American Fireworks News, published by Jack Drewes, 3339 DS Road, Whitewater, Colorado 81527

Eleven issues per year, this journal carries current news of general pyro interest, short technical and craft articles, and regular columns on various pyro subjects.

PGI Bulletin, Director of Publications K. L. Kosanke, Pyrotechnics Guild International, Inc., 3331 DS Road, Whitewater, Colorado 81527

A benefit of membership in the Pyrotechnics Guild International, Inc., this bimonthly journal carries organizational news of the PGI, the reports of its officers to the membership, as well as short technical and historical articles of general pyrotechnic interest.

MICHAEL T. SWISHER

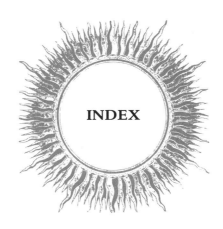

INDEX

Page numbers in italics indicate pictures.

Leopold I, King of Belgium, 217
Let Freedom Ring project, 195
Let Freedom Ring project, 195
Letter shells, 140
Le Vau, 31
Levitt, William, 65–66
Leyendas (slogans), 246
Liber Ignium ad Comburendos Hostes (Book of Fire), 188
Lindsay, John, 49
Line rockets, 203
Lion, fire-belching, *187*
Lisbon, Portugal, Tagus River fireworks show, 166
Little David, 83
Living fireworks, 174
Living set piece, tree as, *185*
Lloyd's Jubilee Fireworks Manufacturing Co., trade catalogue, *118*
Loews Hotel, Monte Carlo, 72, 75
Lomaz, Larry, 121
London
    fireworks at end of World War II, 78
    fireworks for royal wedding, 1981, 38, 41, 155
London Bridge, fireworks at opening in Lake Havasu, Arizona, 78
London *Evening Standard,* 41
London *Gazette,* 36
Lone Eagle brand, 118
Louis XIII of France, 34
Louis XIV of France, 20, 31
    and fireworks at Versailles, 31–34, *32–33*
Louis XVI of France, 206
Lowell, Massachusetts, Whipple Mill explosion, 193
Low explosive, 164
Lübeck, set piece at, *201*
Lucerne, Switzerland, fireworks at Seenachfest, 256
Lully, 34

McCord, David, 91
Ma Cha, Buddhist deity, 256
Machine, 29, 174–75, *28*
    in Italian fireworks, 34–36, *35*
    waterborne, 180

McLaughlin, Mike, 93
Macy's Department Store, 135, 174, 259
Madeira, fireworks at Funchal, 248
Mad lions, 213
Maffettone family, 233
Magnalium spangles *(lente juela magnalium),* 210
Mahanavami Festival, 230
Mailer, Norman, 17–18
Maison Lacroix, La, 226
Mallarmé, 17
Malta, fireworks tours, 243–45, *245*
Mandarin crackers, 117
Man in the Iron Mask, 31
Man in Tuxedi, 163
Mankinds, 163
Mapolle, 115
Marco Polo, 164
Marie Antoinette, 206
    invitation to *Fête Publique, 225*
Maroon, 197
Marsh, Charlie, 160
Martin, Billy, 131
Marutamaya Ogatsu Fireworks Co., Ltd., 61, 77, 91, 99, 100, 131, 163
Massy-Paliseau, fireworks displays, 224
Master Blaster Pastor, 176, *177*
Match heads, 156
    electric, 207
    flare, 167
Mathews, Margaret, 254
Matsushima, Japan, lantern festival, 241
Maxentius, 155
Maximilian of Austria, Emperor of Mexico, 247
Medicine at Work, 165
M-80, 156, 176, 195, 196
Melbourne Royal Show, 217
Memorabilia, fireworks, *119*
Memorial Hall, Cambridge, Mass., 79
    Lampoon centennial dinner at, 90–91
Messina, fireworks display, 236
Meteors, 169
Metropolitan Museum of Art, 204
Mexico, fireworks tours, 245–47
Michelangelo, 48, 169
Mickey Mouse, 218
Mikky Mouse, 163
Milan, fireworks displays, 234–35
Military-Civilian Pyrotechnics (Ellern), 208